Why The Vietnam War?

Why the Vietnam War?

Nuclear Bombs and Nation Building in Southeast Asia, 1945-1961

By Michael Swanson

Why The Vietnam War? : Nuclear Bombs and Nation Building in Southeast Asia, 1945-1961

Michael Swanson

ISBN: 978-1-7341393-5-8

Cover images in black and white in public domain source publications of US government. Cover background of Vietnam War 'style' image of two helicopters flying low over the jungle canopy at sunset time. (Artist's Impression) by Keith Tarrier. Source Shutterstock.

www.campaniapartners.com

First Edition: 2021

"When the Second World War was over we were the one great power in the world, the Soviets had a substantial military machine, but they could not touch us in power. We had this enormous force that had been built up, we had the greatest fleet in the world, we came through the war economically sound, and I think that, in addition to feeling a sense of responsibility, we also began to feel the sense of a world power that possibly we could control the future of the world."

- Clark Clifford, advisor to Presidents Harry Truman and John F. Kennedy, Secretary of Defense for President Lyndon Johnson[1]

---

[1] Heart and Minds, dir. by Peter Davis (1974; Criterion, 2002 dvd)

CONTENTS

CONCEPTION

September 29, 1972, is a date that Robert McNamara never forgot for the rest of his life, because on that evening someone tried to murder him. By that time, the former Secretary of Defense for Presidents John F. Kennedy and Lyndon Johnson had been out of government for over four years, after leaving on the verge of a nervous breakdown. Now he was fifty-six years old. That night he traveled on the V.M Islander, a little steamboat that hustled passengers back and forth from Massachusetts to Martha's Vineyard, an island south of Cape Cod that served as a yuppie colony and vacation getaway for the rich. McNamara had bought a house on the island and loved it. He enjoyed lounging around its restaurants and soaking in its peaceful seaside environment.

McNamara stood on the deck of the steamer talking with a friend until a walking interruption appeared. A twenty-seven year old short bearded man wearing tennis shoes went up to tell him, "Mr. McNamara, there's a phone call for you. Please follow me." McNamara nodded and said to his companion, "Excuse me a minute, I'll get this and be right back." He followed behind this messenger.

"I led him around the wheelhouse," the strange man retold what happened; "he was right behind me. I felt very much in control. I think we were about a mile or two out of Woods Hole. It was very dark. Those can be pretty rough waters out there. Now the pilothouse on the Islander, if you've ever been on the boat, comes around like this, in a kind of hard oval. There's a very narrow walkway on both sides. You're right at the edge of the ferry. All you've got protecting you from the sea is a four-foot railing with a metal grate in it that runs down to the floor of the deck."

"So we're out there on the walkway now, just the two of us, and he thinks I'm leading him to the pilothouse for this nonexistent phone call, and, well, I just turned on him. I was scared as hell, but I think I was pretty calm, too. I didn't say a word, you know, here's to Rolling Thunder, sir, or, this one's for the Gulf of Tonkin, you lying sack of crap. Nope, nothing like that. I just grabbed him. I got him by the belt and his shirt collar, right below his throat. I had him over, too. He was halfway over the side. He would have gone, another couple of seconds. He was just kind of hanging there in the dark, clawing for the railing. I remember he screamed, 'Oh, my God, no.' But only once. Those may have been the only words between us. I'm pretty sure his glasses came off. I suppose the whole thing didn't last a minute," the bearded man said, "he was amazingly strong, I'll give him that."

McNamara had been pushed just inches away from death. "I don't think they would have had a prayer of saving him. We were on the back side of the boat, since we were headed toward the island, so there was a good chance he was going to get sucked underneath, and in that case the propeller probably would have gotten him if he hadn't drowned first," his attacker said.

At that moment, the assailant felt someone grab him from behind his neck. People spilled out of the boat's lunchroom. More hands grasped on to him. Robert McNamara broke free from his attack. The man traveled the boat himself a lot and had friends of his own on it who stowed him away. After the ferry reached its destination, the police came on board trying to find him, but they found nothing. Robert McNamara told the police he didn't want them to try to find him or press charges against him. He wanted it all to go away. He seemed to understand why a random stranger could come out of nowhere and try to kill him.

Why did this man try to kill someone he never had met before? One word - Vietnam. The Vietnam War brought the deaths of over 58,000 American soldiers and over two million Vietnamese. Three-hundred thousand Americans came back from the war wounded. My father joined the army and served as a medical intern at Walter Reed for a few of them. It was a fight that the United States did not win and a war that divided the country. It was a disaster and Robert McNamara was one of the men who helped to create it. Some blamed him for not letting the military do what it needed to do in order to win, while others saw him as helping place the United States into a conflict that it could never win, and should never have gotten into in the first place. Men like Robert McNamara were responsible.

The man who attacked him on the ferry was an artist who lived in Martha's Vineyard. He had never engaged in an act of violence before that night. Nor did he serve in Vietnam. Journalist Paul Hendrickson found out who he was and got his story. The man didn't plan to seek out Robert McNamara and kill him. He just happened upon him and then the feelings he had about the war welled up inside of him to possess him to act. The attacker had two brothers who served in Vietnam. "My mother's brother was an admiral in World War II. He even won the Medal of Honor. A cousin in our family was a major in the Marine Corps. One of my own brothers, the one who went to Vietnam twice, is now a general. There were all these family ghosts in me, that's what I'm trying to say. I saw him there and something happened," he explained.

He said that he just wanted to "confront him on Vietnam. I know it sounds extremist now. But tell me, what good would screaming in his face have done? What I felt about Vietnam was a lot deeper than that. I suppose this arrogance thing came back pretty hard. Here he was, starting out his long privileged weekend on the Vineyard, stretched out against the counter like that, talking loud, laughing, obviously enjoying himself a great deal. It was as if he owned the lousy steamship authority or something. I mean, why isn't he at least sitting down in his car with a ski mask over his face? I guess I began to feel crazy inside. This won't make any sense to you, but it may have been his posture as much as anything that really did it to me."[2]

The Vietnam War made many Americans distrust their government. Over and over again, Secretary of Defense Robert McNamara, President Lyndon Johnson, and the generals that ran the war made statements to the effect that they were winning, that they saw "light at the end of the tunnel," only to be hit by events that proved their statements wrong time and time again. As a result, many Americans came to conclude that they were either liars, or had no idea what they were doing. The war destroyed Lyndon Johnson's presidency, and caused him to announce that he would not run for re-election.

The Vietnam War created more controversy in the United States than any other war in its history. Hundreds of books have been written about it.

---

[2] Paul Hendrickson, *The Living And The Dead: Robert McNamara And Five Lives Of A Lost War* (New York: Alfred A. Knopf, 1996), pp. 7-13.

Some great ones have been written by men who experienced the war firsthand as journalists, or as soldiers, such as Michael Herr's *Dispatches*, Philip Caputo's *A Rumor of War*, Frederick Downs's *A Killing Zone*, Joseph Galloway's *We Were Soldier's Once...And Young*, and Neil Sheehan's *A Bright Shining Lie* to name just a few of them.

I was less than five months old when the United States began its evacuation of Saigon, the capital of South Vietnam, in 1975. I have no personal memories of the war, and have never served in the military, or in combat, so I cannot write about the experience of being in Vietnam, or attempt to do justice to those that sacrificed there. This book is not about that. This book is about the men like Robert McNamara, who made the decisions to go to war in Vietnam. It is a study of how the bureaucrats in Washington make decisions of war and peace that the rest of the country ends up living with. It is about why the Vietnam War happened.

In some ways the distance of time makes it easier to understand why these decisions were made about Vietnam now than in years past. Passions over the war are dissipating, and more records are also available now than there were just a few years ago. In fact, the Vietnam War may now be the most documented war in American history. It provides us with a plethora of presidential records, taped national security council meetings, and the recorded conversations of Presidents Kennedy, Johnson, and Nixon. Since Vietnam and Watergate, the United States government has become much more secretive. Future historians will not have the type of paper trail for today's events that we have for the 1960's today, nor will they have access to the taped conversations of presidents.

You see, one of the lessons successive presidents took from Vietnam is to protect themselves from embarrassment. The most famous source we have on the war are the so-called *Pentagon Papers*. This is an internal Pentagon study that Robert McNamara ordered Defense Department staffers to put together so that they could understand all of the decisions the government had made about the war and prevent future mistakes. The study was supposed to be kept top secret, but a Pentagon consultant named Daniel Ellsberg turned against the war, and leaked it to the press and to Congress.

The documents caused a firestorm, because they revealed that what many of the presidents told the public they were doing compared to what they actually did, and planned, in regards to Vietnam had been two different things. They exposed lies. Yes, it is still true that we will never know everything. There are things surrounding the Vietnam War and Cold War history, that are still secret, and will likely always remain hidden away for the health of the state, but when you put all of the information we do have together it means that the historical record surrounding the Vietnam War is our best window into understanding how the American empire operates.

Senator Mike Gravel of Alaska read the study into the Congressional record. In his words, "the *Pentagon Papers* reveal the inner workings of a government bureaucracy set up to defend this country, but now out of control, managing an international empire by garrisoning American troops around the world." Looking back from the vantage point of today, it is clear that the American government helped to create something akin to an empire after World War II and still defends it today. In fact, the logic, and thought processes, that show up in the *Pentagon Papers* again, and again, still guide American foreign policy.[3]

Although some like to boast that the United States is an empire, because they see it as a force of good in the world, most Americans are uncomfortable with the idea of empire, as the nation was founded in opposition to the British Empire. Most works of history tend to focus on great leaders, and tell stories with an end to them. They tell a story about the United States as a place in which freedom has advanced through the ages thanks to a chain of events, such as the signing of the Declaration of Independence, the Civil War bringing the

---

[3] *The Pentagon Papers, Gravel Edition, Volume 1* (Boston: Beacon Press, 1971), pp. 1, xi.

end to slavery, women voting thanks to the nineteenth amendment, the New Deal bringing social programs, and help, to the masses, and the Civil Rights struggle ending segregation. They see the United States as a force that defeated evil around the world during World War II, and has protected freedom ever since.

However, as the philosopher Friedrich Nietzsche described history over 150 years ago, "every story must have an aim, hence also the history of a people and the history of the world. That means: because there is 'world history' there must also be some aim in the world process. That means: we demand stories only with aims. But we do not at all demand stories about the world process, for we consider it a swindle to talk about it. That my life has no aim is evident even from the accidental nature of its origin; that I can posit an aim for myself is another matter. But a state has no aim; we alone give it this aim or that." In order to willingly make sacrifices for the state we must give it a high purpose.[4]

Most Americans embody the government of the United States of America with the aim of world freedom. It's human nature for people to think like this, because it makes them feel good to believe that their country is a force of pure righteousness.

---

4 Friedrich Nietzsche, "Notes," in *The Portable Nietzsche*, ed. Walter Kaufmann (New York: Penguin Books, 1982), p.40.

Yet, this requires treating the United States as if it is some sort of mystical power never before seen by man, because it ignores the reality of what all governments created by man really are when you get down to it - organized monopolies of force. In order to function in the world, the United States government must engage in violence. The overriding purpose of every state is to maintain its power. Fulfilling the abstract inspirational principles that surround any state is secondary to this primary purpose.

The tough truth is that to act as a world superpower the United States has bases all over the world, has repeatedly engaged in covert operations to overthrow governments it has deemed unfriendly to it, and carried out wars. Today it rains drone strikes down on world hot spots. Yes, it also has made alliances. But in the end, it has acted as every other imperial power in history has that came before it, because it has done what they all have done - interfered with the internal governments of other states to get them to carry out policies that they desire. Such interference in other states is the definition of empire. To bring order to the world the United States must constantly be engaged in some form of warfare somewhere on the planet at all times.

There are almost no history books about the United States that really examines past American wars, such as the Vietnam War, and explains how they fit as an operation of empire. The problem is, as Nietzsche explains, to study an empire means to study "the world process." That doesn't fit into an easy story either. Nor is it a story that has an ending to it, because it is still ongoing today. In fact, "the world process" is not something that can really be understood as a sequence of historical events as one might imagine as a simple chain of causes and effects. In a similar manner, a person's real biography is not really a story either about one sequence of events that explains their life, but instead it is a process of growth and evolution leading to what they become. The artist on the boat who attacked Robert McNamara did not plan on attacking him. There were not three or four or any specific sequence of events that led up to his outburst, but instead, as he explained, it was "family ghosts" and the vision of Robert McNamara suddenly in front of him that served as the conception in his mind that launched him into a physical attack.

We do not even have a vocabulary for the American empire. As a result, the American news media reports on events as if they are all disjointed and random occurrences, with no connection to past ones. The media rarely puts anything in context so it all seems like confusing chaos to the television watcher. So the Vietnam War just looks like an isolated sad tragedy on the History Channel that has no meaning for today. People are taught that it was just a bunch of bad decisions and mistakes, but by focusing on a historical event like the Vietnam

War, in a new way, we can begin to see the "world process," without which history can feel like a trap between two dichotomies. On one hand, when it comes to history, people are presented with jingoistic stories that they are expected to never question, and then if they doubt them they can end up looking for conspiracies they can never get to the bottom of, because as the ancient saying goes, no man steps into the same river twice. It is the river that is important, but you can't see it if you only look up at the clouds, and never look down towards the ground.

Cornelius Tacitus, who was a famous classical historian of the Roman Empire, and served as a Legionnaire Commander, Consul, and Roman Senator, wrote in his *Annals* about the "Arcana Imperii"- secret, mysterious, and hidden authority. He used this phrase to contrast the real motives and techniques of rule by the Roman emperor, and the Roman imperial government, with those presented to the public, and even the Senate. He suggested that the true operations of empire had to be hidden from the Roman masses in order to function. So, the emperors created a ceremonial reality for the public to engage in that they themselves placed their own individual authority in the center of.[5]

---

[5] Tacitus, *The Annals of Imperial Rome*, ed. Michael Grant (New York: Penguin Books, 1989), p.35.

If the physical manifestations of America's empire have been war, alliances, and covert operations, in the end its true power rests on the American people's acceptance of the purported reasons for imperial actions, which are self-defense and to bring freedom to the world, a powerful metaphysical concept that serves as the state religion of the United States. The rationales President Johnson and his advisors gave the public for expanding America's role in Vietnam were much different than those they shared amongst themselves, and so were those of the presidents and officials who came before, and after, him.

This book is a case study of the American empire, how the secretive national security-bureaucracy really views the rest of the world and acts upon it. It is a sequel to my book *The War State: The Cold War Origins of the Military-Industrial* Complex *and the Power Elite*. In that book I traced the origins of today's American empire to the end of World War II, when the world became dominated by two camps, made up of a Soviet Union, with an empire of satellite states in Eastern Europe, and the United States, with its "free" world allies. This Cold War conflict, between two global blocs, led American policy makers to view the entire world in "us versus them" terms. Any country that was not allied with the United States, even if it tried to stay neutral, became a target for intervention.

This policy became codified in national security doctrine once President Harry Truman gave his approving signature to document NSC-68, which declared that "even if there were no Soviet Union we would face the great problem of the free society, accentuated many fold in this industrial age, of reconciling order, security, the need for participation, with the requirement of freedom. We would face the fact that in a shrinking world the absence of order among nations is becoming less and less tolerable." Order has been the watchword for all empires.[6]

America's empire, though, is different than most empires in history, which have sought to control societies in order to exploit them. Rome, for example, grabbed provinces in order to enslave people, and tax them, while the Spaniards killed thousands of South Americans to loot their gold. The United States, however, sought to control societies in order to improve them, in order to incorporate them into the modern capitalist world order through nation building. But becoming an empire changed the United States forever, and led it to fight a disastrous war in Vietnam.[7]

---

[6] Ernest May, ed., *American Cold War Strategy: Interpreting NSC-68* (Boston: Bedford Books of St. Martin's Press, 1993), p.52.
[7] Odd Arne Westad, *The Global Cold War* (New York: Cambridge University Press, 2010), p.5.

Out of the first few years of the Cold War, immediately following World War II, came a massive arms buildup and the erection of a permanent military-industrial complex. This was all new in the American experience, and led to the birth of a network of national security bureaucrats that worked inside of the executive branch of the federal government, inside the military, and in the intelligence community that created American foreign policy, along with influential businessmen connected to the defense industry, and key political leaders. This was a new elite devoted to global empire that did not exist before World War II. Sociologist C. Wright Mills called them "the power elite." By the time John F. Kennedy became president, one of his advisors, Arthur Schlesinger, Jr., referred to this network as a "permanent government."[8]

This is a story I explained in *The War State*, by looking at a broad series of events from the last few months of World War II through the end of Kennedy's presidency. In my view, this period of American history actually transformed the United States into a militaristic war state. It put the country on something it never had been on before, and that is a permanent war footing that continues to this day. This book continues that story, with a close exami-

[8] Michael Swanson, *The War State: The Cold War Origins Of The Military-Industrial Complex And The Power Elite, 1945-1963* (South Carolina: CreateSpace, 2013), p. 246.

nation of the first sixteen years of America's involvement in Vietnam as an in depth case study, to not recount how the American empire came into being, as my previous book did, but to show how it operates. That is the only way to truly understand why America went to war in Vietnam.

When reporter Neil Sheehan first read the Pentagon Papers, he realized that the government of the United States was not what he thought it was. He realized that there was an inner U.S government, what I call the war state, that in his words acted as a "a centralized state, far more powerful than anything else, for whom the enemy is simply not the Communists, but everything else, its own press, its own judiciary, its own Congress, foreign and friendly governments - all these are potentially antagonistic. It had survived and perpetuated itself often using the issue of anti-Communism against the other branches of government and the press, and finally, it does not function necessarily for the benefit of the Republic, but rather for its own ends, its own perpetuation; it has its own codes which are quite different than public codes. Secrecy was a way of protecting itself, not so much from threats by foreign governments, but from detection from its own population on charges of its own competence and wisdom." After the end of the Cold War, the issue of terrorism replaced the issue of Communism to give a justifiable purpose to the power of the war state.[9]

This creates a problem for those whose only frame of reference for America's interaction with the rest of the world is the media images after the 2001 terrorist attacks when it comes to understanding the Vietnam War, because it doesn't fit into the "war on terror" narrative of the past twenty years. As a result, empty explanations of it just being a sad tragedy, or good intentions gone wrong, have begun to dominate the mainstream media by those trying to fit the Vietnam War into that frame to garner the most readers and viewers. The reality is that when most Americans today think of the Vietnam War they think of the time period between the years surrounding 1965 and 1969, because that is when most American soldiers actually went to Vietnam, so it persists in the collective memory of their culture. It is the period portrayed the most in movies about the war, and documentaries too, even though, in reality, the conflict over Vietnam actually began, in 1945, when the communist Democratic Republic of Vietnam was founded, and lasted until its victory over South Vietnam, in 1975.

For instance, the popular Ken Burns ten episode TV series on the war released, in 2017, had

---

[9] David Halberstam, *The Best And The Brightest* (New York: Random House, 1972), p. 409.

only one episode devoted to the time period from 1945 to 1961. The series was more about the culture wars that began during those years of peak American involvement in the war, and less about the causes of the war, much less any real lessons that can be drawn from it; but this is also the period that most books about the war concentrate on too. This book, though, focuses on those years from 1945 to 1961 that have gone down the collective memory hole. If we want to know why the Vietnam War happened, we must first ask ourselves how did the United States first get involved in Vietnam in the first place?

CHAPTER I - OSS AGENT 19 CODE NAME LUCIUS

For a few critical months, Archimedes Patti was the top representative of the American government in Vietnam. An Italian American born in the Bronx, Patti served as a Lieutenant Colonel in the U.S. Army, and the Office of Strategic Services (OSS - the precursor to the CIA), during World War II. During the war, he was sent to what was then called French Indochina to head OSS efforts in Vietnam, which had been occupied by the Japanese.

Following World War II, Patti eventually worked at the highest levels of the U.S. intelligence community on continuity of government plans in case of a nuclear attack. He wanted to write a book about his experiences in Vietnam, but was warned that if he did he "would be subject to disciplinary action," and ruined. The problem wasn't that he wanted to reveal secret information that could harm the United States, but that the leaders of the military, and probably even the White House, worried that if word of what he saw in Vietnam got out to the public that their policies would be put in doubt. So, Patti waited until 1980, five years after the war ended, to publish his book. By then it was all distant history that seemed so far away that no one cared.[10]

Vietnam is a country that is 8,500 miles away from the United States, about the size of Montana, but shaped similar to Florida or California. It rests southeast of China, with a large ocean coastline to its east. To its west it is flanked by two smaller countries, Laos and Cambodia. The three countries together used to make up French-Indochina. In the 1850's, the French occupied Vietnam and turned it into a colony and, by 1900, took control of Laos, and Cambodia too.

The French divided Vietnam itself up into three regions. They called the northern area Tonkin, which was the home to the city of Hanoi, and the port of Haiphong, the middle region Annam, and the southern area where the city of Saigon sat Cochinchina. They also called the Vietnamese "Annamites," which is what the Chinese who controlled Vietnam for almost a thousand years before they did called them.

The French exploited the colony for all they could by creating French monopolies on the sale of opium, salt, and alcohol, and by taxing the people,

---

[10] Archimedes Patti, *Why Vietnam?: Prelude to America's Albatross* (California: University of California Press, 1980), p. xviii.

sending much of the money to France. They operated zinc, copper, and coal mines and ran rubber plantations in the colony. Vietnam was a rural country full of primitive farmers living in small villages tending rice fields. They lived year to year dependent on the size of their crops for survival. A bad season could mean starvation.

The French introduced to them not only the threat of rifle fire for disobedience, but the instruments of colonial bureaucracy, including land surveys, census reports, tax rolls, and new regulations, all with a goal of using the life of the people to generate tax revenue for the home country. In seasons in which crop yields were small, though, Vietnamese villagers got pushed into famine, because taxes were laid on them at fixed rates, with no merciful adjustments made for their empty bellies.

Some responded in such times with rebellion. But more common responses included turning to the thievery of brigandage or making crafts to sell. The French, however, made this difficult with their oppressive monopoly taxes. For instance, rice wine distilling was popular all over Vietnam until the French declared a monopoly on alcohol, thereby making it a major crime to create rice wine.

The French sent inspectors into the countryside, where they recruited informers, to identify people illegally creating rice wine. They then laid fines on them, or jailed them, to stamp out their attempts to make a living. Some villagers went into the forests to make charcoal and cut wood to sell at markets. However, the French made this a crime too. They sent forest agents out with new regulations, and taxes, to line their pockets with. Thousands sunk so far into poverty that they found they now had no choice but to work for a pittance in French owned factories and mines. These workers lived like slaves.[11]

One of them remembered that "each person was issued a numbered piece of wood to hang around his neck like a prison number... Every morning we had to get up at four o'clock to cook our food. At five-thirty we all had to form ranks in the village courtyard so overseers could check the roll. As they did this, some of the overseers would use their batons, whacking the worker's heads as they counted them. There was not one of them who did not play that game. After roll call, the overseers took us out to the work area from six in the morning until six in the evening. We had to toil steadily under the sun, hot as fire, except for fifteen minutes at noon to eat, drink, and relieve ourselves... One's strength today was never what it had been the day before. Every day one was worn down a bit more, cheeks sunken, teeth gone crooked,

---

[11] James C. Scott, *The Moral Economy of the Peasant: Rebellion and Subsistence in Southeast Asia* (New Haven: Yale University Press, 1976), pp. 91-95, 112,135.

eyes hollow with dark circles around them, clothes hanging from collarbones. Everyone appeared almost dead, and in fact in the end about all did die."[12]

The Vietnamese for centuries had fought against the Chinese and throughout French rule continued to engage in periodic rebellions, but France was a great empire and French Indochina wasn't its only colony. It also had Algeria, Tunisia, and what today are the African countries of Mauritania, Guinea, Mali, Ivory Coast, Niger, Congo, Senegal, Benin, and Chad. Then came World War II, and the Nazis. Adolph Hitler defeated France in less than two months. The Nazi regime occupied three-fifths of France, and allowed a new collaborationist French Vichy government to rule the rest of the country. Some French fled to England, where they organized a "Free French" resistance movement under the leadership of General Charles De Gaulle to take their country back.

The French colonies, though, fell under control of the Vichy collaborationists. Japan occupied French Indochina, turning it into its own colony. At first, the Japanese allowed the French to continue to administer the area. That way they could control Vietnam with a small force of men. They needed all

---

[12] Dixee Bartholomew-Feis, The *OSS And Ho Chi Minh: Unexpected Allies In The War Against Japan* (USA: University Press of Kansas, 2006), p.13.

of the men they could get, because they were in a giant war against China, Great Britain, and the United States all at the same time. In Japan militarists had taken control of the country and had gone crazy. The people of Vietnam came to hate both the French and the Japanese.[13]

Japan needed food to feed its soldiers, and for its home islands. So, the Japanese taxed Vietnamese rice growers, demanding that they give them large portions of their crop. As they started to lose the war, and suffer shipping shortages, thanks to the American navy, they ordered scores of farmers in Vietnam to stop planting rice, and to start to grow peanuts and other oil seed crops instead, so that they could use them as byproducts for oil and lubricants in their machinery. All that mattered was their war effort. The result was a widespread famine that killed between one and two million Vietnamese in a silent holocaust. The French officers supervised this misery on behalf of their Japanese masters. They made sure that they themselves were well fed.[14]

One man in Hanoi remembers how the villagers came into the city to try to survive. "They dug in garbage piles, looking for anything at all, banana skins, orange peels, discarded greens. They even

---

[13] Stanley Karnow, *Vietnam: A History* (New York: Penguin Books, 1991), p. 160; also see Neil Jamieson, *Understanding Vietnam* (California: University Press of California, 1995).
[14] Bartholomew-Feis, pp. 29-30.

ate rats. But then they couldn't get enough to keep alive. They tried to beg, but everyone else was hungry, and they would drop dead in the streets. Every morning, when I opened my door, I found five or six corpses on the step," he said.[15]

Then after the Soviets pushed the German army out of Russia, and the allied army under Dwight Eisenhower landed in Normandy, the Japanese decided that they could no longer trust the French, so they took total control of Vietnam. They put the French soldiers in prison. Some of the French managed to escape into China. This was the situation when Archimedes Patti received orders to prepare to travel to Vietnam in order to set up an American intelligence operation to gather information, rescue any downed American pilots in the region, and run sabotage operations against the Japanese.

Patti believed that the United States would do some good in Vietnam. Most Americans were opposed to colonialism, and imperialism, of all sorts. President Franklin Roosevelt told one friend that Winston Churchill had to "understand how most of our people feel about Britain and her role in the life of other peoples... There are many kinds of Americans of course, but as a people, as a country, we're opposed to imperialism - we can't stomach it."

Of course, for FDR winning the war was the top priority, but as the allies came closer to victory he

---

[15] Karnow, p. 160.

thought more, and more, about the future postwar world. He told Soviet Foreign Minister Vyacheslav Molotov "that an end to colonial possessions would serve world peace by preventing postwar struggles for independence and that international trusteeships should be set up for former colonies until they were ready for self-government." Even before America entered the war, he got Churchill to sign the Atlantic Charter, which stated that as allies "they respect the right of all peoples to choose the form of government under which they will live; and they wish to see sovereign rights and self-government restored to those who have been forcibly deprived of them."

Roosevelt explained to Churchill that he needed this to be an official war goal in order to get the support of the American people. He also thought it was the best way to win the war, as it "helped elevate the Allied cause among the colonial peoples because it would have shown that the war's goal was not to reestablish European empires." The top American commanders in China, Generals Joseph Stilwell and Albert Wedemeyer, both believed colonialism was wrong and that the colonial governments were too weak to fight against Japan anyway. John Davies, an adviser to Stilwell, said they thought, "Why should American boys die to recreate the colonial empires of the British and their Dutch and French satellites?"

Roosevelt didn't push Churchill too hard on Britain's colonies. However, he had disdain for France's position. As for French Indochina, he told his son, "the Japanese control that colony now. Why was it a cinch for the Japanese to conquer the land? The native Indo-Chinese have been so flagrantly downtrodden that they thought to themselves: Anything must be better than to live under French colonial rule! Should a land belong to France? By what logic and by what custom and by what historical rule? I'm talking about another war, Elliot... I'm talking about what will happen to our world, if after this war we allow millions of people to slide back into the same semi-slavery!"

President Roosevelt told Secretary of State Cordell Hull that "France has milked it for one hundred years. The people of Indo-China are entitled to something better than that." The Allies came up with a plan for Vietnam, after they defeated Japan, Chinese Nationalist forces would occupy the northern half of the country while forces from England would take over the lower half of the country. After a period of time, they could leave, and make the country independent.[16]

The United States needed its own men in Vietnam. Archimedes Patti traveled to an OSS operations base in Kunming, China, their closest station to Vietnam. In peacetime, Kunming was connected

[16] Bartholomew-Feis, pp. 39-44.

to Hanoi by a day long train ride. Patti's orders from William Donovan, the head of the OSS, were to "use anyone who will work with us against the Japanese, but do not become involved in French-Indochinese politics." There were lots of French officers in the area. Patti could work with them as long as he didn't help them restore their colony, which they all wanted to do.[17]

Lieutenant Colonel Patti decided he needed to find people in Vietnam that could provide the United States with intelligence and "carry out operations." He came up with a plan to send two small groups of armed men into Vietnam to make contact with resistance groups in the country and give them radios to communicate with him. He gave the groups code names Cat and Deer, and worked out a deal with two French officials to train a hundred Vietnamese troops, and ten French officers, that would be led by two Americans.

The French agreed to join in the mission, but then backed out. They demanded money, saying that they would not take orders from the Americans in a "sit-down strike." Patti threw up his hands, concluding that working with the French would be a waste of time. So, he turned to piles of intelligence information about a native resistance group given to him on his arrival.[18]

---

[17] Patti, p. 21, 31.
[18] Patti, pp. 107-118.

A year before, a gang of Vietnamese men led by a man named Ho Chi Minh came to Kunming with Lieutenant Rudolph Shaw, an American pilot who had been missing for a month after being shot down over Vietnam. The OSS offered Ho money as a reward, but he turned them down. Instead he wanted the honor of meeting the famous general of the Flying Tigers Claire Chennault. The general wasn't around, so Ho just left.[19]

Shaw gave the OSS a report, which recounted that "as soon as I touched the ground a young Indo-Chinese came along smiling and warmly shaking both my hands and making signs to me to follow him. I handed him 600 Indo-China dollars. He absolutely refused to take the money and looked rather offended. I was surprised by his attitude and thought that he considered the sum insufficient. It was a great mistake on my part! What I first thought to be a greediness is in reality a common virtue of the Indo-Chinese patriots. They help us not for our money, but for love and friendship. They know that we are fighting not only for America, but also for the freedom and democracy of the world, hence for their country also. For that reason, they consider it is their patriotic duty to help us - their allies."

The first Vietnamese he encountered took him to a hiding place. More arrived. Neither could

[19] Bartholomew-Feis, pp. 111-112.

speak the other's language. The Vietnamese said to him, "Viet Minh! America! Viet Minh! America!" Shaw answered back, "Viet Minh! Viet Minh!" This made them "very pleased." The men found his plane, eying Japanese and French troops taking it apart.

Then "for 30 days, playing hide and seek with the French and the Japs, the patriots," Shaw wrote, "brought me from one hiding place to another. They did their best to make me comfortable. Whenever and wherever they could the villagers, men and women, boys and girls, hold secret meetings to welcome me. When the speakers finished, I always replied with a brief and simple speech: Viet Minh! US! The meetings ended by an all around handshaking."

Shaw flew back home to the United States. General Claire Chennault sent a report to General Wedemeyer telling him that Shaw's "immediate welfare and ultimate escape" came thanks to "a native organization called The League for Indochina Independence." "I am heartily in favor of maintaining good relations with any organization in French Indochina that will effectively aid in escape the US military personnel likely to require aid in that country, regardless of their local political affiliations," he wrote.[20]

---

[20] Bartholomew-Feis, pp. 150-153.

Charles Fenn, a British born American OSS agent based in Kunming, followed up with the fifty-five year old Ho a few months later. He arranged a meeting with him on March 17, 1945. The French had warned the Americans that Ho was a "long-standing rebel, anti-French, of course, and strictly a Communist." Fenn asked Ho about his allegiances, and he replied that the French said anyone who wants independence is a Communist. Fenn asked Ho what he would want in return for helping the OSS. "Arms and medicine," he replied. Fenn recorded that he was "impressed by his clear-cut talk; and Buddha-like composure."

Fenn decided to send Ho back to Vietnam with a radio operator and Frank Tan, a Chinese American born in the United States, to assess the situation. Before they left, he granted another request from Ho to meet with General Chennault. Fenn recorded in his diary that, "Chennault told Ho how grateful he was about the saved pilot. Ho said he would always be glad to help the Americans and particularly to help General Chennault for whom he had the greatest admiration. They exchange talk about the Flying Tigers. Chennault was pleased the old man knew about this. We talked about saving more pilots. Nothing was said about the French, or about politics. I heaved a sigh of relief as we started to leave. Then Ho said he had a small favor to ask the general.... But all Ho wanted was the general's photograph. There's nothing Chennault likes more than giving his photograph. So he presses the bell and in comes Doreen [Chennault's secretary] again. In due course, it's some other girl who produces a folder of eight-by-ten glossies. 'Take your pick,' says Chennault. Ho takes one and asks would the general be so kind as to sign it? Doreen produces a Parker 51 and Chennault writes across the bottom."

Fenn created an OSS file for Ho, and labeled him Agent 19 code name "Lucius." In spy parlance Ho had become an "asset" of the OSS, meaning someone with whom the intelligence agency has a relationship with. It doesn't mean they had control of him, but that they could get information from him, and work with him. Fenn taught Ho the basics "about SI, SO, MO, X2, and particularly about weather reports, which were, indeed, almost the top of the list, since without them our planes couldn't fly." Ho asked for one last thing, six Colt .45 automatic pistols in their original U.S. army issue wrappings. Fenn went, and got them for him. Fenn used Ho to create a network of radio operators in Vietnam. He called this operation the QUAIL PROJECT.[21]

When Archimedes Patti came to Kunming, and took over OSS operations for Vietnam, he got the files for the QUAIL PROJECT. It must have looked good. He undoubtedly would have read the reports written by Frank Tan, who had taken a two week

---

[21] Bartholomew-Feis, pp. 155-159.

long trip into Vietnam along with Ho, and twenty of his men, who came to protect them from any Japanese or bandits that they might encounter. "We set out dressed as border smugglers with all equipment carried in bamboo baskets so as to arouse normal suspicion of being illicit border traders," Tan reported. Along with them was Mac Shin, a Chinese radio expert working with the OSS. Shin brought a basket full of radios he planned to show Ho's men how to use.

The trek took the men through the jungles, and mountains, of Vietnam with little food and water. Tan almost gave out, but Ho kept him going, telling them that they could not stop. "Mac, remember, the salt is better than gold," Ho told Shin. They had to eat their horses. Shin finally got in touch with Fenn over the radio, and got some food parachuted into a safe spot.

After they got out of the mountains, the journey got easier. They began to encounter more, and more, friendly people. The people would try to give them food, but "Ho Chi Minh still said that we had some money and we can pay, and we understood that Ho Chi Minh was very concerned about some kind of suspicion that might arise that the liberation soldiers just take the things from the people," Tan wrote.

When they made it to their destination, it was a "mere hut" in the entrance of a cave. It served as the "headquarters" of the Vietminh. "I don't know how to classify VM," Tan wrote back, "I guess they are what they are thru circumstances. The country where I am is very poor. They couldn't afford to pay taxes and still exist. As near as I can judge, this League is quite powerful and has several hundred followers."

Tan found that "the gang all salute me and do everything they can to help us, and they worry if we can't eat their food. Mac is teaching them radio technique and say they all love him. They are very military-conscious and have military drill every day. The fact that we brought a sizeable amount of guns and ammo has really paid dividends." Vietnamese regularly came to him with "letters, maps, documents, Japanese leaflets and other MO material." For the men in Kunming, this was an intelligence breakthrough.

Ho got sick, disappearing for a while. When he came back, "he invited all the top leaders to a conference, not his own people, but rivals working for other groups, who had used his absence to push themselves forward. He told them he had now secured the help of the Americans, including Chennault. At first nobody really believed him. Then he produced the photograph of Chennault signed 'yours sincerely.' After this he presented the automatic pistols and gave one to each of the leaders. The leaders considered Chennault had sent these presents personally. After this conference there was never any talk about who was the top leader," Charles Fenn recounted.

Tan told Ho of regrets of having left a girl behind in Kunming. In response Ho told him his life story of how he left Vietnam as a young man to travel the world to work to make Vietnam its own country. He left a young girl behind too and never married. "I began to see him as the man he was - a man who dedicated his life to win freedom for his people. He was a man who I felt was a lonely person, bereft and denied all the normal comforts of happiness of life. Such a sacrifice left him nothing but to think and act for one thing only. Hence, the inconsistency that caused some to describe him as a communist, or conversely as a patriot," Tan recalled.

"For Mac, who was young and looked younger," Tan said, "Ho seemed to look on him as something of a son. He said that if Mac wanted to return after the war he would help him get settled on a nice piece of land, but to leave it to Mac to find a nice wife."

Tran Trong Trung, one of the Vietminh radio operators, "noticed that Mr. Mac Shin and Mr. Frank Tan were very fond of Ho Chi Minh. And Mr. Mac Shin himself in the course of his instruction, his radio lessons, he said that 'Our Ho is a great man.' This is a real honor for you guys to be here with Ho Chi Minh, that's why you guys have to try and master all these technologies so that you can best serve Ho Chi Minh."[22]

Patti decided that he needed to meet Ho for himself, so the two arranged a meeting at a tea house on the China border. Ho was chain-smoking a brand of local cigarettes. When he ran out of them "I offered him a Chesterfield," Patti wrote, "his eyes lit up with pleasure as he reached with his long delicate fingers for one, adding apologetically that smoking was one of his more serious vices. And that, I found later, was the truth. When his state of health was precarious in the tense days of August and September, he was still enjoying my Chesterfields. Even with a racking cough he smoked. It seemed to be his one indulgence and I never had the heart to preach as he enjoyed my cigarettes."

The two talked for several hours sizing each other up. "I realized he was searching my motives and trying to discover my attitude toward the Vietnamese as a people, and in particular," Patti remembered, "whether I represented colonial interests or Roosevelt's anti-colonialism."

"Ho's sincerity, pragmatism, and eloquence made an indelible impression on me. He did not strike me as a starry-eyed revolutionary or a flaming radical, given to clichés mouthing a party line, or bent on destroying without plans for rebuilding.

---

[22] Bartholomew-Feis, pp. 163-169.

This wisp of a man was intelligent, well-versed in the problems for his country, rational, and dedicated. I also felt he could be trusted as an ally against the Japanese," Patti concluded.

Ho explained that the Vietminh were organized in small groups, with each one led by a "cadre" leader. Each unit could operate on its own or together as needed. He said he was ready to align himself with the Americans whenever they needed anything.

Patti had operated in Europe, where he found that underground groups would make big claims, and ask for arms and money. In contrast, Ho revealed that he had some captured weapons, and asked for no money. After midnight passed, Patti left impressed by Ho. The Vietnamese leader said he had up to one thousand "well trained" men to use in any plan the Americans may have against the Japanese.[23]

Patti poured over his intelligence data, thinking about Ho and the Vietnamese. He could see the war coming to an end. He came to the conclusion that the Viet Minh movement "was real, dynamic, and bound to succeed." "I had determined from solid evidence that it was well organized and had specific objectives and popular endorsement," he later wrote, "in my reports to Heppner, Wedemeyer, and Hurley, I emphatically refused to

---

[23] Patti, pp.85-88.

accept French allegations that there was no real movement for independence in Indochina, that a few agitators fomenting discord were 'communist expatriates' aided and abetted by Moscow, Yenan, and Chungking or that the 'natives' were loyal, dependent people waiting patiently for the return of the French to shelter and protect them from Chinese and Thai overlordship. On the contrary, I had concluded that the independence movement was only a medium for a first cause - the instinct for survival. If national independence could assure a Vietnamese of survival, he saw the Viet Minh as the answer. It mattered not to him whether the medium was democratic, socialistic, or communistic."

"I confirmed in my reports that French colonialism in Indochina had been one of the worst possible examples of peonage, disregard for humans' rights, and French cupidity and that for more than three-quarters of a century the Vietnamese had been cruelly exploited, brutally maltreated, and generally used as French chattel," Patti wrote. He saw the famine as a turning point.

In Patti's view, the Japanese and French collaborators had demanded farmers "impossible quotas in requisitioning foodstuffs." It not only caused "nearly two million people" to die, but "had also fanned their hatred for the Japanese and French oppressors and strengthened the people's determination to fight and win back the right to live," he wrote, "the right to live - survival - that was the first cause of the revolution. Accordingly, the Indochinese Communist Party adopted the slogan, 'seize paddy stocks to save the people from starvation.'"[24]

Patti gave his approval for OSS teams DEER and CAT to go into Vietnam in order to train Ho's Vietminh forces to fight the Japanese. Both teams brought American weapons with them, and spent several weeks training the Vietnamese in how to use them.

Major Allison Thomas, who headed the DEER team, and his men parachuted into Ho's camp. The Vietminh leader wasn't there. Instead, a man named Vo Nguyen Giap was in charge. He had been born into an upper class Vietnamese family. As a boy, Giap learned French in colonial schools, and his mother taught him patriotism. His father gave him a Vietnamese history book. "In that book I discovered our forebears, our martyrs, our duty to expunge our past humiliation," he said.

Giap studied the anti-colonial writings of Ho and French translations of Karl Marx. "I spent my nights reading them, and my eyes opened," he remembered, "Marxism promised revolution, an end to oppression, the happiness of mankind. It echoed the appeals of Ho Chi Minh, who wrote that downtrodden peoples should join the proletariat of all countries to gain their liberation. Nationalism

---

[24] Patti, pp. 131-133.

made me a Marxist, as it did so many Vietnamese, especially intellectuals and students. Marxism also seemed to me to coincide with the ideals of our ancient society, when the emperor and his subjects lived in harmony, when everyone worked and prospered together, when the old and children were cared for. It was a utopian dream."

Giap got a law degree in Hanoi and then became a school teacher. He read everything Ho wrote. "I tried to imagine this man," he remembered, "I looked forward to meeting him one day." As fate would have it, he got his chance, leaving Hanoi to meet Ho in China. "Here, was this legend, but he was just a man, like any other man," he said. When Giap came back home, he found that his sister and brother-in-law had been executed by the French for treason. To top it off, his wife had been arrested by the French too. She died in prison. Giap told some French officials he was friends with that their government "destroyed my life."

Now he was in charge of Ho's army fighting for revenge, and liberation. Giap was about thirty years old when the DEER team met him. Wearing western clothes, and a fedora on his head, while nearly all Viet Minh wore peasant clothing, he stood out. He usually wore a suit and tie in public. According to Allison Thomas, "he had a very strong feeling against the French. He was an intense man, no question about it. The French called him a snow-covered volcano. He was always in control of himself, and obviously very bright and well educated. His troops looked up to him. I liked him."

The DEER team was told that Ho was laid up sick in a nearby village. After a few days, two Americans went to find him in a hut. Rene Defourneaux recalls that "the man was shaking like a leaf and obviously running a high fever. When my eyes had become accustomed to the darkness, I noticed the long scraggly goatee hanging from a pointed chin."

Paul Hoagland, an OSS medic, took a glance at him and said, "this man doesn't have long for this world." Hoagland figured that he had malaria, dengue fever, and dysentery. He gave him sulfa drugs, quinine, and "looked after him periodically." After ten days, he was up and about the camp. Thomas thought that without their help he would have died.[25]

On August 6, 1945, news of the atomic bombing of Hiroshima circulated throughout the camp. A week later, Thomas wrote in his diary, "wild hilarity to-day. 9 AM heard by our radio that negotiations for final surrender were almost finished." But many of his men were disappointed, because they were proud of the training they had been given and wanted to get into a little bit of the fight. "The Vietnamese," one of the Americans wrote, "were fascinated by these strangers who dropped from the sky

[25] Bartholomew-Feis, pp. 207-208; Karnow, pp. 154-156.

with tons of western equipment, maintained constant contact with great sources of power in the outside world, often insisted on walking around bare-chested (completely unlike the sartorially conscious French colonials), and showed every sign of wanting to kill 'Japs' the minute the training program was concluded."[26]

Ho left to go to a "National Insurrection Committee." Sixty delegates representing various political parties, religious groups, and factions attended. They resolved "to wrest power from the hands of the Japanese and the puppet government before the arrival of the Allied troops in Indochina, so that we, as masters of the country, would welcome these troops coming to disarm the Japanese." Tens of thousands, perhaps hundreds of thousands, joined the revolt as starving peasants took over Japanese granaries.

One country villager remembers that where he lived "a man in brown pants and a cloth shirt climbed onto a chair, and guards armed with machetes, spears and sticks surrounded him. He delivered a speech, saying that the Japanese had capitulated to the Allies, and that the time had come for the Vietminh to seize power. I was just a teenager in ragged clothes, and I asked a school mate,

---

[26] Bartholomew-Feis, p. 213.

'Now that we've seized power who will be the mandarin?' He replied, 'get this. The mandarin is just a peasant - really ordinary.'"[27]

In some villages people who collaborated with the Japanese or the French were put to death, but in other places the situation was very peaceful, because, with the war over, the Japanese did not fight. They simply stayed in their barracks. In Hanoi they withdrew from the city administration buildings and Giap took them over. The only place the Japanese guarded was the Bank of Indochina, which they charged a protection tax to "in payment of expenses incurred in maintaining law and order and for the protection of the French." They still had thousands of French prisoners of war, and a few Americans, in custody.

This created a new mission for Patti - go to Hanoi, arrange the Japanese surrender, investigate any potential war crimes they may have committed, get them to free their prisoners, and continue to collect intelligence information. He traveled by plane to the city, along with French Major General Jean Sainteny, who was on orders from the new Free French De Gaulle government to "feel out" the different groups in Vietnam, ahead of a possible French reentry into the country, and also check on the prisoners of war. Patti had strict orders not to assist the French in taking over Vietnam, or to give

---

[27] Patti, pp. 134-135; Karnow, pp. 160-161.

even the appearance of supporting any such plans.[28]

"When we landed we caught the Japanese by surprise," Patti recalled, at the airport "they were all fully armed and they had tanquettes and they were all quite shocked to see us come in. They hadn't been warned. And, frankly, I was shocked too. As a matter of fact, not only shocked, but I was scared. I could just see them starting, opening up, with their little submachine guns out there and it would be a massacre." Patti, though, at this instant didn't realize that he was more than just a man, because to arrive at this moment, the way he did, representing what he was representing, meant that he was almost like a God who for some meant salvation. "In the background, behind the Japanese, I saw a huge mob," he said.

Inside the mass of people were men holding up the British Union Jack flag, the Dutch flag, and the American flag. "Now, who were these people? They were the prisoners of war," Patti said, "they were Indian prisoners of war. They were British prisoners that had been captured at, in Malaya earlier in the war in '42." Patti was worried about the Japanese. "I probably bluffed my way a little bit by saying that we had come to accept the surrender for Chiang Kai-Shek and that didn't sit so well with them. In fact, it was a major who approached me

---

[28] Patti, pp. 142-146, 163.

and he didn't like it one bit, but, nevertheless, they were very correct. They were absolutely perfect from the military viewpoint. They saluted and they bowed and they maintained their stance and they were in every respect soldiers," he remembered.

"Unfortunately, I had taken with me five Frenchmen," Patti said, "one of them being Major Sainteny, the Chief of the Intelligence Service in China. And, he started to make demands immediately for the use of the Bach Mai radio station, demands to have a car, demands for this, the other, and that, and I tried to calm him down, and tell him to wait until we see someone in authority, that these people weren't the people to talk with. They were only field soldiers, but we succeeded, and finally, we were brought into a small hut where the Japanese treated us rather well. They gave us ice cold towels to dry our brow, which was pretty hot at that time, and they provided us some excellent Japanese beer, which I dare say was good as I've ever had."

Patti and Sainteny got into the back of a car together, and headed into Hanoi. The streets were peaceful, but there were flags flying everywhere. Most of them were "a red flag where they, with a gold star in the center. That was the Viet Minh flag. Then there were also banners run across the streets, which said Vietnam to the Vietnamese. Out with the French. Welcome the Allies," Patti remembered.

Then Patti turned and said, "Jean it doesn't look like it's gonna be very good, is it? And, he shook his head and was absolutely stunned by the display of anti-French sentiment, and also by the display of the red flag with the gold star."

The two arrived at the Hotel Metropole to find one hundred French women and children. "When they saw the French uniforms, of course, they went out of their minds. They really were elated. They were happy. They were joyous, and there was a lot of embracing and a lot of kissing, and handshaking, patting on the back," Patti said. However, once they realized that Sainteny only had a few men with them, they got despondent. Some Japanese came, telling Patti that it might be best if the French went to the Governors General Palace where they could be protected, because Giap had taken control of the city with his army, running the utilities, and keeping order.

They all agreed it would be best if the French used the palace as their fortress. According to Patti, the "Vietnamese had been upset by the initial reaction of the French. The initial reaction being that of being aggressive, and I'd like to say pushy. They were shoving them around. They were again starting to talk about the boys. The boys being a pejorative term for the Vietnamese. Also, referring to them as the Annamites, which they didn't like, and so on. So, there was some turbulence there that had to be kept under control."[29]

Patti soon discovered that the "OSS team had immediately become a center of Allied authority to which everyone with a cause or a desire for prestige brought himself to be heard. The French came to complain, make demands, and play conspiratorial games. The Vietnamese came to be seen with the Allies, and acquire status in the eyes of their adversaries, creating an image of insiders with the American mission. Other nationalities came for various self-serving interests."[30]

One such visitor came from Russia. Stephane Solosieff presented himself "as some sort of Soviet liaison to the Japanese political offices in Hanoi, Hue, and Saigon with the task of looking after the interests of Soviet citizens in Indochina," Patti wrote. The Soviet agent claimed that there were about five hundred such Russians in the region.

He told Patti that he had heard from the French that Ho Chi Minh, and the Vietminh, were under OSS "protection" and wanted to know if that were true. Patti told him that they had worked together

---

[29] Archimedes Patti interview, 1981, *Vietnam: A Television History Program: Roots of War*, http://openvault.wgbh.org/catalog/vietnam-bf3262-interview-with-archimedes-l-a-patti-1981, accessed 1/02/2014.
[30] Archimedes Patti, *Why Vietnam?: Prelude to America's Albatross* (California: University of California Press, 1980), p. 162.

in clandestine operations against Japan before they surrendered, but now that the war was over the United States "had made no commitment to interfere in the internal affairs of Indochina."

Patti knew that Ho had gone to the Soviet Union, when he was younger, for training, and came out as a Comintern agent. So, he wanted to know if the Soviets were now going to work with Ho. Solosieff said that the days of French colonialism were over, but the Russians weren't in any position to help anyone. They needed to rebuild from the war. What is more, he thought that Soviet interference in French, and British, interests would not be in his country's best interests at the time. He thought with French, and American, help the Vietnamese could be given independence in a few years. To Patti this sounded like President Roosevelt's trusteeship concept.[31]

A Vietnamese delegation came to Patti, asking him to see Giap. The two met for coffee. Giap didn't know what all was happening. He wanted to know if the Chinese Nationalists, and the British, were going to occupy Vietnam as had been planned originally, or if now the French were going to come with their army. He wanted to know why Patti brought a bunch of Frenchmen with him on the plane.

---

[31] Patti, pp. 178-179.

Patti told him that as far as he knew there was no change in plans. He expected the Chinese to come, and then for there to be some formal surrender on the part of the Japanese. He told him that the French just came with him to help any POW's, and French civilians, but were being confined or protected by the Japanese, in the French Governor General's Palace.

Once the two talked for an hour, Patti realized that the Soviet Union had not made any contact with other Vietnamese. "Giap arose and with a warm smile," Patti wrote, "which I found as I knew him better to be a rarity, and said, 'the people wish to welcome you and our American friends. Would you and your staff oblige us by coming to the front gate?'"

As they went outside, Patti saw a huge ceremony. A fifty-piece military band stood across the street in front of him, with five giant flags waving in the wind, representing the United States, Great Britain, the Soviet Union, China, and Ho's Democratic Republic of Vietnam. To his left were a hundred men standing at "present arms." Giap told him these are "my troops who have just arrived from the mountains."

Suddenly, all of the flags dipped, except the Stars and Stripes. "The band struck up the 'Star Spangled Banner' and it was the best rendition I heard in the Far East," Patti wrote. He stood at attention and saluted the flag. The troops marched by Giap, and Patti, for review. Then a parade of civilians, ten abreast, walked by with more flags, and placards, welcoming the United States, and praising independence. And then another tune began to play.

General Giap told Patti, "this is the first time in the history of Vietnam that our flag has been displayed in an international ceremony and our national anthem played in honor of a foreign guest. I will long remember this occasion." With a small ragtag army, and a flag, Ho and Giap created a nation. The Japanese surrender created a power vacuum that they took advantage of, they simply marched into history.[32]

Patti then met with Ho in a two story house in an old section of Vietnam. "I was pleased to see him again, but thoroughly shocked," Patti wrote, "Ho was only a shadow of the man I had met at Chiu Chou Chieh four months to the day earlier. I reached for his hands, and he seemed very unsteady on his sandaled feet. The thin, bony legs supporting his frail frame made a startling contrast with the large head and the radiant smile on his face. His clothes, a high-collared brown tunic and trousers, hung loosely, accentuating his wasted condition."

---

[32] Patti, pp.196-199.

Malaria and intestinal ailments had weakened Ho. But, they didn't stop him from hosting dinner, and talking for several hours. He was preparing to issue a declaration of independence, and wanted to know what the United States would do.

Patti told him that he couldn't speak for the United States government, but could only keep the people back home informed of events. Ho tried to explain that he was not a communist, or "an agent of the Comintern." He admitted that he was a socialist, and had worked with French, Chinese, and Vietnamese Communists. He told him how he had traveled to the Soviet Union, but explained "who else was there to work with?" He labeled himself a "progressive-socialist-nationalist."[33]

Patti brokered a meeting with Giap and Sainteny, who chose to meet the Vietnamese in the French palace. Patti arrived first, meeting the Frenchman in one of the largest rooms in the giant building. "His choice of setting could be construed as showing suitable respect for a visitor of importance and mark of distinction or as exhibiting a not very subtle desire to overawe the Vietnamese. I did not know which," he wrote.

Giap arrived with an assistant. As they entered Sainteny's large room, they walked over half way towards the Frenchman before he got up to greet them. Patti, sensing tenseness, decided to speak

---

[33] Patti, pp. 199-203.

first, introducing everyone. The group then walked in silence all of the way across the giant room to a bunch of chairs arranged for the meeting.

Sainteny began with complaints about "Annamite" behavior. He wanted to know why they had the gumption to make a proclamation to "let the world know that French presence in Indochina was no longer welcome." Without pausing to hear a reply, he told them that he "would keep a watchful eye" on their provisional government.

According to Patti, "in perfect French and with absolute self-control, Giap said he had not come to be lectured nor to justify the actions of the people of Vietnam, but had come at the invitation of one he believed to be a representative of the new French government, and that he was prepared to engage in an amicable exchange of views. For the first time in his life Sainteny was meeting face to face a Vietnamese who dared to stand up to a Frenchman."

Sainteny softened up a little, saying that now that France was "a free and liberal nation" under De Gaulle the "old ways" would be discarded. Giap pressed him for specifics, but he said he couldn't give any at the moment. He spoke in generalities. Giap "sat stolidly," and did not seem "willing to concede that France might have any say in Vietnam's future." There didn't seem to be much more the two could say to one another.[34]

As the meeting broke up, Sainteny asked Patti to stay behind. "He said, very confidentially, that the Paris government had laid aside a huge sum of money in francs for the exclusive use of the American commercial interest, financial interest with whom could he get in touch with? With whom could he pursue this offer? I was seething, of course. I was very unhappy. I was mad, I was...I didn't say a word. I just could barely speak," Patti remembered.

Patti said, at "that moment I realized what he was doing. He was offering the American officials a bribe not to interfere in French interests in Indochina. And, I as much as told that to Sainteny. In fact, I said, I don't think there's anyone in Kunming or in Washington or in Chongqing who'd be willing to accept an offer such as you are making. However, it is my duty to report it and I'll do that. I'll let you know. And, I did. The answer came back within hours from Kunming and Chongqing both from the embassy and from the military headquarters saying have no part of this. Stay completely

[34] Patti, pp. 207-210.

out." Patti could not be corrupted and neither could any of his OSS colleagues.[35]

The Chinese Nationalist army, and the British forces, divided Vietnam in half at the 16th parallel to oversee the Japanese surrender, with the Chinese coming in from the north. For the Chinese getting involved in Vietnam for a short period of time was a way for them to become players on the world stage. The situation in Hanoi remained quiet. Patti attended a Japanese surrender ceremony as a representative of the United States. The Japanese stayed peacefully armed the whole time and after the surrender ceremony they eventually left Hanoi on their own to go back to Japan.

Right before the Chinese came into Vietnam, Ho and Giap held a large ceremony of their own proclaiming the independence for their country, much of it almost copied word by word from the American Declaration of Independence. On the eve of this gathering, Patti walked around the city to try to get a feel for what the Vietnamese really thought. He walked up to one man, asking him if he knew that the Viet Minh were communists? The man had never seen a photograph of Ho or knew where he had come from. "He seemed confused and embarrassed, then confessed he did not really

---

[35] Archimedes Patti interview, 1981, *Vietnam: A Television History Program: Roots of War*, http://openvault.wgbh.org/catalog/vietnam-bf3262-interview-with-archimedes-l-a-patti-1981, accessed 1/02/2014.

know what I meant by communist," Patti recalled, "I did not pursue the point, but could not help but observe that in speaking of Ho Chi Minh his answers exuded a proprietary pride, as though Ho were a member of his own family. I was to experience this phenomenon many times in the weeks I spent in Hanoi." Ho had become a prophet for his people.

As for the Chinese, according to Patti, "they undertook to assume control of all the Vietnamese assets and properties in the area—both in the bank of Indochina, which had already been pretty well depleted, by the Japanese to start with, and later they took over what was left. They also bought all of the cinemas, the bars, the hotels they could lay their hands on that belonged to the Vietnamese, and to the French, at a price next to nothing, so that before they were finished, they really had full control of all the financial, and banking, assets in not only Hanoi, but in Haiphong and in other nearby centers." The Japanese occupation caused the economy of Vietnam to collapse. Millions starved. Those that survived World War II were destitute with no money. That made for opportunities for the Chinese.

Something truly horrible, though, happened in the southern part of Vietnam, and in Saigon, where the British, under Major General Douglas Gracey, arrived, with a mixed battalion of Indian Gurkhas and Englishmen. All Gracey knew about Vietnam when he came was a one page summary of the political situation given to him by the French. Gracey worked as a colonial officer in India, Burma, and Malaya and expected the Vietnamese to behave like subjects. He saw his mission as serving as a stop gap for a French return.[36]

The United States sent OSS operative Lieutenant Colonel Peter Dewey into Saigon to check on any American prisoners of war and gather intelligence. Only twenty-eight years old, Dewey was the youngest son of Congressman Charles Dewey. He had graduated from Yale, with a double major in French and history. He served in North Africa from October 1942 to July 1943, where he completed "eight or more intelligence missions" and became "well acquainted with many high ranking [French] persons." He led a team in southern France in August of 1944, on which he "sent back valuable intelligence on the eve of the Allied landing on the Riviera, then worked with local resistance forces in capturing 400 Nazi prisoners and destroying three enemy tanks." The French awarded him the Croix

[36] Archimedes Patti, *Why Vietnam?: Prelude to America's Albatross* (California: University of California Press, 1980), pp. 240, 307-209; Archimedes Patti interview, 1981, *Vietnam: A Television History Program: Roots of War*, http://openvault.wgbh.org/catalog/vietnam-bf3262-interview-with-archimedes-l-a-patti-1981, accessed 1/02/2014.

de Guerre. Yes, you could say that he was a war hero, with a great career in front of him.[37]

When General Gracey first arrived in Vietnam, he came out of the sky in a plane. After he landed, he ignored a small group of Viet Minh delegates that were on the tarmac to greet him and instead walked straight up to some Japanese officers that were on hand. As he left, he brushed off the Viet Minh again and headed to Saigon by car. He had no idea who they were.

General Gracey was informed that the city was "fairly quiet, and half under the control of the Japanese who only acted when they felt like it," while the Viet Minh claimed to control the city, but had no power. An intelligence report, based on French sources, told him that the Viet Minh were an "Annamite government army" that consisted of a "very large hooligan element out to make mischief, many of whom were criminals of the worst type."

General Gracey received reports that Peter Dewey was running around the city talking to all sorts of groups, including the Viet Minh. He was collecting intelligence as ordered. A British historian later wrote that "the activities of the OSS detachment were so blatantly subversive to the Allied command that within forty-eight hours of his arrival Gracey felt compelled to summon its chief, Lieutenant-Colonel Peter Dewey, to appear before

[37] Bartholomew-Feis, pp. 268-269.

him." The General berated him, insisting to be informed of all of his activities.

With a small contingent of 1,800 men, General Gracey began to get nervous. So, he decided to give guns to 1,400 French POWs. As they received these weapons, they were told to go to a designated rendezvous point for orders. Instead, they decided to release their pent up angst by going to the center of Saigon, where, armed with guns, they looted Vietnamese homes and stores. They were tired of taking orders, and feeling controlled, all the time by foreigners. Filled with drink, they then raised the French flag over public buildings and attacked Vietnamese in the streets in a vicious French riot. [38]

General Gracey declared martial law, proclaiming a death penalty for any acts of sabotage, or disorder. He shut down all Vietnamese newspapers, but let the French newspaper keep printing and the French radio station keep playing. The Vietnamese planned mass demonstrations in protest. The French, though, beat them to the punch as French soldiers took over the police stations, treasury, and telegram offices in a French coup. They went to the city hall, shooting down Viet Minh sentries outside of it, and took over.

---

[38] Bartholomew-Feis, pp. 280-285; Archimedes Patti, *Why Vietnam?: Prelude to America's Albatross* (California: University of California Press, 1980), pp. 315-317.

"The French who had lived in fear for three weeks rejoiced their moment of victory had arrived, so also their moment of revenge. Instantly they reacted as one savage mob on the rampage. Banding in gangs of three, four, six, and even more, French men and women roamed the streets of Saigon in search of Vietnamese. They found many still unaware of the French coup and set upon them savagely with sticks and fists," wrote Patti, "for most victims the beatings were severe, some were maimed for life. In general, after the beatings, the victims were pushed and shoved into cars or trucks and sent to the nearest jail for the crime of being Vietnamese."

General Gracey did nothing, and said nothing, but Associated Press reporters witnessed the spectacle and made it headlines all over the world. Peter Dewey sent a note to General Gracey in protest. The British General ignored him, so, Dewey then sent notes to his superiors. In response, Gracey declared Peter Dewey persona non grata, ordering him to leave Saigon, as soon as possible.

Mortars exploded throughout Saigon, as the whole city descended into chaos, and an insurrection began in the surrounding countryside. The Viet Minh stormed the prison and freed everyone. In London, a senior Foreign Office diplomat saw a huge problem. He did not want to back the French in Vietnam in fear of alienating China and fueling anti-colonial opinion in the United States. Nor did he want to retreat. So, he proposed "to get French troops into southern Indochina with upmost dispatch, and, after turning it over to them, to withdraw our forces as soon as possible."[39]

An American reporter announced that he was "returning immediately to Hanoi to inform the American commission there on what is happening in the south to avoid bloodshed in Tonkin. The French are following a bad road and as for the British they have lost their heads to have done what they have done."

Peter Dewey made arrangements to flee by plane. Then he dispatched a note to his superiors stating, "Cochinchina is burning, the French and British are finished here, and we ought to clear out of Southeast Asia." He then jumped in a jeep and headed for the airport with Herbert Bluechel, an OSS team member under his command.

Dewey encountered a barricade of two logs blocking the road. The jeep had enough room to get by, so he slowed down to drive around it. A machine gun opened fire. Bullets tore thru Dewey and he slumped in his seat dead. The jeep swerved to the right side of the road and flipped over. Dewey's body landed on top of Bluechel, who jumped from the wreckage and was able to run away and escape.

---

[39] Karnow, p. 165; Patti, pp. 309-320.

They had been attacked by the Viet Minh by mistake. Bluechel filed a report stating that Dewey "was ambushed and killed through being mistaken of a nationality other than American. If the jeep in which he was riding at the time of the incident had been displaying an American flag I feel positive that the shot would not have been fired. A flag was not being displayed in accordance with verbal instructions by General Gracey."[40]

In Patti's view, "Gracey seemed to be a man without a plan. He merely reacted to events as they occurred, neither anticipating them nor appreciating their impact after the fact. His reaction in the case of Dewey's death was to order the arrest of Field Marshal Count Terauchi, not because the Japanese were responsible for the incident, but because Gracey had to react."

As the situation deteriorated, the British, though, asked the Japanese army to help them fight back the Viet Minh. They agreed. General Douglas MacArthur told a reporter, "If there is anything that makes my blood boil, it is to see our allies in Indochina and Java deploying Japanese troops to reconquer these little people we promised to liberate. It is the most ignoble kind of betrayal."

Soon a new French general arrived, with an army, and the British went home. The Chinese Nationalists handed over their occupied part of the

---

[40] Bartholomew-Feis, pp. 289-295.

country to them. With World War II over, men like Archimedes Patti went back home, but not before Ho warned him that if the French want to return to Vietnam "as imperialists to exploit, to maim and kill my people" they will face a "scorched earth to the end." The OSS itself disbanded. The French fought a war against Ho Chi Minh and Giap for almost ten years and lost. [41]

Things could have gone very differently. "Ho Chi Minh was on a silver platter in 1945," remembered Archimedes Patti, "we had him. He was willing to, to be a democratic republic, if nothing else. Socialist, yes, but a democratic republican. He was leaning not towards the Soviet Union, which at the time he told me that USSR could not assist him, could not help him because they just — won a war only by dint of real heroism. And they were in no position to help anyone."

"So really, we had Ho Chi Minh, we had the Viet Minh, we had the Indochina question in our hand, but for reasons which defy good logic we find today that we supported the French for a war which they themselves dubbed 'la sale guerre,' the dirty war, and we paid to the tune of 80 percent of the cost of that French war and then we picked up 100 percent of the American-Vietnam War," said Patti.

"In my opinion, the Vietnam War was a great waste. There was no need for it to happen in the

---

[41] Patti, pp. 4, 322, 325.

first place. At all. None whatsoever," Patti said, "during all the years of the Vietnam War no one ever approached me to find out what had happened in 1945 or in '44. In all the years that I spent in the Pentagon, Department of State in the White House, never was I approached by anyone in authority. However, I did prepare a large number, and I mean about, oh, well over fifteen position papers on our position in Vietnam. But I never knew what happened to them. Those things just disappeared, they just went down the dry well, as far as I was concerned, even though I was in a high-level position to be able to see that they got to the right people."

In 1973, he was able to contact the Central Intelligence Agency and get a hold of his old reports on Vietnam that he sent to the United States. He could tell that "they had never been opened, they had never been looked at. So then the question arises from time to time as to whether or not the same situation doesn't apply to Iran, to Afghanistan, to El Salvador, to any other trouble spot in the world," Patti said, "that perhaps there are people who may know the causes that actually led to what followed, and have never been approached, or asked to give at least, if not their views, at least to give what facts they have. That is a question."[42]

[42] Archimedes Patti interview, 1981, *Vietnam: A Television History Program: Roots of War*, http://openvault.wgbh.org/catalog/vietnam-bf3262-interview-with-archimedes-l-a-patti-1981, accessed 1/02/2014.

The war state bureaucrats had their own plans for Vietnam, and didn't feel a need to learn anything about the history of Vietnam, or discover what the wishes of the people of Vietnam were when they made their decisions. They didn't even bother to glance at the intelligence reports that the men that were there in Vietnam, such as Lt. Colonel Patti, sent home to them. They made their decisions, and that was that. And their decisions brought death and disaster, even though they did have a peculiar logic to them. One day Robert McNamara would make his bombing recommendations. Decades afterwards, as an old man at eighty-five years of age, he would look back on the Vietnam War and explain, "How much evil must we do in order to do good? We have certain ideals. Certain responsibilities. Recognize that at times you will have to engage in evil, but minimize it."[43]

---

[43] *The Fog of War: Eleven Lessons from the Life of Robert S. McNamara*, dir. by Errol Morris (Sony Pictures Home Entertainment, 2004 dvd)

CHAPTER II - THE FRENCH "RATHOLE"

Before John F. Kennedy became president of the United States, he served in the United States Senate for the state of Massachusetts. And before that, he was a congressman. In 1951, he took a Congressional trip to Vietnam, with his brother Robert Kennedy, his sometimes sidekick, who a year later would work as a tough prosecutor, and also help him win his Senate seat.

By 1951, the French had been fighting Ho and Giap for over five years of fierce bloody combat in a colonial war to control Vietnam. By the end of that year, they would suffer 90,000 casualties, including both the dead and injured, in the conflict. In China, Mao Zedong and his communist army had beaten Chiang Kai-shek's Nationalist army for control of that country. Laos and Cambodia remained firmly in the hands of governments tied to France, while Chiang Kai-shek fled to Taiwan, where he formed the Republic of China.

Harry Truman was president at the time, and under his leadership, the United States had emerged out of World War II as one of the world's two superpowers, along with the Soviet Union. Together the two nations had split the world in half in a Cold War confrontation. The United States was funding France's war in Vietnam, and would end up financing 78% of its effort, while several hundred thousand American troops were fighting Chinese and North Korean troops in the Korean War in defense of South Korea to a stalemate at the 38th parallel.

As soon as the thirty-four year old bachelor John Kennedy, and his brother, stepped off the airplane that took them to Saigon, they heard what sounded like gunfire. Kennedy asked what the sound was. "Small arms fire. Another attack by the Viet Minh," he was told. Robert and John Kennedy discovered that Vietnam was a war zone. They were told not to leave Saigon by car, because at night the Vietminh controlled all of the roads outside of the city.

In fact, as soon as the war started, the French lost control of most of the country. The French occupied cities along Route 1, the main national road that went up and down the coast of Vietnam, but could not go far off of that route safely. They recalled some Vietnamese noncommissioned officers who had served with the French military before 1945 to form a small officer corps, as there had been no such officers before. Most such Vietnamese were organized into auxiliary units that manned fortified outposts along the main roads, while the French did the larger fighting.

But, almost the entire Vietnamese population opposed them, and the Vietminh had complete control of the countryside. Tran Ngoc Chau, who fought against the French, recalled that "this fight went on openly in the country, secretly in the French-controlled cities. We received all our supplies and intelligence from deep inside areas supposedly under the rule of France. Groups of people from those French-controlled areas often visited us. Our military intelligence personnel infiltrated such locations regularly, disguised as normal civilians. They often talked to French soldiers, usually in restaurants and bars. Many bar girls and prostitutes worked for our cause."

Constant harassment against the French with grenades, mines, sniper fire, and ambushes took place. Unable to stop this resistance, "French reaction after these ambushes and attacks was merciless. They burned houses and killed or captured Vietnamese unlucky enough to be found. Women and young girls routinely were raped; many suffered group rape and died or were traumatized for the rest of their lives. Some were killed as they tried to escape the horror," wrote Chau.

People tried to live normally inside the cities, but when the Kennedy brothers came to Saigon they quickly noticed anti-grenade nets over terraces and restaurants. People were nervous everywhere. The Viet Minh had bases just twenty-five miles outside of Saigon, launching attacks on towns all around it. After they settled into the fancy French Majestic Hotel, the next morning John Kennedy sought out Associated Press Saigon bureau chief Seymour Topping to get his take on the war.

Topping told him that the French were losing, with, probably, no chance of winning. He told Kennedy that Ho Chi Minh was the leading Vietnamese nationalist and had an unlimited supply of men. Whenever the French killed his soldiers new ones just took their place. He also controlled the borders with China and was getting supplies from Mao Zedong. Kennedy asked Topping what the Vietnamese thought of the United States. The journalist told him that, at the end of World War II, the Americans were popular everywhere, but now that they have supported the French they were hated.

Kennedy then talked with Edmund Gullion, the American Charge de Affairs of its Saigon embassy, who pretty much confirmed to him the reporter's description of the situation. He then met with U.S. minister Donald Heath and the commanding French General Jean de Lattre de Tassigny, who both talked of victory. Kennedy was skeptical, though, and Tassigny sent a formal complaint against him to the American embassy for expressing his doubts.

When he came back home, Kennedy gave a speech to the Boston Chamber of Commerce in which he declared that "in Indochina we have allied ourselves to the desperate efforts of the French regime to hang on to the remnants of empire. There is no broad general support of the native Vietnamese government among people of that area. To check the southern drive of communism makes sense, but not only through reliance on the force of arms. The task is rather to build strong native non-communist sentiment within these areas and rely on that as a spearhead of defense rather than upon the legions of General de Tassigny. To do this apart from and in defiance of innately nationalist aims spells foredoomed failure."

Kennedy had not just stopped in Vietnam, but toured the rest of Asia and India also. In a radio interview, he said that what was clear to him from visiting these countries was that colonialism was going to become a thing of the past. The way he saw it, "this was an area of human conflict between civilizations striving to be born and those desperately trying to retain what they have held for so long." In places like Vietnam, "in which the fires of nationalism so long dormant have been kindled are now ablaze... Here colonialism is not a topic for tea-talk conversation; it is the daily fare of millions of men. This is also an area of revolution, which manifests itself at times in bloody riots and assassinations, in bloody guerilla war... and pitched battles and full-scale modern war."

Robert Kennedy told their father that Vietnam "doesn't seem to be a picture with a very bright future." He said that their trip had made a huge impact on his brother, John Kennedy, because it showed him "the importance of associating ourselves with the people rather than just the governments, which might be transitional, transitory; the mistake of the war in Indochina; the mistake of French policy; the failure of the United States to back the people."[44]

The war wasn't popular in America, nor in France by then either. The United States came into history as thirteen British colonies that declared their independence from England. Americans had a tradition of opposing colonialism. Many that went to fight in World War II did so with the goal

---

[44] William Gibbons, *The U.S. Government and the Vietnam War, Part I: Executive and Legislative Roles and Relationships* (New Jersey: Princeton University Press, 1986), p. 93; Fredrik Logevall, *Embers of War: The Fall of an Empire and the Making of America's Vietnam* (New York: Random House, 2012),pp. xi-xiv; Tran Ngoc Chau, *Vietnam Labyrinth: Allies, Enemies, & Why The U.S. Lost The War* (Lubbock: Texas Tech University Press, 2012), pp.34-37; Arthur Schlesinger, Jr., *Robert Kennedy And His Times* (New York: Ballantine Books, 1978), pp. 99-100; Richard Mahoney, *JFK: Ordeal in Africa* (New York: Oxford University Press, 1983), pp. 14-15.

to not only defeat the Axis enemy of Japanese, Germans, and Italians, but to create a better world, one in which a global war, such as World War II, would never be fought again. They were liberators, who sought to make colonial and imperial rivalries a thing of the past, but in Vietnam the United States government was supporting French colonialism, in what seemed to be a contradiction to American values.

In the closing months of World War II, the situation in Vietnam was fluid. OSS men Archimedes Patti and Peter Dewey held true to the deceased President Roosevelt's anti-colonial sentiments. State Department experts Abbott Low Moffat and Edwin Stanton argued that Indochina served as a key "source of raw materials, a potential market for exports, and a strategic base in the Far East" and thought that a restoration of French colonialism "would poorly serve American interests."

In 1946 Moffat, who was head of the Division of Southeast Asian Affairs in the United States Department of State, went to Vietnam and visited with Ho Chi Minh. He reported back that "Ho spoke of his friendship and admiration for the United States and the Americans he had known and worked in the jungles." "Before I left, Ho gave me letters to President Truman and the Secretary of State, the usual kind of stuff that he handed to everybody," he remembered, "I brought them back and did what you'd expect me to do: I filed them away, because our government was just not interested."[45]

His superiors above him simply didn't know much about Vietnam or care about it. As the war came to a close, French Premier Charles De Gaulle insisted that the United States back its venture in Vietnam. He told the U.S. ambassador to France, Jefferson Caffery, that "if the public here comes to realize that you are against us in Indochina there will be terrific disappointment and nobody knows to what that will lead. We do not want to be Communist; we do not want to fall into the Russian orbit, but I hope that you do not push us into it."[46]

The men at the top of the State Department decided that the United States had to fall in line with France. "We in Southeast Asia division and the Far Eastern office," Moffat said, "on the other hand were very conscious of the tremendous surge of nationalism that had taken, was taking place, had already started before the war, and now had been thrust forward at accelerated speed during the war. That was disregarded by the, ah, European division, I think, or they discounted it. I remember one senior official saying to me one day, 'Why are you fussing with Indonesia? That's nothing but a Dutch

---

[45] Dixee Bartholomew-Feis, The *OSS And Ho Chi Minh: Unexpected Allies In The War Against Japan* (USA: University Press of Kansas, 2006), pp. 303-304.
[46] Gibbons, p. 18.

colony,' and another one was talking about this nationalist movement and he said, 'Oh, well that's just the result of Japanese propaganda.'"

Moffat had read the OSS reports on Ho Chi Minh and saw that "all the reports were very, very, favorable. We knew he was a communist, but we also felt, as they did, and the way anybody who has known, ever met Ho Chi Minh, who I've ever talked with had the same feeling - he was first a nationalist, and second, a Communist. That is, he was interested in getting the independence of his people and then he felt probably the best thing for them was the communist type of government. But he was a nationalist first and foremost."[47]

"With French forces back in Indochina and with all potential leverage gone, there was little that the United States could do to alter the outcome," said Moffatt. So, the United States could only observe the situation. Then on March 6, 1946, Ho Chi Minh and France came to an agreement. The Vietnamese agreed to "welcome amicably" the return of the French army to northern Vietnam, while France agreed to recognize the "Democratic Republic of Vietnam" as a "free state" in the French empire.

[47] Abbott Moffatt interview, 1982, *Vietnam: A Television History Program: Roots of War*, , http://openvault.wgbh.org/catalog/vietnam-8a2551-interview-with-abbott-low-moffat-1982,accessed 1/02/2014.

It became nothing more than a cease fire. Negotiations broke down over the meaning of independence, so France shelled the port of Haiphong killing 6,000 people. Ho and Giap in turn attacked French forces in Hanoi, as the French occupied the city, and then disappeared into the countryside. Ho Chi Minh told Jean Sainteny, "you will kill ten of my men while we kill one of yours, but you will be the ones to end up exhausted." These events marked the start of what would be known as the "First Indochina War."

Ho predicted to an American that "it will be a war between an elephant and a tiger. If the tiger ever stands still the elephant will crush him with his mighty tusks. But the tiger does not stand still. He lurks in the jungle by day and emerges by night. He will leap upon the back of the elephant, tearing huge chunks from his hide, and then he will leap back into the dark jungle. And slowly the elephant will bleed to death. That will be the war of Indochina." In 1947, the French talked former puppet emperor Bao Dai into coming back to the country to lead a new government of their own creation.[48]

Some Americans nicknamed Boa Dai the "night club emperor" who, according to the Pentagon Papers, "for all practical purposes, remained outside

[48] Gibbons, p. 26; William Duiker, *Ho Chi Minh: A Life* (New York: Hyperion, 2000), pp. 379-380.

the process of government." One American diplomat who got to be friends with him thought, "Bao Dai, above all, was an intelligent man," but "he was too congenial, and he was almost pathologically shy, which was one reason why he always liked to wear dark glasses. He would go through depressive cycles, and when he was depressed, he would dress himself in Vietnamese clothes instead of European ones, and would mince no words about the French. His policy, he said to me on one of these dour occasions was one of 'grignotage,' or 'nibbling,' and he was painfully aware of it." This official thought the French had control of him thanks to "some blackmail on him, about his relationship with gambling enterprises in Saigon and his love of the fleshpots."[49]

As for Ho Chi Minh, in the first years of the war he had about 60,000 troops, and a million local guerilla fighters, led by Giap. The Viet Minh general saw the war taking three stages. During the first stage he would remain on the defensive in order to build his strength, in the second, as his forces began to equal those of the French, he would launch surprise attacks on enemy troops, and installations, and suddenly retreat to attack again, and then, in the final stage of the war, he planned to launch a general offensive to drive the French forces into the ocean, but he got very little help

49 *The Pentagon Papers*, Gravel Edition, Volume 1 (Boston: Beacon Press, 1971), pp. 59-60.

from the outside world in the beginning of the war. [50]

Ho Chi Minh acted as an international diplomat for the Viet Minh, but he had no direct contacts with the Soviet Union in the first few years of the war. The Russians were too busy rebuilding their country, and consolidating their position in Eastern Europe, to care much about what was happening in Vietnam. What is more, Joseph Stalin simply did not trust Ho, because he didn't think he was an orthodox communist that would readily obey his dictates. The fact that he tried to ally himself with the United States at the end of World War II was evidence to Stalin that Ho was not someone he could count on. The Soviet dictator did not even grant diplomatic recognition to Ho Chi Minh's "Democratic Republic of Vietnam."

Ho Chi Minh finally traveled to Moscow in 1950, as Stalin and Mao Zedong signed a treaty of alliance, but, after Ho suggested to Stalin that they should sign a similar treaty together, Stalin told him that it would not be possible since Ho was on a "secret" mission to Moscow. Ho said that the Russians should then get a helicopter and fly him to their airport to give him a lot of publicity, so his trip would be known throughout the world. Stalin brushed him off by saying, "Oh, you Orientals. You have such rich imaginations."

---

[50] Duiker, p. 394.

According to Nikita Khrushchev, Stalin treated Ho in an "offensive, infuriating" manner. At a later meeting, Stalin pointed to two chairs in a room and said, "Comrade Ho Chi Minh, there are two chairs here, one for nationalists and one for internationalists. On which do you wish to sit?" Ho replied, "Comrade Stalin, I would like to sit on both chairs."

Stalin was a mass killer and a notorious negotiator. Harry Truman called him "smart as hell." Mao told his people that "getting something from Stalin is like taking meat from the mouth of a tiger." Stalin would finally grant diplomatic recognition to Ho's government shortly after he formed his alliance with China. He told Ho, "our surplus materials are plenty, and we will ship them to you through China. But because of limits of natural conditions, it will be mainly China that helps you."

As promised, China kept the Viet Minh army well supplied with arms and a spattering of soldiers to serve as advisors. In contrast to the more pragmatic Ho Chi Minh, Mao Zedong was a hardcore Stalin style communist, who would starve and murder tens of millions of people in an attempt to modernize his country in what he called a "Great Leap Forward" and "Cultural Revolution" with not an ounce of sympathy for those that suffered. His advisors would have a huge impact on the leadership ranks of the Viet Minh by spreading his ideas to them.[51]

The United States understood, early in the war, that Ho Chi Minh was not acting under the control of Joseph Stalin. However, as the Cold War began, officials in the government began to view the entire world in "us versus them" terms. At the end of World War II, the collapse of colonial powers, such as England and France, and the destruction of the Axis Powers, created power vacuums throughout the world. The Soviet Union created a series of buffer states in Eastern Europe, while the United States shored up the rest of Europe through aid programs such as the Marshall Plan, covert activities in Greece, Italy, and Turkey, and alliances such as NATO to prevent the Soviet Union from gaining influence over other countries in Europe.

This strategy became known as the "containment" policy, and was announced to the public in a speech by President Harry Truman, in March of 1947, known as the "Truman Doctrine." In it Truman explained that he was giving aid to Greece and Turkey in order to "support free peoples who are

---

[51] Duiker, pp. 421-423; Michael Swanson, *The War State: The Cold War Origins of the Military-Industrial Complex and The Power Elite, 1945-1963* (South Carolina: CreateSpace, 2013), p. 63.

resisting attempted subjugation by armed minorities or by outside pressures."[52]

Before World War II, the United States did not have a policy of intervening throughout Europe, much less the rest of the world, nor did it have a Central Intelligence Agency, with the authority, under "plausible deniability," to interfere in the internal affairs of other governments. Nor did it have a sizable military or devote a massive portion of its budget to a military-industrial complex.

World War II transformed the United States and its position in the world. It in effect became not only a global superpower, but also an empire. Few Americans today understand this turning point in the history of their country, and it's a story that I explain in great detail in my earlier book *The War State: The Cold War Origins of the Military-Industrial Complex and The Power Elite*.

Yes, it is true that the United States had fought in several major wars before World War II, but after all of these previous wars ended it demobilized its forces. For example, in the 1930's, before the start of World War II, the entire U.S. army consisted of only 140,000 soldiers. In 1934, the military budget for the war department was only $243 million dollars, and the whole army only owned eighty semiautomatic rifles with most soldiers using out of date 1903 bolt-action Springfield rifles.

[52] Gibbons, p. 27.

In 1935, supplies were so low that Army Chief of Staff General Douglas MacArthur set a "hopeful" goal of stockpiling enough ordinance for a thirty-day supply of ammunition. In 1940, the military only had eighty tanks and forty-nine bombers.

By the end of World War II, the United States produced over 88,000 tanks and self-propelled guns, 257,000 artillery pieces, 2 million machine guns, 97,000 bombers, 99,000 fighter aircraft, 22 aircraft carriers, 8 battleships, and over 400 destroyers and cruisers. The enormous war production brought an economic boom to the United States that took the unemployment rate down from 14.6% in 1940 to 1.2% in 1944. At the end of the war, the United States had spent over $840 billion dollars in constant 1940 dollars or $13.59 trillion in inflation adjusted 2012 dollars. Defense spending also reached 36% of GDP and 86% of all federal government spending by 1944. The huge military spending created a whole new class of corporate business elite tied into the defense industry and dependent on government outlays.[53]

All of the American forces that fought in World War I came home after the war ended, but, after World War II, the United States formed permanent military bases in Europe and stayed as Joseph Stalin kept his armies in control of Eastern Europe. By 1949, the United States had succeeded in creating a

---

[53] Swanson, pp. 13-16.

recovery in Europe and had also succeeded in "containing" the Soviet position there.

George Kennan, one of the top experts on the Soviet Union in the Department of State, had first come up with the "containment" doctrine, even inventing the phrase. But, he saw it as a way to simply respond to Soviet expansionism after World War II, not as a concept that should apply to the entire world, or be used to justify unlimited military spending. He objected to the "sweeping nature of the commitments" applied by the "Truman Doctrine" speech.[54]

Instead, a group inside of the Truman administration, led by Secretary of State Dean Acheson, decided to consider every single country in the world as either an ally of the Soviet Union or as an ally of the United States. They left no room for a country to decide to be neutral, believing that a neutral nation should be considered as a potential enemy whose government should somehow be turned towards the United States.

Dean Acheson made empire the official policy of the United States in NSC-68, a secret document he commissioned, signed by President Truman on April 15, 1950, and declassified in the 1970's, which stated that that "even if there were no Soviet Union we would face the great problem of the free society,

[54] Gibbons, p. 28.

accentuated many fold in this industrial age, of reconciling order, security, the need for participation, with the requirement of freedom. We would face the fact that in a shrinking world the absence of order among nations is becoming less and less tolerable." The document called for a new arms build-up and portrayed the entire world as one of an arena of competition between that of the Soviet Union and the ideology of communism versus the United States and the forces of freedom.

By 1953, three-fourths of the entire federal budget became earmarked to national security programs. Defense spending came to equal eighteen percent of the nation's entire gross national product, a full one-third of the country's business activity. In the first two decades of the Cold War, the country put sixty-percent of its federal budget into defense spending.

These policies turned the United States into an imperial world power, transforming it into a war state. These changes happened slowly, behind the scenes, so they didn't really hit public consciousness until President Eisenhower warned about them in his famous farewell address about the military-industrial complex. Not much has changed today. In fact, the military-industrial complex and the war state are more powerful than ever. Today's American national security officials simply talk about preventing terrorism and general world disorder as a reason for their active intervention throughout the planet and their support of the federal government's giant military budget instead of a communist threat. Their methods and means are basically the same, even though their justifications for them have changed.[55]

In the 1950's they spoke of a battle for the future of the "Third World." Like the words "Cold War," the words "Third World" were never used before World War II either. After the war, the phrase was used to describe the parts of the world in Africa, Asia, and Latin America that had formerly been colonies of one of the European powers. American officials claimed to be in a battle with the Soviet Union for the future of these "Third World" nations as they jettisoned their colonial past to become independent nations, a process that went on till the 1970's, with the final states being formed in Africa out of the collapse of colonialism.

The United States sought not to crudely exploit areas of the world, like the European colonial powers before them did, but, as the historian Odd Arne Westad put it, to "control and improve" them. Those that did not go along with the program were declared to suffer from communist subversion, whether real or imaginary. They became marked for intervention, usually by the Central Intelligence Agency, while compliant allies were given foreign aid.

---

[55] Swanson, pp. 85-91.

American war state bureaucrats believed that the destiny of the entire world lay in their hands. In 1955, State Department official Joseph Jones rhetorically asked "what indeed are the limits of United States foreign policy? The answer is that the limits of our foreign policy are on a distant and receding horizon; for many practical purposes they are what we think we can accomplish and what we think are necessary to accomplish at any given time."[56]

After World War II, the United States government knew that Ho Chi Minh "seemed to have no visible ties with Moscow." In 1948, the State Department gave an official appraisal to the American ambassador in China, which stated that the "Dept has no evidence of direct link between Ho and Moscow but assumes it exists... Ho seems quite capable of retaining and even strengthening his grip on Indochina with no outside assistance other than continuing procession of French puppet govts."[57]

Using binary logic, the State Department assumed Ho was working for Stalin, because he was not working for the United States and by then he was fighting against France, which was an ally of the United States. In the battle for the "Third World" he was not in the right camp. Once the Soviet Union formally acknowledged Ho Chi Minh's

---

[56] Odd Arne Westad, *The Global Cold War* (New York: Cambridge University Press, 2010), pp. 1-5, 25.
[57] *The Pentagon Papers, Vol 1.*, pp. 33-34.

government, Secretary of State Dean Acheson declared, "The recognition by the Kremlin of Ho Chi Minh's communist movement in Indochina comes as a surprise. The Soviet acknowledgement of this movement should remove any illusions as to the 'nationalist' nature of Ho Chi Minh's aims and reveals Ho in his true colors as the mortal enemy of native independence in Indochina."[58]

David Bruce, the U.S. Ambassador to France, cabled home that it was now time to deal with Vietnam "in a completely cold-blooded fashion." A State Department "working group," put together by Dean Acheson, declared that the United States had to now support France's effort in Vietnam "or face the extension of Communism over the remainder of the continental area of Southeast Asia and, possibly, further westward." Harry Truman promptly gave diplomatic recognition to the Bao Dai government in Vietnam and sent France $10 million dollars in military assistance in 1950. It would soon fund 78% of its war expenses in Vietnam to the tune of a billion dollars in 1954.

To provide the strategic rationale for these policies, President Harry Truman approved NSC-64, which declared that "the neighboring countries of Thailand and Burma could be expected to fall under Communist domination if Indochina were controlled by a Communist-dominated government.

---

[58] *The Pentagon Papers, Vol. 1*, p. 51.

The balance of Southeast Asia would then be in grave hazard." Back in Saigon, Edmund Gullion warned that if the Viet Minh won then "most of [the] colored races of [the] world would in time fall to Communists sickle."[59]

This type of thinking became known as the domino theory. Its clearest articulation is in NSC 124/2, which claimed that in the region "the loss of any single country would probably lead to relatively swift submission to or an alignment with communism by the remaining countries of this group. Furthermore, an alignment with communism of the rest of Southeast Asia and India, and in the longer term, of the Middle East (with the probable exceptions of at least Pakistan and Turkey) would in all probability progressively follow. Such widespread alignment would endanger the stability and security of Europe."[60]

Assistant Secretary of State Dean Rusk summed up the situation this way, "it is generally acknowledged that if Indochina were to fall under control of the Communists, Burma and Thailand would follow suit almost immediately. Thereafter, it would be difficult if not impossible for Indonesia, India, and others to remain outside the Soviet-dominated Asian bloc."[61]

---

[59] Gibbons, pp. 62-67.
[60] *The Pentagon Papers, Vol. 1*, pp. 83-84.
[61] Gibbons, p. 88.

A debate hidden from the public broke out inside the government over NSC 124/2. A first draft for NSC 124/2, created by the State Department, stated that if China intervened in Vietnam, and put the French position in danger, then the United States should go to the United Nations and send troops of their own, just like they did in Korea to bolster the French forces. The Joint Chiefs of Staff objected to this policy, claiming that they would not be able to win such a limited war in Vietnam if China sent troops in.

The Joint Chiefs of Staff responded to the State Department with a position paper that claimed that in order to intervene with any success in such a scenario they would have to take the war directly to China. That could mean nuclear weapons. If they had to do such a thing alone then the "political, economic, and military costs - would be tremendous - and the decision would strongly affect future U.S. global strategy." It wouldn't be worth it. They were not itching for a dangerous general war. So, the chiefs recommended that if China were to intervene in Vietnam it might be best to only help the French evacuate from the area. To get everyone on board policy directive NSC 124/2, Dean Acheson had its final version focus on the internal situation in Vietnam as the "primary threat," with military aid to the French as the answer.[62]

When asked by a reporter why the United States was supporting the French in Vietnam, President Dwight Eisenhower explained, "you have broader considerations that might follow what you would call the 'falling domino' principle. You have a row of dominos set up, you knock over the first one, and what will happen to the last one is the certainty that it will go over very quickly. So you could have a beginning of a disintegration that would have the most profound influences." This is how the importance of Vietnam was explained to the public.[63]

President Eisenhower, and successors Kennedy, and Johnson, all invoked the domino theory at times in speeches in support of American involvement in Vietnam. After the war, many writers argued that the domino theory led the United States to support the French, later sending troops of their own, and escalating the war in Vietnam into disaster. The domino theory made the assumption that if Vietnam went communist it would automatically become a satellite of the Soviet Union and China,

---

[62] Doris Condit, *History of the Office of Secretary of Defense: Volume II, The Test of War, 1950-1953* (Washington, D.C.: Department of Defense, 1988), pp. 214-217, http://permanent.access.gpo.gov/gpo21475/OSDSeries_Vol2.pdf, accessed 1/04/2014.
[63] *The Pentagon Papers, Vol 1.*, p. 597.

with other countries would following suit. However, nations are not bowling balls. They are individual entities with their own unique historical dynamics. What happens in one nation does not automatically create new conditions in another one. In fact, after the Vietnam War was over, China launched a border war against it in 1979, thereby making a mockery of the idea that the Viet Minh were merely Chinese puppets.

Yes, some who argued against the domino theory also held some mistaken beliefs as well. To believe that adherence to the faulty domino theory caused the Vietnam War suggests that American officials simply had bad ideas when it came to the world, operating under a set of rigid ideological assumptions that came to be rejected once the war was over. If they didn't believe in the domino theory then the Vietnam War would have never happened this argument would lead you to believe, it was just bad mistakes.

However, the real reasons for American intervention in Vietnam is more complicated than that, because there is plenty of evidence to prove that none of the policies of the presidents was actually motivated by the domino theory, and, in fact, as you will see in the course of this book, all of them at one time or another actually repudiated it in public or in private. Dean Rusk, who went on to become secretary of state and a war hawk, said in 1968 that he "never used the domino theory," while

McGeorge Bundy, who served as the national security advisor for both Presidents Kennedy and Johnson would state that when it came to dominos "I never believed that."

It was a theory presidents used to explain their policies to the public and a rationale used by war state bureaucrats to push for their own national security policies in the maintenance of empire and the credibility of American military power. It was pure power politics. The political scientist Robert Jervis sees the "domino theory" as the result of "motivation bias." By this he means a way to rationalize a policy for reasons that are too painful to acknowledge, or would not seem to be legitimate to the public.[64]

Those in government who believed it simply believed it because they liked what it meant for them. The world is a complex place and it is impossible to know everything about it or to predict the future. Most people in the United States, including those in the Pentagon and the State Department, had never been to Southeast Asia or Vietnam. They really had no idea what was really going on there. A concept like the domino theory allowed them to see themselves, and the United States as an extension

---

[64] Gareth Porter, *Perils Of Dominance: The Imbalance Of Power And The Road To War In Vietnam* (Los Angeles: University of California Press, 2005), pp. 230-241; Robert Jervis, *Perception And Misperception In International Politics* (Princeton: Princeton University Press, 1976), pp. 390-391.

of themselves, as simple defenders of freedom locked in an end of the world defensive struggle, instead of as power expansionists. For those that really believed in the domino theory, they did so not because of any real evidence for it, but because it was attractive to them. It served as an abstract principle that provided an easy explanation for a complex world, and gave them a righteous role in it, but it wasn't the real reason for the country's engagement in Vietnam.

To put things another way, the domino theory did not cause the United States to carry out a massive arms build-up, station troops throughout the world, or to finance France's war in Vietnam. The United States first supported France, because it was its ally. It wanted to make sure it stayed within the orbit of its NATO alliance. It also did so as part of its imperial struggle for control of the "Third World." The domino theory was just a simple rationale for all of these policies put together after the fact.

Robert McNamara and McGeorge Bundy later made their recommendations to escalate the war in Vietnam to President Lyndon Johnson for more unsavory reasons. The truth is foreign policy decisions are rarely made for one single reason, but instead are generally sold to the public with a single slogan. As Dean Acheson put it, "leadership requires understanding, responsibility, discipline.

The flatulent bombast of our public utterances will lead no one but fools."[65]

However, American leaders were uneasy about supporting Bao Dai, and the French, because to do so meant to associate the United States with the stigma of colonialism, which they saw as a dying fragment of the past. This led John Kennedy to doubt the French effort as a young congressmen visiting Saigon in 1951. Such concerns were widespread throughout the Congress.

During a Senate hearing for the 1952 bill to aid the French in Indochina, Senator Theodore Greene said that he thought the "principal ambition" of the Vietnamese was to "get rid of the French." He thought "the problem that faces us is can we, without the expenditure of an enormous military force of money and men, ever subdue this feeling of nationalism?"[66]

On November 18, 1952, Dwight Eisenhower met with Harry Truman and his advisors before succeeding him as president of the United States. They discussed many subjects, but when they got to Vietnam Dean Acheson told him that the war in Indochina wasn't going so well. He said that even though the French lacked "an aggressive attitude from a military point of view in Indochina," the "central problem" there was "fence-sitting by the

---

[65] Swanson, p. 73.
[66] Gibbons, p. 119.

population." Many doubted that the Vietnamese would ever go with the French, unless they were truly granted independence. President Eisenhower and his Secretary of State John Foster Dulles, who was the brother of CIA Director Allen Dulles, sought to support the French and take steps to shore up an anti-communist movement in Vietnam in case the French withdrew.

President Eisenhower told his men at a National Security Council meeting that he had "the firm belief" that unless the French appointed an effective military commander, and told the Vietnamese that they were going to give them their independence, that "nothing could possibly save Indochina, and that continued United States assistance would amount to pouring our money down a rathole." Vice-President Richard Nixon, agreed.

The next day, Ike told the Prime Minister of Canada that "the only chance of preserving South East Asia lay in making sure of the support of native peoples. He went on to say that regulars can't win against guerrillas who have indigenous support."

Air Force Chief of Staff General Hoyt Vandenberg relayed to the State Department, and the CIA, that the Joint Chiefs of Staff reported "that the French have not really been taking the native people into their confidence. They don't seem to trust the native forces enough to want to use them in large units and they only plan on using native forces in very small units. The whole French position seems to be a defensive one and one of not really wanting to fight the war to a conclusion. I feel that if the French keep up in this manner, we will be pouring money down a rathole."[67]

However, the Eisenhower administration saw no alternative to supporting the French. When they presented a 1953 bill for $400 million in aid to Indochina it quickly passed the House, but provoked a storm of controversy in the Senate. Republican Senator Barry Goldwater of Arizona presented an amendment to the bill that required the French to make "an immediate declaration" to set a target date for the "complete independence" of the countries in Indochina before they could get the money.

Goldwater explained that he had become convinced that the war could only be won if the Vietnamese were given their freedom. He said that the people of Vietnam "have been fighting for the same thing for which 177 years ago, the people of the American colonies fought," and "yet here today, on the floor of the United States Senate, we are proposing to support a country, France, that has colonial intentions; we are going against the wonderful second paragraph of our Declaration of Independence... We are saying to the great men who penned that document and whose ghosts haunt these walls,

---

[67] Gibbons, pp. 120-127.

that we do not believe entirely in the Declaration of Independence, that perhaps all men are not created equal, that perhaps they are not endowed by their Creator with certain unalienable rights, and that perhaps we have a right to support countries which wish to enslave other peoples."

Senator Goldwater said he was worried that, if the Vietnamese were not given freedom, the French would lose and then the United States would take their place and send troops to Vietnam. If the Vietnamese were not granted independence, then "as surely as day follows night our boys will follow this $400 million," he claimed.

Senator Everett Dirksen agreed. He asked of the Viet Minh, "What makes them so tough? What is the force that makes them resist? It is an ideological force. It is the nationalism which they preach. They do not preach communism. They preach nationalism and freedom. If they can do that, does anyone believe that sending additional planes, or $400 million worth of equipment there, is likely to do the job, when there are still so many official fence-sitters who believe that Ho Chi Minh will win, and who are waiting for that day?"

The Senate Republican and Democratic leaders came together to block Goldwater's amendment on the grounds that they should not interfere with the executive branch when it comes to foreign policy decisions and feared that it would discourage the

French and cause them to leave Vietnam. Republican Majority Leader William Knowland demanded that Barry Goldwater withdraw his amendment, telling him that even if it was voted on and defeated that it would show to the Vietnamese that "we did not hope that ultimately they might gain their freedom."

Senator John Kennedy agreed with Goldwater's thoughts, so he came up with a substitute amendment that ordered that all money sent to Indochina "shall be administered in such a way as to encourage through all available means the freedom and independence desired by the people of the Associated States, including the intensification of the military training of the Vietnamese." It was defeated 17-64 after assurances by Eisenhower administration officials that they would work towards these goals without it.

Some in the administration wanted the United States to get more involved in Vietnam, but people feared it would be "another Korea." According to Admiral Arthur Radford, who became Chairman of the Joint Chiefs of Staff in 1953, "officials of State and Defense estimated that there was no indication that public opinion would support a contribution to the Indochina war other than the current aid program. American military participation, they said, would not be acceptable to the public."[68]

---

[68] Gibbons, p. 129-134.

Nonetheless, the French position in Vietnam got worse and they came to Washington asking for more money. They wanted an additional $385 million for 1953 on top of the $400 million that had already been earmarked for them with the goal of using it to launch a giant offensive against the Viet Minh under the command of General Navarre. The general informed his own government in a secret report that he did not think he could actually win the war, but hoped to cause a stalemate.

President Eisenhower's National Security Council approved the aid. When they informed members of the Senator Foreign Relations Committee some of them went through the roof. Thurston Morton, the Assistant Secretary of State for Congressional Relations, remembered when he told Senator Richard Russell about it the Senator said, "You are pouring it down a rathole; the worst mess we ever got into, this Vietnam. The President has decided it. I'm not going to say a word of criticism. I'll keep my mouth shut, but I'll tell you right now we are in for something that is going to be one of the worst things this country ever got into."[69]

The money did not help and the Navarre offensive turned into a disaster. Giap began his third and final phase of his war against the French by massing 50,000 of his men around a garrison of 16,000 French troops stationed at Dien Bien Phu, a

[69] Gibbons, pp. 137-139.

valley deep in the mountains of northwestern Vietnam near the Laotian border. The Chinese supported Giap with advisors, 200 trucks, 10,000 barrels of oil, 100 artillery pieces, and 1,700 tons of grain. Thousands of supporters traveled up, and down, the mountains to carry the supplies to Giap's men by bicycle and by foot.

Chinese General Wei Gouqing told Giap that he should do a giant "human wave" assault on the French position, like the Chinese used against the Americans in Korea. They massed their forces against the French ready to attack on January 26, 1954, but then Giap had a change of mind. The night before the attack was to begin, he couldn't close his eyes. He got hit by a terrible headache. He didn't want to waste men. Ho had told him to attack if he thought he could win, otherwise do nothing.

The next morning, he told General Gouqing "if we fight, we lose." He ordered his troops to pull back from their attack positions and prepare to obey a new directive of "Steady Attack, Steady Advance." Some of the Chinese complained that Giap lacked "Bolshevik spirit." But, as Giap later wrote, "in taking this correct decision we strictly followed the fundamental principle of the conduct of a revolutionary war; strike to win; strike only when success is certain; if it is not, then don't strike."

Giap decided to trap the French army with a siege to destroy them. It took weeks to prepare. He ordered his troops to dig a network of several hundred miles worth of tunnels, and trenches, surrounding the French position so they could move at will without exposure to French firepower. At the same time, he had giant artillery pieces disassembled, then secretly carried all of the way up to the top of mountains by hand, and into caves, where they were reassembled to rain shells down on the French position.[70]

The Central Intelligence Agency gave the White House a National Intelligence Estimate, which predicted that, even if the Navarre campaign turned out to be a success, it would fail "to achieve a complete military victory in Indochina." The best that could be hoped for was to "aim at improving their position sufficiently to negotiate a settlement."[71]

The Eisenhower administration was split on what to do. Secretary of State John Foster Dulles, Vice-President Richard Nixon, and Joint Chiefs of Staff Chairman Admiral Radford talked of using the United States military to support the French. The other Chiefs of Staff disagreed. General Matthew Ridgeway, the Army Chief of Staff, gave the

---

[70] Duiker, pp. 453-454; Fredrik Logevall, *Embers of War: The Fall of an Empire and the Making of America's Vietnam* (New York: Random House, 2012), pp. 420-424.
[71] Gibbons, p. 148.

National Security Council a position paper that argued that it would take hundreds of thousands of American soldiers to make a difference in Vietnam and it "is not militarily desirable." He claimed that even if they dropped an atomic bomb on Giap's forces near Dien Bien Phu they would still need to send all of these troops to Vietnam to control the country. Such a drain on forces would require pulling men out of Europe, thereby weakening American power in a more vital area.

As Giap began to move his forces into position, according to notes of a National Security Council meeting, President Eisenhower said that he "simply could not imagine the United States putting ground forces anywhere in Southeast Asia, except possibly in Malaya, which one would have to defend as a bulwark to our off-shore island chain. But to do this anywhere else was simply beyond his contemplation. Indeed, the key to winning this war was to get the Vietnamese to fight. There was just no sense in even talking about United States forces replacing the French in Indochina. If we did so, the Vietnamese could be expected to transfer their hatred of the French to us. I cannot tell you, said the President with vehemence, how bitterly opposed I am to such a course of action. This war in Indochina would absorb our troops by divisions!"[72]

---

[72] *The Pentagon Papers, Vol. 1*, pp. 89-93; Gibbons, p. 153.

President Eisenhower ordered his advisors to prepare for the possible withdrawal of the French from Vietnam. To do that they had to make the "loss" of Indochina acceptable to the public, so they began to repudiate the domino theory. Speaking at an executive session of the Foreign Relations Committee, Under Secretary of State Walter Bedell Smith said, "I want now to retract the statement that I thought of Southeast Asia, as like one of those house of cards that children build, and if you knock one of them out, the whole structure collapses. Well, I do not believe that now, that is, I am not prepared to and I would not say that now. I think that, even at the worst, part of Indochina might be lost without losing the rest of Southeast Asia. One can think of the possibility of an area defense pact which might include Thailand as the bastion, Burma, and possibly Cambodia."[73]

Giap began his attack on the French on March 13, 1954, with a massive artillery barrage and attack on a French fortification. It was destroyed in a flash. The artillery barrage took the French by complete surprise, because they never imagined that the Vietnamese would be able to move their artillery pieces up the mountain. The French artillery commander found that he was unable to counter fire on the Vietnamese artillery position. Believing

[73] Gibbons, pp. 156-157.

he had dishonored the French army, he went into his dugout, and killed himself with a grenade.

So many shells rained down on the French airstrip that it became almost impossible to land planes on it for resupply. The French position grew precarious as the siege continued on for weeks. General Paul Ely, the French Chief of Staff, went to Washington to plead for help at the invitation of Admiral Radford.

As soon as he arrived in Washington, Radford invited him to his house for dinner. Among those there were John Foster Dulles, his brother CIA director Allen Dulles, and Vice-President Richard Nixon. These men would lobby to get the United States military involved in the war. Richard Nixon met with a group of editors from the American Newspaper Association, telling them, in what amounted to a trial balloon for war, that "if this government cannot avoid it, the administration must face up to the situation and dispatch forces." In a National Security Council meeting he asked whether it might be wise to use atomic bombs to save Dien Bien Phu. He was told it would take three to wipe out the Viet Minh forces surrounding the French position, but President Eisenhower said he doubted they could actually win a war there after using them.[74]

---

[74] Logevall, pp. 492-493, 499.

Right before General Ely left the United States, Admiral Radford held a final one on one meeting with him to tell him that he had a plan he called Operation Vulture. The Admiral said it would be up to the President, but he could get "as many as 350 aircraft operating from carriers" brought into battle within forty-eight hours. He hoped to blow Vietnam and the Viet Minh forces to bits.[75]

The New Yorker magazine reported that Secretary of State Dulles was now conducting "one of the boldest campaigns of political suasion ever undertaken by an American statesmen." Congressmen, reporters, and television talking heads were being "rounded up in droves and escorted to lectures and briefings on what the State Department regards as the American stake in Indochina." Dulles was telling them "we should not flinch at doing anything that is needed to prevent a Communist victory."

Admiral Radford polled his fellow Joint Chiefs of Staff on whether the United States should bomb the Viet Minh. All four of the other Chiefs said no. Only Radford wanted to do it. Army General Mathew Ridgway refused to answer the question in writing, saying that it was only right for the President to ask it and he thought the poll inappropriately "involved the JCS inevitably in politics."

John Foster Dulles drew up a draft Congressional resolution to give President Eisenhower the

---

[75] *The Pentagon Papers, Vol. 1*, p. 97; Gibbons, pp. 172-173.

authorization to use the military to "assist the forces which are resisting aggression in Southeast Asia." When Dulles showed it to the President, Ike said that he would sign it only if he took it to the Congressional leadership and got them to develop it first.

Admiral Radford presented the Joint Chiefs of Staff with a new document asking them whether they wanted to intervene in Vietnam. This time he told them it came from Secretary of War Charles Wilson. Once again, they said no. This time, General Ridgway presented him with a position paper that stated, "From the military viewpoint, the outcome of the Dien Bien Phu operation, whichever way it might go, would not in itself decisively effect the military situation there. If recommended and executed, intervention by United States armed forces would greatly increase the risk of general war."

General Shepard, the Commandant of the Marines, said the Viet Minh "simply do not offer us a target which our air will find remunerative." General Twining said it only made sense to intervene if the French granted "true sovereignty" to the Bao Dai government and agreed to let the United States "train and organize indigenous forces and indigenous leadership."

Dulles and Radford met with Senate leaders armed with Dulles's draft resolution. General Ridgway showed up. Senator Albert Gore, Sr., recalled "that Admiral Radford was strongly in favor of intervention, as were Mr. Dulles and others. But the one strong opponent from within the administration was the then head of the U.S. Army, General Ridgway. He strongly opposed it, and utilized some of what may have been, within the military circles, rather trite phrases about the unwisdom of the United States becoming involved in a land war in Asia."

After Radford outlined a plan for an air strike, Senator Clement asked if the other members of the Joint Chiefs of Staff approved it.

Admiral Radford answered "no."

"How do you account for that?"

"I have spent more time in the Far East than any of them and I understand the situation better."

Senator Lyndon Johnson asked John Foster Dulles if he had consulted with Great Britain or any other allies on this? He said he hadn't.

According to a Washington Post story titled "The Day We Didn't Go To War", "in the end, all eight members of Congress Republicans and Democrats alike, were agreed that Dulles had better first go shopping for allies. Some people who should know say that Dulles was carrying, but did not produce, a draft of the joint resolution the President wanted Congress to consider."[76]

President Eisenhower then met with Radford and Dulles and told them that there was no way he was going to war in Vietnam without allies, without "active British Commonwealth participation," and without Congressional approval. The Army gave President Eisenhower a Planning Board report that said that they would have to send 500,000 men to Vietnam to be effective there and that "the use of atomic weapons in Indochina would not reduce the number of ground forces required to achieve a military victory." His chief of staff Sherman Adams later said, "having avoided one total war with Red China, the year before in Korea when he had United Nations support, he was in no mood to provoke another one in Indochina by going it alone in a military action without British and other Western Allies."[77]

Nevertheless, rumors spread on Capitol Hill that forces inside the Eisenhower administration were still moving towards war. Several Senators walked into the Senate to give a series of speeches in opposition. Senator John Kennedy led the group stating, "I am frankly of the belief that no amount of military assistance in Indochina can conquer an enemy which is everywhere and at the same time

---

[76] Gibbons, pp. 182-194.
[77] *The Pentagon Papers, Vol. 1*, p. 101; Gibbons, p. 199.

nowhere, an enemy of the people which has the sympathy and covert support of the people." He said that he hoped that John Foster Dulles "will recognize the futility of channeling American men and machines into that hopeless and internecine struggle."

Several Senators congratulated John Kennedy for his speeches, including Republican Senate Majority Leader William Knowland. Other Senators said they would support sending troops to Vietnam, but only if they went with the British in a show of "United Action." Even more important than this public debate, though, was one held in private.

At a closed-door meeting of the Senate Democratic Policy Committee, chaired by Lyndon Johnson, it became clear that the Democratic Party as a whole was lined up against intervention. George Reedy, Jr., an assistant to Lyndon Johnson, said, "It was a fascinating meeting. Walter George was there, and very obviously there to play devil's advocate, and to argue that we should go into Indochina. Of course, Walter George was a very commanding personality in the Senate. Nobody liked to be disrespectful to him. I have never seen a group of men explode like that, especially [Senator] Bob Kerr. George said something like, 'if we don't go in we will lose face,' and Bob slammed that fist of his down on the table saying, 'I'm not worried about losing face; I'm worried about losing my ass.'"

Lyndon Johnson told Eisenhower about the opposition to war.[78]

In one final gambit, John Foster Dulles, though, flew to Great Britain to try to get them on board a plan of "United Action" for Vietnam, but failed to sell them on it. Not wanting war, Ike may have purposely given Dulles an impossible task. British Foreign Secretary Anthony Eden thought it was a stupid idea. First, he thought that bombing would not cause China "to withdraw her support from the Viet Minh," and, after it failed, we would have "to withdraw ignominiously or else embark on a warlike action against China." Secondly, British intelligence reports claimed that the United States was giving more aid to the French than China was to the Viet Minh and, therefore, even if China stopped its support of the Viet Minh, it wouldn't make much of a difference anyway. Nor did he think Vietnam mattered much in the big picture, arguing that the domino theory held no validity.[79]

On May 7, 1954, the remaining French forces at Dien Bien Phu surrendered. Close to 12,000 of them became prisoners of war. The garrison represented ten percent of France's manpower in the war. Thirty-six years later, Giap looked back on the battle and what would have happened if the United States had intervened with bombers. "No doubt we

---

[78] Gibbons, pp. 205-207.

[79] *The Pentagon Papers, Vol. 1*, pp. 101-103; Logevall, pp. 483-484.

would have had problems," he said, "but the outcome would have been the same. The battlefield was too big for effective bombing. Only a lunatic would have resorted to atomic weapons, which in any case would have devastated the French troops."[80]

Two days after the fall of Dien Bien Phu, Secretary of State John Foster Dulles held a morning meeting at his home. His assistants, Robert Bowie and Douglas MacArthur II, attended, along with Admiral Radford and his aide George Anderson. Undersecretary of Defense Robert Anderson also came. The topic was the Vietnam situation and what it meant in the big picture.

It wasn't mere dominos that were at stake. The situation wasn't just the idea that if Vietnam were to go Communist then reds inside Thailand, or any other neighboring country, would seize power. What was at stake was much bigger than that, it was nothing more than the destiny of billions of people in Asia and the Pacific. Who would be the dominant power in that giant area of the globe? Would it be the United States or China? At the moment, the United States had an overwhelming strategic superiority over China. It had nuclear weapons, while China had yet to successfully detonate an atomic bomb, and wouldn't until October 16,

---

[80] Stanley Karnow, *Vietnam: A History* (New York: Penguin Books, 1991), p. 214.

1964. This gave the United States a large freedom of action in the region for the time being and the men in the room knew it.

According to notes taken at the meeting, Admiral Radford said that "the only military solution was to go to the source of the Communist power in the Far East, i.e. China, and destroy that power. The point was made that the true source of the power of the international Communist conspiracy was Russia, to which the Admiral assented, making the point that three or four years from now the balance of military power between the Soviets and the U.S. will have shifted in the former's favor because they will then have sufficient stockpile of nuclear weapons which, although numerically less than the U.S. stockpile, will give them the necessary capability to initiate and carry on general war on favorable terms. The Admiral indicated that he did not believe we would at any point in the future be confronted with as clear-cut a basis for taking measures directly against China as was the case now in Indonesia." In 1971, Admiral Radford would tell a reporter that his real purpose in pushing for Operation Vulture was to provoke a military reaction from China that would draw the United States into war with it while the time was right. The potential to deploy bombers armed with nuclear weapons gave the United States a clear advantage against China. These bombers represented total power.

Dulles said he was now looking to build alliances against China and communists in the region that would deter war, because the political environment made war inconceivable. Although the other members of the Joint Chiefs of Staff were not in support of Admiral Radford's views, there were elements inside of the Pentagon bureaucracy that were in synch with them. Army Brigadier General Charles Bonesteel, who served on the National Security Council Planning Board, put together a position paper which stated that if war is to come it would be best to consider it now, because of "the steadily increasing Soviet capabilities in nuclear warfare and the consequent steady diminution of the present military advantage of the U.S. over the U.S.S.R., these increased risks can more surely and safely be accepted now than ever again." Bonesteel argued that the Soviets and Chinese were getting stronger in terms of military power with each passing month, so the point would eventually come in which the United States would no longer be able to carry out threats against them. "Asia could thus be lost," he declared.[81]

Some on the inside found such war talk very disturbing. Robert Stevens, the Secretary of the

[81] John Prados, *Operation Vulture* (New York: I Books, 2002), pp. 253-254; *The Pentagon Papers, Vol. 1*, p. 506; Leslie Gelb and Richard Betts, *The Irony of Vietnam: The System Worked* (Washington, D.C.,: The Brookings Institution, 1979), p. 57.

Army, sent a memo to the Secretary of Defense saying, "I am becoming increasingly concerned over the frequency of statements by individuals of influence within and without the government of the United States that air and sea forces alone could solve our problems in Indo-China, and equally so over the very evident lack of appreciation of the logistics factors affecting operations in that area." It would require untold numbers of army troops to provide base protection for such forces. He then went on to go into great detail why he thought to wage such a war "would be a basically faulty military decision." It would mean trying to win a conflict against a "large native population, in thousands of villages, most of which are about evenly divided between friendly and hostile."[82]

On May 9, 1954, John Foster Dulles announced at a press conference that he no longer thought that the domino theory was valid when it came to Vietnam. He said that, if Vietnam were to fall to the Viet Minh, it would not necessarily lead to the spread of communism throughout Southeast Asia and into the South Pacific. He now thought that "Southeast Asia could be secured even without perhaps Vietnam, Laos, and Cambodia." He said that the latter two countries were "important, but by no means essential," because they were such poor countries with small populations, and he did not

---

[82] *The Pentagon Papers, Vol. 1*, pp. 508-509.

want people to think that neither he nor the president were going to "give up in despair."[83]

Vietnamese, French, British, Korean, American, and Chinese diplomats convened in Geneva, Switzerland to approve an official cease fire for the Korean War and to negotiate a settlement between the French and the Viet Minh over Vietnam. Despite the fact that the Viet Minh had defeated the French on the battlefield, Soviet and Chinese diplomats pressured them into agreeing to a partition of the country.

The Vietminh would take control of Vietnam north of the 17th parallel, while the government supported by France would control the area south of the line. The two sides would then agree to vote, in July of 1956, to reunite the country. Both parties signed the agreement, with the Viet Minh forces retreating to the north, while the French went south. The United States acknowledged the agreement, but refused to put its signature on it.

Secretary of State John Foster Dulles did not want the United States to sign something that amounted to a defeat to communism. He also wanted to give the United States the freedom to take steps to support the forces in South Vietnam and later "roll back" the Viet Minh. He had no intention of allowing the Geneva elections to occur, because, as Walter Bedell Smith predicted, if they

[83] *The Pentagon Papers, Vol. 1*, p. 106.

did Ho would get over 80% of the vote "as Bao Dai was corrupt and the French still continue to impose colonialism."

At a National Security Council meeting, Dulles said that it would be "best to let the French get out of Indochina entirely and then to try to rebuild from the foundation" ourselves. The secretary of state claimed that they could "salvage something from Southeast Asia, free of the taint of French colonialism." He thought in the South "it would be necessary to build up indigenous forces, and to give some economic aid."[84]

As the dust settled from Geneva, people inside the national security bureaucracy took a big picture look at the real strategic meaning of Vietnam for the United States. The NSC planning board wrote a position paper for President Eisenhower's consideration titled "Statement of Policy Proposed by the National Security Council on Review of U.S. Policy in the Far East" going through various scenarios for the country and how the United States should now deal with the reality of a North and South Vietnam. It argued that the division of Vietnam made for a victory for China, and a "loss of prestige" for the United States, that threatened its power throughout Asia and the Pacific.

---

[84] *The Pentagon Papers, Vol. 1*, p. 165; Gibbons, pp. 240, 251-252.

It recommended, among other things, that a warning should be issued to China that, if it were to interfere in South Vietnam, or other nations in the region, such a move "will not be tolerated and that its continuance would in all probability lead to the application of military power not necessarily restricted to conventional weapons against the source of the aggression." The paper also said that South Vietnam, and other nations in Southeast Asia, should receive any assistance necessary if they encountered "local subversion." It advocated going to Congress so that the president could get a blank check "to attack Communist China in the event it commits such armed aggression" with full "U.S. freedom to use nuclear weapons."

It then listed a range of actions from trying to engage with China, and separate it from its alliance with the Soviet Union, to making threats of war "to confront the regime with a clear likelihood of U.S. military action against China proper unless Communist China takes public action to change its belligerent support of Communist expansion." The president would then have to be "be prepared and determined to carry out the threat of military action unless China backs down on the issue involved," even though "this means general war."[85]

---

[85] Document 283, *Foreign Relations of the United States, 1952-1954. East Asia and the Pacific: Volume XII, Part 1,*

President Eisenhower used this position paper to convene a full meeting of the National Security Council to debate the proper course of action for the United States to take in Southeast Asia and unite the entire national security bureaucracy together under one policy on August 18, 1954. Among those at the meeting were John Foster Dulles, Vice-President Richard Nixon, CIA Director Allen Dulles, a representative of the Treasury Department, and Admiral Radford of the Joint Chiefs of Staff.

This was not a meeting for press releases and the public. Vague concepts for the public imagination such as the domino theory, democracy, and human rights were not discussed. It was a top-level meeting in which the reality of world power politics were seen to be in play and openly discussed. It focused on the question of whether China would end up in control of Asia in a few decades or if the United States and its free world allies would.

President Eisenhower began the meeting by saying that he thought that, if "local subversion" began in South Vietnam, it would be difficult for the United States "to intervene" with any success, but "if such subversion were the result of Chinese Communist motivation" that he "would be quite

---

U.S. Department of State; accessed 4/7/2014 http://history.state.gov/historicaldocuments/frus1952-54v12p1/d283#fn13.

right in seeking Congressional authority for the United States to intervene."

His national security assistant, Robert Cutler, said that the Joint Chiefs of Staff saw China as the "heart of the problem for U.S. policy in Asia" and not the Soviet Union or some small local communist group. It was China that was the big competitor for the future control of Asia. Cutler then went through the several alternatives outlined in the position paper used as the basis from the meeting from a "soft policy," which he described as "representing the objective of peaceful coexistence," to "tougher" policies designed "to prevent by force any further expansion of Communist control in Asia."

Cutler said that most of the Joint Chiefs of Staff recommended "alternative C," which called for warning the Chinese that force would be used to stop any further expansion of communist influence in Asia, and then reacting to any such move they make with force. He noted, though, that Army Chief of Staff General Matthew Ridgeway was displeased with this recommendation. Recommendation D called for risking general war.

Secretary of State John Foster Dulles argued that at this point in time it would be impossible to carry out the most belligerent of recommendations that carried the risk of war with them, because they simply had no allies who would support such moves.

Joint Chiefs of Staff Chairman Admiral Radford said that, despite what Ridgeway has stated, all of the chiefs are united in the view that no "piece-meal" war in Asia is possible. "The heart of the problem confronting U.S. policy in Asia was how to handle Communist China. A solution of that problem by all odds provided the best planning basis for the Joint Chiefs of Staff," he said.

According to notes of the meeting, Radford said that he "was very skeptical of any policy based on trying to split Communist China and the Soviet Union. We had been trying to do precisely this ever since 1950, and with very scant success. He thought that the tie-up was something religious in nature, and he doubted the possibility of breaking it. Accordingly, if China continued to be Communist and continued to increase its power in mainland Asia, Japan would soon have no other course than to accommodate itself to Communism. In short, there would be no way to prevent all Asia from going Communist if Communist China's power continued to expand. With regard to our allies, it was, said Admiral Radford, obviously important to have them with us, but it might be necessary, in defense of the vital security interests of the United States, to act without our allies."

"As for the soft policy in Alternative A, continued Admiral Radford, this appeared to him as merely an invitation to Communize all Asia. As for Alternatives B, C and D, so far as he could see they really didn't differ a great deal from each other, since if the United States undertook to carry out the policies in Alternative B or C, the situation envisaged in Alternative D would almost certainly come to pass, whether we liked it or not." Radford in essence thought peace with China was impossible and war one day was inevitable, because China was an expanding power in Asia that would eventually control the whole region and displace the United States unless it was destroyed first. The only way to do that right would be to go to war before it developed atomic weapons of its own.

Radford said what he and the rest of the Joint Chiefs of Staff wanted to know was "whether it is the national aim of the United States to have a friendly non-Communist China, or whether it is the aim of the United States to accommodate to a Communist China over a long period of time?"

President Eisenhower responded by saying, "there was no argument in his mind at all. In his view, it was hopeless to imagine that we could break China away from the Soviets and from Communism short of some great cataclysm. In any event, we should not count on such a split, although history did seem to indicate that when two dictatorships become too large and powerful, jealousies between them spring up. Then, and only then, is there a chance to split them apart."

Secretary of State Dulles said, he was "inclined to believe that over a period of perhaps 25 years China and Russia would split apart because of the pressure of basic historical forces and because the religious fervor of Communism would have died down. The Chinese were very proud of their own history, and Chinese did not like Russians. In the end, therefore, they would split apart; the problem for us was whether we could play this thing for 25 years. Could we afford to wait that long for a split between these two enemies?"

Vice-President Richard Nixon said that he "was at least convinced that China was the key to Asia. It was the great dynamic force in Asia and for that reason we could well afford to take a month to make up our minds finally on how to handle Communist China."

Ultimately, though, Nixon thought "we would have to face the final decision whether to adopt a hard or a soft policy toward Communist China. Personally, he did not believe that any soft policy would work over the period of the next 25 or 50 years. On the contrary, he believed such a soft policy would result in complete Chinese Communist domination of Asia. All that, however, was a problem for the experts to decide. Let the current policy stand as it is until Secretary Dulles and other experts in the field can come up to the Council with a considered judgment, perhaps in a month or so."

"What preoccupied him," Secretary Dulles responded, "was to avoid getting the United States into a war which the whole world would believe we were wrong to be in. This did not mean, of course, that we should run away from anything or everything that might involve us in war with Communist China." "On the other hand," Secretary Dulles reiterated that he "did not wish to see the United States become involved in a major war where world public opinion would be wholly against the United States, because that," he said, "was the kind of war you lose. World public opinion was a tremendous force which must be reckoned with."

President Eisenhower agreed, saying that the United States "could not afford to become involved in such a war even if the rest of the world would declare simply for neutrality."

As the meeting neared its end, President Eisenhower, and those who attended, agreed to policy recommendation C, which consisted of warning the Chinese not to expand into other nations in Asia and to react with force if it did.[86]

---

[86] Document 305, *Foreign Relations of the United States, 1952-1954. East Asia and the Pacific: Volume XII, Part 1,*

President Eisenhower had little interest in getting the nation involved in a war in Asia or Vietnam. He said at a national security meeting just days before this one that defense spending in the United States had already reached a maximum point. The nation had to be careful "to stick to a system of defense that could be sustained for 40 years if necessary, in order to avoid transforming the U.S. into an armed camp," he said. If defense spending led to huge budget deficits inflation could explode and the nation would be turned into a garrison state that demolished private enterprise as a result. He said he was "frankly puzzled by the problem of helping defeat local subversion without turning the U.S. into an armed camp." Aid to nations encountering local subversion was one thing, but getting the United States involved in another war made him very uncomfortable.[87]

Although many in Washington were not happy with Geneva, neither were the leaders in North Vietnam either. Ho, Giap, and the Viet Minh had defeated the French on the battlefield and splitting Vietnam in two was a bitter pill for them to swallow, but their Chinese and Soviet allies gave them

---

U.S. Department of State; accessed 4/7/2014 http://history.state.gov/historicaldocuments/frus1952-54v12p1/d305.
[87] Document, 297, *Foreign Relations of the United States, 1952-1954. East Asia and the Pacific: Volume XII, Part 1*, U.S. Department of State; accessed 4/7/2014 http://history.state.gov/historicaldocuments/frus1952-54v12p1/d297.

no choice. Stalin had died and new Soviet leaders wanted to try to bring about a thaw in the Cold War. They didn't really care too much about what happened in Vietnam and believed that creating a buffer state out of North Vietnam would be enough to secure China's security needs.

Nikita Khrushchev, who became the premier of the Soviet Union, just didn't spend much time thinking about Indochina. He went to Indonesia once and that was enough for him. He said he "found the climate almost unbearably hot, damp and sticky. I felt like I was in a sauna the whole time. My underwear stuck to my body, and it was almost impossible to breathe." So, he never accepted a trip to North Vietnam.

Khrushchev said that he liked Ho. "I've met many people in the course of my political career," he explained, "but Ho Chi Minh impressed me in a very special way. Religious people used to talk about holy apostles. Well, by the way he lived and by the way he impressed other people, Ho Chi Minh was like one of those holy apostles." The problem for the Soviets was that he was getting old and younger leaders in the Viet Minh were becoming more powerful. They tended to be closely aligned to Chinese style communism and wouldn't blindly take Soviet advice.

By 1958, Ho went into semi-retirement and began to act more as a figurehead and a diplomat than as a government decision maker in Vietnam. Vietnamese newspapers began to refer to him as Uncle Ho and play up China. At the same time, Soviet relations with China began to grow worse behind the scenes as Khrushchev, and the Soviet Presidium, tried to implement a policy of "peaceful coexistence" with the West.[88]

Zhou Enlai, who served as Premier of China under Mao, explained to Giap and Ho that they could not repeat in Vietnam what happened in Korea. Once the Americans intervened there, they had to send over a million troops to fight to a draw. "The central issue," he told them, "is to prevent American's intervention" to "achieve a peaceful settlement." The Chinese convinced Ho that the best he could do is form a new state in North Vietnam and hope for a collapse in the south, otherwise he risked American intervention.[89]

Ho replaced the Viet Minh war slogan "Resistance to the end," with "Peace, unity, independence, democracy." The new state of the Democratic Republic of Vietnam formed behind the footsteps of the Viet Minh Army. The state and the army were now both united together with the ideological glue of communism and nationalism. At their top

---

[88] *The Pentagon Papers, Vol. 1*, p. 134; Aleksandr Furensko and Timothy Naftali, *Khrushchev's Cold War* (New York: W.W. Norton & Company, 2006), 324-328.
[89] Logevall, p. 597.

existed a ruling Central Committee. Ho sat on it, but younger men came to dominate it.

By 1957, Le Duan, who had served as a leader of the Viet Minh forces in the southern part of Vietnam during the war, became the acting General Secretary, which made him the most powerful person in the North Vietnamese communist government. The younger leaders sought to create a strong state by creating a land reform program, which they said should take the form of a Maoist "class war." They believed that if they could destroy "feudal elements" in their society, mainly large landlords, the former peasants would become absolutely devoted to the state and to them personally as their leaders.

Over twenty-thousand militants, under the training of Chinese advisors, went to "work with, eat with, and live with" the peasants. They forced large landowners off their land and executed thousands of others, some of whom had supported the Viet Minh, for treason. The rich had the option of going with the program or being killed for their disobedience to the state. "In my uncle's village, people persecuted him with zeal to show how ardently they supported land reform and to be in the good graces of the militant peasants now holding power. Others who had envied his wealth and influence now took pleasure in humiliating him," one person remembered.

Ho supported land reform, but said "it cannot be said of a group of people that they are all good or bad; to know who is good and who is bad, you must rely on the masses." He became troubled by the violence. He wrote in a government newspaper that certain militants, "are still committing the error of using torture. It is a savage method used by imperialists, capitalists, and feudal elements to master the masses and the revolution. Why must we, who are in possession of a just program, and a just rationale, make use of such brutal methods?"

The Central Committee members declared at a March, 1955, meeting that being too soft on land reform was riskier than being too harsh in carrying it out. At the end of the meeting, Ho said he was unhappy with the decisions being made. He said land reform is like hot soup, something that is best drunk slowly. One of his friends thought Ho had become appalled at what had turned into an indiscriminate campaign of terror, but was afraid to go against the Chinese officials now in North Vietnam and Mao Zedong himself. Ho had led the Viet Minh against the French and had been instrumental in creating the new Democratic Republic of Vietnam, but he did not rule the new North Vietnamese state. [90]

Secretary of State John Foster Dulles, and CIA Director Allen Dulles, had their own plans for

---

[90] Duiker, pp. 460, 474-480.

South Vietnam. Few people in Congress knew it, and probably not even everyone on the National Security Council did either, but the two brothers had been working with the "native leadership" of South Vietnam for years. A few weeks after the Geneva accords were signed, they ordered CIA agent Colonel Edward Lansdale to travel to Saigon as head of the CIA Saigon Military Mission. The charge of affairs in Saigon, Robert McClintock, told Washington that they should get rid of Bao Dai and get "regents" who "would in fact be figureheads and we would write their constitution." "To objections that this program is injurious to the theory of sovereignty I would reply," he wrote, "that Vietnamese will be far worse off under government presided by Ho Chi Minh and that in case of bankruptcy we now confront, bankers have right to organize receivership."

The Dulles brothers decided to make a man named Ngo Dinh Diem the Prime Minister of South Vietnam. Diem had been living in New Jersey, at a Catholic seminary, for the past three years, while touring up and down the east coast of the United States, lobbying to become the new ruler of Vietnam. They told him to pack his bags.

Diem hopped in an airplane and first made a stop in Paris, where he met with officials of the American embassy. "On balance we were favorably impressed," Ambassador Dillon cabled back, "but only in the realization that this Yogi-like mystic could assume the charge he is apparently about to undertake only because the standard set by his predecessors is so low." "We think one of the main weapons to use in driving Bao Dai into action is control of his Exchequer. Nothing impresses him as much as gold and we should endeavor to arrive at arrangement with the French on controlling that portion his income we can in order to enforce our objectives," he suggested.

Bao Dai agreed to appoint Ngo Dinh Diem Prime Minister of South Vietnam and faded into the shadows of history after Diem said that the Geneva agreements meant nothing, since he had never signed them himself and held a referendum to make South Vietnam into a Republic, with him as its president. Diem won by capturing 98% of the votes, including 380,000 votes more than the total number of registered voters, evidence of total voting fraud. The French withdrew their forces from Vietnam.

The Eisenhower administration invited Diem to Washington, to shore him up and show its support. President Eisenhower waited for him as he got off the plane. It was a gesture he had made only once before to greet a head of state and the two leaders held a news conference where Eisenhower declared, "You have exemplified in your part of the world patriotism of the highest order." Diem got a state dinner, addressed a joint session of Congress, and spoke to the National Press Club. The American news media raced against one another to praise him. The Washington Evening Star called Diem "Vietnam's Man of Steel," while the New York Times said he was "an Asian liberator, a man of tenacity of purpose, a stubborn man... bent on succeeding, a man whose life - all of it - is devoted to his country and his God." They called him a "miracle man."[91]

Robert Amory, then deputy director of the CIA, later said, "You know who first put Ngo Dinh Diem in power? This goes way back to 1954. I was at an after-theater party in Martin Agronsky's house - pleasant, a couple of scotches and some canapes - and got off in a corner with Mr. Justice [William O.] Douglas, and Douglas said, 'Do you know who's the guy to fix up in Vietnam? He's here in this country, and that's Ngo Dinh Diem.' Well, I wrote it down in my notebook on the way out as you know, Z-I-M Z-I-M. I came back and asked the biographic boys the next morning, 'dig me up anything you got on this guy.' 'We ain't got anything on this guy.' And the next morning meeting I said to Allen Dulles and Frank Wisner, 'A suggestion out of the blue...' But Wisner picked it up and looked at the thing. And that's how 'Ngo Zim Zim' became our man in Indochina."

[91] Logevall, pp. 674-676.

Through Diem, the two Dulles brothers planned to create a new nation that would stand in contrast with the communist state in North Vietnam and serve as an example of freedom on planet earth. They sought to control, and improve, the people of Vietnam in the struggle for mastery of the "Third World." Some would call this "winning hearts and minds." Communists called Diem a puppet of the United States, but as events unfolded the miracle man would prove to have a mind of his own.[92]

[92] Gibbons, pp. 259-262.

CHAPTER III - THE MANDARIN

Ho Chi Minh had a lot of respect for Ngo Dinh Diem. Bui Tin, a North Vietnam leader who went on to accept South Vietnam's surrender in 1975 at Saigon's Independence Palace, said, "although we criticized Ngo Dinh Diem publicly as an American puppet, Ho Chi Minh adopted a more sober appraisal. He realized Diem was a patriot like himself, but in a different way. Later many other people came to accept and value Diem as a leader who was imbued with the spirit of nationalism, and who lived an honest and clean life, and, like Ho Chi Minh, was unmarried."

Diem hated the French and spent much of World War II organizing a group called the "Association for the Restoration of Great Vietnam." After Ho Chi Minh took over in Hanoi, in the aftermath of the Japanese surrender, Diem got arrested by his forces. Diem had to have been frightened, because the Viet Minh had killed his anti-communist brother for opposing them.

"Why did you kill my brother?" Diem asked Ho as soon as he saw him.

"It was a mistake," Ho replied, "the country was all confused. It could not be helped." Ho asked him to join his government as his minister of the interior.

Diem said he might, but only if he was going to be let in on all of his decisions. Ho wouldn't agree to that. "I see it is useless to discuss matters with you while you are so irritable, but stay around awhile," Ho told him. The Viet Minh leader let Diem go out of respect. Later, he would say it was one of the biggest mistakes he ever made.

Why did Ho ask him to join him? The answer is Diem's personal history. Diem became minister of the interior for Bao Dai in 1933, at the age of 31, and was the son of the famous mandarin Ngo Dinh Kha, who was the headmaster of the National Academy in Hue, with family roots that went back hundreds of years to the first king of Vietnam. As a youngster, Diem was a serious student who never missed a day of school. He took from his father the lessons of nationalism and the Catholic faith. He made a vow of chastity and joined a monastery to become a priest, but dropped out. One of his brothers became a leading archbishop.

Diem became a district chief in Bao Dai's colonial Vietnam. In that position he dressed in a mandarin's robe while supervising construction projects and settling disputes among peasants. Most people of such authority took bribes, but Diem took none. As a result, his reputation grew, he found himself promoted to provincial chief, and then became the minister of interior. "You will lead this country one day," one man told him.

He only served a few months, though, as minister of interior. Bao Dai put him in charge of reforms, but when the French refused to delegate any real power to Vietnamese officials to be able to do anything he resigned his post. A French officer stripped him of all of his titles and academic credentials as punishment. "Take them! I don't need them, they are not important," Diem yelled back at him.[93]

Diem then returned to his hometown, where he spent the next few years reading books, going to church, and talking with anti-colonial nationalists. He fed his mind with a mixture of Catholicism and Confucianism. After World War II, he did not want to support the French, or the Viet Minh, so he waited for the emergence of a "Third Force" that would be independent of both. The French called people like him a "fence-sitter," while Ho's men claimed they were "hiding under a blanket."[94]

---

[93] Mark Moyar, *Triumph Forsaken: The Vietnam War, 1954-1965* (New York: Cambridge University Press, 2006), pp. 11-18.

[94] Edward Miller, *Misalliance: Ngo Dinh Diem, the United States, and the Fate of South Vietnam* (Cambridge: Harvard University Press, 2013), p.32.

In 1950, he found out that the Viet Minh had issued orders for his assassination. He left the country, traveling to Japan, France, and Italy trying to organize his own "Third Force," but had little success. So, he went to America. He had some help from an American political scientist named Stanley Fishel, whom he had once met in Tokyo. Fishel was conducting research there and also working for the military intelligence division of the U.S. Far East Command. Fishel would become one of Diem's biggest supporters in the United States.

Ngo Dinh Diem went to Washington, D.C., for meetings at the State Department. He gave them a proposal to create a Catholic militia to form the core of a new anticommunist army. The men he talked to were interested, but unimpressed. One wrote a report that said that they thought Diem was more interested "with furthering his own personal ambition than solving complex problems facing his country today." The man didn't understand Diem.

He spent a lot of time living in Catholic seminaries, and monasteries, building a network of Catholic supporters in the United States. He spent two years living in Maryknoll Seminary in New Jersey. Father John Keegan, who helped run it, later said, "We didn't know quite exactly what he was all about. He didn't seem to us to be very important. He did dishes with us, and people of importance didn't do that; students did that, or brothers did that, and here was Diem doing dishes at the tables with the rest of the students."

Diem was austere; once he became the leader of South Vietnam he owned only two suits and, despite living in a palace, slept on an army cot. He got to know Francis Cardinal Spellman of New York, Supreme Court Justice William Douglas, and Senators Mike Mansfield and John Kennedy, impressing them all. After Mansfield first met him, he left "with the feeling that if anyone could hold South Vietnam, it was somebody like Ngo Dihn Diem." He lived like a man who wanted to be known as a great incorruptible leader.

Stanley Fishel joined the faculty of Michigan State University and got Diem a job with the college as a consultant. It was starting a foreign aid project with the United States government. With the right American connections, he ended up on a plane back to South Vietnam to become its new premier. Bao Dai was still officially "Head of State" of the new country of South Vietnam, but lived in France as a figurehead. He appointed Diem to be his prime minister. Diem knew that to play that role properly he would need people to obey him.[95]

On June 25, 1954, Diem stepped off an airplane at Tan Son Nhut airport to a welcoming ceremony. Among those to greet him was the head of the

95 Miller, pp. 36-41; Moyar, p. 12.

French colonial army that was now in South Vietnam after the Geneva Conference, a member of Bao Dai's family, and Donald Heath, America's ambassador to South Vietnam. Reporters noted, though, that there were only a few hundred people that came to see him. The French general introduced him, but Diem didn't say anything after he spoke. He just got into a waiting limousine and took off. One reporter thought he looked nervous.

CIA agent Colonel Edward Lansdale, who would become one of Diem's closest collaborators, had planned to be at the airport to meet Diem, but noticed on his way there that the road to the airport was lined with people waiting to see him. He decided to stop to mingle with the crowd. When his limo came by the windows were closed. "The 'let down' feeling [among the crowd] was something tangible, obvious." Lansdale worried that Diem "had no instincts at all of politics and the people he was going to lead." He would spend hours advising him. Stanley Fishel came to help him too.

Lansdale had traveled around Saigon asking Vietnamese he knew what they thought about Diem before Diem arrived in Vietnam. "A number of them knew a great about him," Lansdale said, "and they either liked him fully and no holds barred, a hundred percent for him or a hundred percent against him. He was a man of controversy. Those who were for him said that he was a very honest person, very acceptable to them as being a person of intensely high morality. Those who didn't like him said he's stupid. So, they wouldn't fault him for anything other than they felt he didn't know enough. They felt that he wouldn't be corrupt, that he wouldn't condone graft - that he was a stickler, morally. But they all knew him."

Lansdale thought Communists could spread rumors that Diem was homosexual, since he was not married, so he thought he would try to fix him up. "I asked about the girlfriends he knew when he was growing up," Lansdale later said, "Yes. There was one girl he had been very much interested in. I made him promise he would call on this girl, take her for a boat ride down the Perfume River. When he came back, I said did you see her? Well, he replied, I went by and look at her house but couldn't get enough nerve to go to her door. Imagine. This man was president of his country. He was number one. He could have gone with armed guards and broken his way in if he wanted to. But with all that power, he was a shy, modest sort."

As Lansdale got to know Diem better, he found that he was "a man with a delightful sense of humor. Here he had been pictured all along as a remote mandarin type and he had a delightful wit. His humor was so dry that you'd have to look at him sometimes to catch whether he was pulling your leg or being sort of stupid about something, and I'd catch that little glint in his eye and...which reminds me, the man had a tremendous look of intelligence and spark of life in his eyes, they were the most important part of his features. There was always a sparkle and little gleam there and he'd catch the humor and so forth when he'd find something very funny and was holding himself in and sort of laughing inside at something."

"But the main thing about him was that he was getting over some habits that had been with him all of his life. I think that he mostly wanted to be a student-monk. To live in a monastery someplace and to do research and studies, with probably history was his major subject," Lansdale said, "his main work in those days at the Palace was done not in his office, not in any of the formal rooms of the administrative palace where he was, but in a little tiny alcove off of his bedroom, which...a place that two of us when we talked our knees would touch together."

"But he had all sorts of books, and official documents, and everything stacked from the floor to the ceiling, and he had a little tiny clear space on the table where he could do some writing," Lansdale said, "but so crowded in by books, and papers, and so on, that you hardly see how the man could work there. And I thought, well this is his monastery, this little monk's alcove, this is part of the man, the shy retiring person who has been forced into the limelight, and to the foreground, and doesn't really like it, but he's happiest when he's in a place like this."

Lansdale presented Diem with a giant desk ornament inscribed with the words "Ngo Dinh Diem - The Father of His Country." Colonel Fletcher Prouty, who worked in the Pentagon, recalled that Lansdale told him to go into Washington, D.C., and "purchase the biggest, gaudiest, and grandest desk ornament ever made... I went into the city and found what he wanted. As I recall it cost about $800.00, which I paid. Ed was delighted with the gift and promised to repay me as soon as he returned." "Diem needed to be George Washington," Lansdale recalled, "and I told him as much."

American journalists in Vietnam would go on to portray Diem as totally isolated from the people, and his reception by them at the airport when he first arrived as evidence of this fact. While he had spent years outside of the country, and the masses didn't know him, Diem was not alone. His brothers had built a familial power base for him in his absence. His brother, Ngo Dinh Thuc, was South Vietnam's most powerful religious leader as archbishop of Hue. Another brother, Ngo Dinh Can, was a powerful warlord in central South Vietnam in control of Phan Thiet Province up to the 17th parallel, where he had his own secret police network.

His most important brother was Ngo Dinh Nhu. He had been working for years preparing for

Diem's return. After Diem left the airport, he arrived at the prime minister's palace. There a crowd of several thousand had been waiting for him. They included civil servants, trade unionists, and a network of activists tied to Nhu and his wife Madame Ngo Dinh Nhu, whom American reporters first compared to Joan of Arc, but would later turn on and deride as the "Dragon Lady." Her father became Diem's ambassador to the United States and her uncle served as his minister of foreign affairs. To these people Diem exited his limo to a "vibrant ovation." He shook hands with the crowd as he walked up to the front of the palace to give a speech.

To this crowd he announced, "In this critical situation, I will act decisively. I will move with determination to open a path to national salvation. A total revolution will be implemented in every facet of the organization and the life of the nation." Many of the ideas for what he wanted to do in Vietnam he got from his brother Nhu.[96]

---

[96] Miller, pp. 1-5; Seth Jacobs, *Cold War Mandarin: Ngo Dinh Diem and the Origins of America's War in Vietnam, 1950-1963* (New York: Rowman & Littlefield, 2006), p. 89; Jonathan Nashel, *Edward Lansdale's Cold War* (Boston: University of Massachusetts Press, 2005), 59, 117, 242; Edward Lansdale interview, 1979, *Vietnam: A Television History Program: America's Mandarin*, http://openvault.wgbh.org/catalog/vietnam-f1001a-interview-with-edward-geary-lansdale-1979-part-1-of-5; accessed 8/11/2014.

Ngo Dinh Nhu considered himself to be the leading intellectual in his family. He earned degrees in literature, and studied paleography and librarianship, at the Ecole des Chartes in Paris during the 1930's. He then became a director of the National Library in Hanoi. He moved to the southern highlands of Vietnam to a small town, where he spent time raising orchids and reading.

He became attracted to the theories of Emmanuel Mounier, a French Catholic philosopher. Mounier argued against the capitalism and liberalism of the west, claiming that they led people to become alienated from society, exploited, and immoral. However, he also claimed that communism brought people oppression and caused them to lose their identity to the state. He advocated for a third way between the two that would be a new order that would focus on a person's individual needs and the community at the same time. It would be a way of life that would focus on "spiritual" considerations first. It all meant creating the right moral order. He called it "personalism."

The ideas of "personalism" inspired Nhu to create a regular seminar in Vietnam, attended by roughly twenty people, in which he and a Catholic priest devoted the discussion to the philosophy. One participant remembered that "few spoke, but many listened." To Nhu "personalism" represented a way to create a "third path" alternative to national development different from colonialism or communism.

Nhu published a journal for these ideas. In a talk he said, "These are great undertakings, and they can be summarized as a politico-economic revolution, aimed at making the Person the focus of concern. I say revolution, because it will be a great waste if we try to patch over the fissures in a creaky house, when what is needed is to transform the entire internal structure of the house."

He was vague in describing what this would mean in practice, but successful in gathering followers. Nhu created the "Revolutionary Personalist Workers Party," known as the Can Lao in Vietnamese, that met clandestinely, but attracted Vietnamese of importance with its brand of anti-communism and nationalism. New members had to kiss a picture of Ngo Dinh Diem, while swearing loyalty to him. Catholics and army officers joined.[97]

Diem lived inside the presidential palace, with his brother Nhu and his wife Madame Nhu. According to John Dam, Diem's bodyguard, the President worked around the clock and spent almost all of his waking hours in his office. His bedroom had bare wood floors and consisted of a simple straw

---

[97] Miller, pp. 41-48; Max Boot, *The Road Not Taken: Edward Lansdale And The American Tragedy In Vietnam* (New York: Liveright Publishing Corporation, 2018), p.283.

mat. He often spent days inside eating every meal at his desk by himself. Every morning he drank coffee with sugar and ate rice porridge with small fish. His lunch and dinner was almost always just as simple. He never drank alcohol, but smoked so many cigarettes that his fingers turned yellow.

The five-feet tall and ninety-six pound Madame Nhu served as the hostess of the palace for Diem. "She is charming, talks to him, relieves his tension, argues with him, needles him, and, like a Vietnamese wife, she is dominant in the household," said Diem's chief of staff. John Pham, though, thought she "look like a hot lady, talk too big," but Diem put up with her, because he didn't want to trouble his brother.

Madame Nhu kept a diary. In it she wrote of a loveless marriage. The problem was Nhu spent little time with her even though she was still young and attractive. American magazines told their readers about her, always with photos. The photos were important. Upper class women throughout Asia began to copy her hairstyle and fashion of dress, but Nhu was always busy with politics and plotting. They had four kids together, but he made her miserable. She was made to feel invisible to him in the palace, completely ignored by him. She discovered that he was cheating on her with a woman she named the "creature." When she confronted Nhu about it he claimed that it was because "you scare me." As Catholics they would never divorce, but they agreed it was best for them to stay more apart.[98]

Few people in Washington thought that Diem and his brother could succeed in creating a strong state in South Vietnam. As Diem set up office inside the prime minister's palace, his government only really controlled a few blocks of Saigon. His army was ruled by a chief of staff, with his own ambitions, General Nguyen Van Hinh, who had greater loyalty to the French than to Diem. The Saigon police force was operated by a mafia group, while Diem had practically no control of a countryside that was wracked by war and home to several armed religious groups, with hundreds of thousands of their own followers.[99]

A National Security Council Working Group found, "In Free Vietnam there is political chaos. The Government of Prime Minister Diem has only one virtue - honesty - and is bereft of any practical experience in public administration. The Vietnamese National Army has disintegrated as a fighting force. Cochin-China is the seat of three rival private armies and the security services of Free Vietnam have, by decree of Bao Dai, been handed over to a gangster sect, the Binh Xuyen, whose revenues are derived from gambling, prostitution, and extortion.

---

[98] Monique Brinson Demery, *Finding the Dragon Lady* (Public Affairs: New York, 2013), pp. 98-99; 107.
[99] *The Pentagon Papers, Gravel Edition, Volume 1* (Boston: Beacon Press, 1971), p. 219.

It must not be forgotten that Vietminh elements throughout Vietnam are working with hot haste to take over the entire country by cold war means before national elections are held two years hence."

Secretary of Defense Charles Wilson told President Eisenhower, and Secretary of State John Foster Dulles, that he thought it might be best to just "get completely out of the area." All these groups should be "left to stew in their own juice." Eisenhower disagreed, saying that the United States needed to "try to get the French out of the Indochina area." "To the President's point Secretary Wilson replied that if we had ever been in control of Indochina, as we had once been in the Philippines, he would feel differently about it. As matters stood, however, he could see nothing but grief in store for us if we remained in the area," records the minutes of an October 26, 1954, National Security Council meeting.

Secretary of State Dulles told his men at a State Department staff meeting that, in his view, if the Viet Minh began an "out-out" attack on South Vietnam, "he foresaw American bombing of Tonkin and probably general war with China. Our concept envisages a fight with nuclear weapons rather than the commitment of ground forces." He could not see a scenario where the United States would send hundreds of thousands of troops to defend South Vietnam, but since China had yet to develop an atomic bomb, he thought they had a free hand to use nuclear weapons instead if they decided to do so.

But Dulles didn't expect things would come to that, because the great strategic nuclear advantage the United States had over China made it unlikely to support an invasion of South Vietnam. As evidence, it already compromised at Geneva. The real danger was internal subversion. With the proper assistance, South Vietnam could become a model to the world for the successful transition away from colonialism to American supported development in the battle for the future of the "Third World."

General John W. O'Daniel, the head of the small United States military advisory group in Saigon, wrote, "I feel this is [a] great opportunity [for the] U.S. [to] assist in pointing Vietnam right direction. This area can be used as [a] testing ground to combat - the warfare communist could hope to employ everywhere including US. I personally feel that consideration should be given to make effort toward establishing US strongly here."

Dulles got the approval for hundreds of millions of dollars' worth of aid for South Vietnam to build an army to defend itself and build a new nation. As he approved the program, President Eisenhower said, "In the lands of the blind, one-eyed men are kings," so what he wanted "was a Vietnamese force which would support Diem. Therefore let's get busy and get one."

Ironically, at the moment Eisenhower was holding this meeting, the U.S. Ambassador to South Vietnam sent a cable to Washington claiming that "Diem must go," because "everyone in embassy is convinced that Diem cannot organize and administer strong government." He claimed that even though "he does represent an ideal and he enjoys certain prestige and confidence among masses of population, he has largely lost course continuing deadlock, prestige and confidence of literate, articulate sections of Vietnamese community."[100]

The Joint Chiefs of Staff were uneasy about the prospects of success. They thought that the "chaotic internal political situation within Vietnam is such that there is no assurance that the security forces visualized herein can be developed into loyal and effective support for the Diem Government, or, if developed that these forces will result in political and military stability within South Vietnam. Unless the Vietnamese themselves show an inclination to make individual and collective sacrifices required to resist communism, which they have not done to date, no amount of external pressure and assistance can long delay complete communist victory in South Vietnam."[101]

[100] William Gibbons, *The U.S. Government and the Vietnam War, Part I: Executive and Legislative Roles and Relationships* (New Jersey: Princeton University Press, 1986), pp. 269-270, 285-286.
[101] *The Pentagon Papers, Vol. 1*, p. 218.

The problem was that Ngo Dinh Diem's government was trying to rule in a sea of anarchy. In comparison, the new government of the Democratic Republic of Vietnam, above the 17th parallel appeared, to be strong and popular with its people. Columnist Joseph Alsop had been in areas that the Viet Minh had taken from the French during their war. "It was difficult for me," he wrote, "as it is for any Westerner, to conceive of a communist government's genuinely 'serving the people.' I could hardly imagine a communist government that was also a popular government and almost a democratic government. But this was just the sort of government the palmhut state actually was while the struggle with the French continued. The Viet Minh could not possibly have carried on the resistance for one year, let alone nine years, without people's strong, untied support."

When the Viet Minh "liberated" an area they took the land from the French, and large landowners, and gave it to small farmers and villagers for free. As a result, the masses of peasants become thankful to the Viet Minh and supported their new government. So, it had a firm rule over North Vietnam.[102]

In contrast, Ngo Dinh Diem scarcely controlled even Saigon. The Binh Xuyen gang of 6,000 gangers, led by Bay Vien, controlled vice in the city and

---

[102] *The Pentagon Papers, Vol. 1,* p. 308.

surrounding area. They ran the national opium trade, made money by charging people "road safety taxes," and also owned the Saigon police force, thanks to a payment of $1.2 million to Bao Dai. They also operated the Grande Monde, the biggest casino in Southeast Asia, and an elegant prostitution palace called the Hall of Mirrors. The French had made Bay Vien a brigadier general in their army, paying him $85,000 a year for his services.

At the same time, two armed religious sects named the Cao Dai and Hoa Hao had control of one third of the territory and population in South Vietnam. The Hoa Hao had an army of 20,000 men and over a million followers. The Cao Dai was even larger in size. One of its leaders said that its organization "is that of a modern state. It does not lack ambitions which, however, remain within the realm of possibility: to make Cao-Daism into a religion of the state, into the national religion of Vietnam."[103]

What did they believe in? The Cao Dai mixed Confucianism, Buddhism, and Taoism all together in a synthesis and believed in a coming day of judgment. The group organized itself like the Catholic Church with its own Pope and Holy See. It even

---

[103] *The Pentagon Papers, Vol. 1*, p. 220; Jessica Chapman, *Cauldron Of Resistance: Ngo Dinh Diem, The United States And 1950s Southern Vietnam* (United States: Cornell University Press, 2013), pp. 21, 74.

had its own pantheon of saints that included Jesus, Victor Hugo, Joan of Arc, and Charlie Chaplin.

Founded in 1926, the group grew to over five million members by World War II. Many people came to the religion partly for help. In the 1930's, many peasants fell into starvation, as a few bad harvests brought them small rice crops, while the French maintained fixed taxes on them without mercy. World War II brought total famine and a societal collapse. The Cao Dai met the needs of the masses with charitable houses. With rifles they took control of entire sections of the countryside and laid taxes on the people, but used the money to help them instead of simply sending it to France or Japan.

The organization grew so big that many of the Cao Dai leaders became high ranking Vietnamese in the colonial bureaucracy. To the masses in the villages, they said, "Let's be brothers." They preached equality and a future in which wealth would be redistributed and everyone taken care of.

The Hoa Hao was also a peasant based religious movement that combined Buddhism with a fierce anti-colonialism. The communists, though, assassinated its leader in 1947. They chopped his body into three pieces, burying each part in a different grave to prevent him from reincarnating. His organization then split up into four groups with four military bosses to outlive their leader.[104]

All of these groups were threatened by Diem and wanted to play a role in his new government. Their leaders sought cabinet posts in his new administration, while the French officials left in Vietnam told him it would be best to listen to them, but he wouldn't. He wanted there to be no question of who really had power now even though South Vietnam was not a fully realized nation state. Another third of the countryside also was in the hands of Viet Minh units left over from the war with France.

Diem also faced a formidable challenge from General Nguyen Van Hinh, the Chief of Staff of the Vietnamese National Army, with a lot of allies in France. Hinh got in contact with Bay Vien and a few leaders from the religious groups and began to plot to take over. He then got the backing of some top French officials.

In mid-August, US Ambassador Donald Heath found out about the plotting at a party held by a high-ranking French diplomat. At the event were men from the Binh Xuyen and General Hinh. One of them came up to the ambassador and bluntly

---

104 Samuel Popkin, *The Rational Peasant: The Political Economy of Rural Society in Vietnam* (Los Angeles: University of California Press, 1979), pp. 193-213.

asked, "Is it all right to go ahead and change the government?" The next day, the French High Commissioner Paul Ely told him he thought Diem should be removed.

General Hinh started boasting to his friends that once he took Diem down he was going to take Madame Nhu as his concubine. When Madame Nhu saw Hinh at a party she came up to him and said, "You are never going to overthrow this government, because you do not have the guys. And if you do overthrow it, you will never have me, because I will claw your throat out first." Speechless, the general didn't know what to say, because he couldn't openly admit to his scheming.

Ambassador Heath warned Diem that his government was in an "extremely parlous situation" and that he needed to "come to terms" with these various groups and "broaden" his government. It's best to make potential enemies into friends. Diem wouldn't take that advice, so, Heath sent a cable to Washington saying that "we must keep our eyes open for another leader."

Diem found out about Hinh's plotting and ordered him to go to France for a six-month "study mission." Hinh defied those orders by riding a motorcycle throughout Saigon in shirt sleeves so everyone could see him. He even put a placard on the motorcycle mocking Diem. Hinh then went to his house and surrounded it with guards and two armored cars. He dared Diem to do something about it. The religious groups and police were protecting him, so Diem couldn't do anything.

Ambassador Heath told Washington that "with every day Hinh continues to stall and appear [to] get away with his defiance, influence, and prestige of civil government are diminishing." He told Diem to compromise. "I would lose all my followers," Diem told him, "who would accuse me of being without honor or courage."

Instead, Diem isolated the general. He brought some members of the Cao Dai and Hoa Hao into his cabinet as figureheads. Bao Dai once again told Diem to bring Hinh into his government. This encouraged Hinh to up the confrontation. He told Ambassador Heath that within forty-eight hours he would remove Diem from power if he didn't comply with Bao Dai's instructions.

General Lansdale helped Diem out by asking Hinh if he would "like to visit the nightclubs of Manila." When he said he was too busy, Lansdale got some of his top men to go with him. With the men gone, "General Hinh told me ruefully that he had called off his coup," Lansdale later wrote, "he had forgotten that he needed his chief lieutenants for key roles in the coup and couldn't proceed while they were out of the country with me. I never did figure out how serious Hinh was with his talk.

Diem got General Hinh to meet with him and fooled him into thinking that he was negotiating with him. As talks with the general went on, he had some agents hand Bao Dai dirt on General Hinh. Americans leaned on him too. Bao Dai issued an edict summoning him to Paris to talk to him. The general found he had no choice, but to comply, because he was basing his authority on the notion that he was acting to carry out Bao Dai's orders. Diem's brother, Nhu, told a CIA officer that the Ngo's were now confident that Vietnam's national army "were in hand and loyal" and next they planned to destroy the power of the Binh Xuyen, while holding the Hoa Hao and Cao Dai in a delicate balance. Instead of bringing the different groups of Vietnam into their government, they planned to divide them and then destroy them one at a time.[105]

President Eisenhower had become so concerned about the situation in South Vietnam that he recalled Ambassador Heath and sent General Lawton Collins to temporarily replace him to give him his personal assessment of things. Collins had been one of Ike's senior staffers who helped him plan the D-Day invasion and got the nickname "Lightning Joe" for his efficient style of command. Ike trusted him.

---

[105] The Pentagon Papers, Vol. 1, p. 219; Moyar, pp. 42-44; Miller, pp. 102-107; Gibbons, p. 289; Demery, p.83.

Collins worked on a "crash program" of aid to the Vietnamese National Army and helped to form the U.S. Military Advisory Assistance Group in Saigon to supervise its training. The United States would take the place of the French in assisting his army. At first Collins got taken in with Diem, calling him "the best available Prime Minister," but, after a few months in Vietnam, he got frustrated with him too. He began to believe that Diem was too stubborn to listen to his advice, just as Ambassador Heath had come to conclude, and he did not like that.

Collins suggested to Diem that he appoint Dr. Phan Quat to a cabinet post. He had been a former defense minister who had a reputation for being highly competent. General Collins got along with him well. Diem, however, pretended to take the suggestion seriously, but ignored it. Diem knew that the Cao Dai and Hoa Hao leaders he was working with held grudges against him. Collins didn't know that, though. Collins told Washington that “Diem wishes to do everything himself.” It seemed that “none of his subordinates is delegated sufficient authority to work.” Collins was right about that.

For years the French had been paying the Cao Dai, Hoa Hao, and Binh Xuyen leaders millions of dollars of piasters every month, but could no longer afford the payments. With Lansdale's help, Diem decided to pay some of the religious leaders and incorporated them into his army. As for the Binh Xuyen, he announced that he would shut down their casino.

Bay Vien and the Binh Xuyen could see what was coming, so they joined up with the official Cao Dai "pope" and formed a coalition called the "United Front of Nationalist Forces." They demanded that Diem bring some of them into his cabinet. He used the same tactic which proved effective against General Hinh, he stalled for time by pretending to negotiate with them.

They gave him a deadline of March 26, 1955, to cave to their demands. Instead, on that morning, Diem announced that the Binh Xuyen would no longer have any control over the Saigon police force. Binh Xuyen commandos lobbed mortar shells on to the prime minister's palace. Skirmishes broke out around the city between the opposing sides. General Collins and Paul Ely worked out a truce between the parties. It held for a month.

During that time, Diem believed that he had gotten the bulk of the Cao Dai forces to secretly switch to his side. Many observers came to conclude that Diem was provoking a confrontation. Some of his cabinet ministers resigned in protest. General Collins thought Diem was losing control of his government and came to conclude that he was too obstinate and stubborn to ever be an effective leader.

The prime minister wouldn't listen to his advice. Collins sent a cable to President Eisenhower, and Dulles, saying that Diem is now "almost entirely isolated" and is "operating practically [a] one-man government with his two brothers Luyen and Nhu as principal advisors." He recommend that he be replaced, perhaps with Bao Dai.[106]

Secretary of State Dulles replied to Collins by informing him that he talked with Eisenhower and they both were "disposed to back" any decision Collins made, but saw two problems. First, if Diem went "we will be merely paying the bill and the French will be calling the tune" with Bao Dai. What is more, "there will be very strong opposition in the Congress to supporting the situation in Indochina generally and Vietnam in particular if Diem is replaced under existing circumstances. We do not say that this opposition may not in the last instance be overcome, particularly if you personally can make a case before the Congressional committees, but Mansfield who is looked up with great respect by his colleagues with reference to this matter, is adamantly opposed to abandonment of Diem under present conditions."

President Eisenhower brought Collins back to Washington, who gave him an endless list of reasons why Diem was unsuitable. “The net of it is,” Collins said, “this fellow is impossible.” After this

---

[106] Gibbons, p. 289; Jacobs, p. 67; Miller, pp. 108-116.

meeting, the President decided it was time for Diem to go. Collins and the Secretary of State then met with Senator Mansfield and CIA Director Allen Dulles and they both now agreed too. A cable was then sent to Paris and Saigon with new orders. It said that officially the United States would support Diem "until and unless Vietnamese leaders develop alternate proposal which Bao Dai would support." "While the Vietnamese in Saigon should appear to be the framers of a new government, Collins and Ely will probably have to be in practice the catalysts. This may result in stories regarding a new Collins-Ely 'formula,' but we should make every attempt to keep the Vietnamese label." If the Vietnamese can't come up with a new name "then Ely and Collins will have to recommend a name for Bao Dai to designate to form a new government." Collins would "urge Diem to serve in a new capacity, if he will, and provide full support for the new government. If Diem refuses, the program should nevertheless be carried out."[107]

Four hours after these instructions were received by the Americans in Saigon, small gunfire erupted at a Binh Xuyen command. An hour later, mortar shells landed near Bay Vien's headquarters. Incited into action, Bay Vien launched an attack on

[107] Jacobs, p. 74; Gibbons, pp. 294-296.

the Vietnamese National Army headquarters building and began mortar fire on Diem's palace. A battle for Saigon began.

Ngo Dinh Diem called Paul Ely to tell him that the Binh Xuyen had broken the truce and he was going to order a counterattack if they did not stop shelling his palace. After Ely told him that he would hold him responsible for any bloodshed, Diem hung up the phone on him. Fighting went on for several days and nights. Entire city blocks burned down to leave 20,000 homeless, but the Binh Xuyen were pushed out of the city. Their Grande Monde casino burned to the ground. Five hundred civilians got killed as the tactics of both sides consisted primarily of mortar and artillery barrages in a war of attrition fought over a square mile of the city.

The battled ended the Washington plans to replace Diem. Right after it started, Secretary of State Dulles had sent a "blocking cable" telling the American embassy "to take no action whatsoever" on the earlier messages. Colonel Lansdale had sent Dulles a few memos earlier in the day recommending that they stick with Diem. It now made no sense to replace him with a battle raging. Some authors believe that Lansdale had tipped Diem off to the plans to do away with him, so he was able to act before they were implemented. Someone in Washington probably told Lansdale what was going on there.[108]

American and French officials in Vietnam told Diem to focus on building up his army and to cut some deals. He ignored them and sent Colonel Duong Van Minh, who the Americans nicknamed "Big Minh" for his impressive height, into the countryside to destroy the remaining Binh Xuyen forces. Hundreds of them surrendered and those that didn't were broken up after a four-week siege. Bay Vien, along with his closest men, escaped with their wealth to live the rest of their lives in France. Some of the Cao Dai and Hoa Hao units went to Diem's side and joined the Vietnamese National Army. Diem defeated their remnants and captured the leading Hoa Hao general Ba Cut. He had him brought to Saigon, where he had his head lopped off, with a guillotine, in public.[109]

Ngo Dinh Diem and his brothers had survived and beaten their enemies when most thought they would fail. They had learned that even though the Americans were their allies, and they depended on them for money, that they didn't always know what they were doing. Men in Washington on the other side of the world had little understanding of what

---

[108] Miller, pp. 120-123; Jacobs, p.76; Moyar, p. 49.
[109] Miller, p. 162; Chapman, pp. 124-128.

was really going on in Vietnam and could not always be trusted.

Now Senator Mansfield proclaimed that all aid to South Vietnam should be cut off if Diem were to be overthrown. Senator Hubert Humphrey stated that "Premier Diem is an honest, wholesome, and honorable man. He is the kind of man we ought to be supporting, rather than conspirators, gangsters, and hoodlums." Congressman Thomas Dodd said that Collins should be fired and "replaced by someone who measures up to the needs of the hour." Diem's victory over "Binh Xuyen gangsters," Life magazine proclaimed "immensely simplifies the task of U.S. diplomacy in Saigon. That task is, or should be, simply to back Diem to the hilt."[110]

In May of 1957, Diem took a twenty-one day trip to the United States. President Eisenhower met him at the Washington National Airport. The American press now gushed over Diem. Life magazine called him "the tough miracle man of Vietnam." The New York Times said he was "an Asian liberator." Senator Mike Mansfield argued that "the chief credit for holding back the Communist aggression not only in Vietnam, but, because of that, in Southeast Asia as well, lies in the determination, the courage, the incorruptibility, and the integrity

[110] Jacobs, p. 77.

of President Diem, who has shown such great ability and has accomplished so much against tremendous odds."

New York City gave Diem a parade from Lower Broadway to City Hall. Mayor Robert Wagner said, the Premier is a “man to whom freedom is the very breath of life.” Henry Luce chaired a dinner for Diem at the famous Park Avenue Ambassador Hotel with Cardinal Spellman, John D. Rockefeller, Eleanor Roosevelt, and Senators Mansfield and Kennedy. Diem teared up as he stood up and said, “The word *friends* should be my theme tonight. Looking at newspapers since I have arrived in your country, one would think that everybody in America is now a friend of Vietnam.”

During Diem's trip, one of his men let slip to an American official that Diem wasn't sure that the United States would really defend South Vietnam if it were attacked from the north. Admiral Felix Stump, the commander-in-chief of the U.S. Pacific command, went to Diem to reassure him. He told him that if communists invaded any non-communist territory President Eisenhower, and Secretary of State John Foster Dulles, intended to attack them with nuclear weapons. The United States would not drop nuclear weapons on population centers in Vietnam, but "if we are unable to stop the communists in Vietnam or nearby territories in connection with any hostilities, we will not hesitate to use all weapons at our disposal on such areas as the [Chinese] Canton military complex in order to bring about the defeat of the communists. The United States now has military capabilities which can stop and defeat any communist military thrust."[111]

Now that Diem was in control of Saigon, and of his army, he spent the next few years consolidating his power, trying to build a new nation in South Vietnam, with the ideology of personsalism and a land reform program that he hoped would tie the individual peasant to his state. He believed that this would be key to his long-term success. One of the first things he did when he became prime minister was to encourage close to a million people in North Vietnam to emigrate to South Vietnam. Most of them were Catholics who feared communism. They would serve as cadres in his brother's Can Lao political party and in the army.

The Geneva Accords had contained provisions to allow people to regroup immediately after the war with France. Two-hundred thousand Viet Minh supporters went from South Vietnam to North Vietnam, while 900,000 people came down into the south. Through Operation EXODUS, the United States navy helped transport 300,000 of these people. Lansdale encouraged the movement of as many of them into South Vietnam as possible, with propaganda and a $100 bonus stipend, which

[111] Jacobs, p. 103; Moyar, pp. 77-78.

at the time was about as much as a Vietnamese made in an entire year. The Americans figured these people would become dependent on Diem's new state and thus loyal to him. They also provided wonderful stories for newspapers in the United States and images in newsreels and on television. The American people needed to be trained to support Diem too. Their television sets taught most of them everything they knew about Vietnam.[112]

Now Diem took his first real step in consolidating political power by announcing a national referendum for the people of South Vietnam to choose between being ruled by a national monarchy, with Bao Dai as king, or a Republic, with Diem as president. U.S. advisers told him that he should not make the election results too lopsided, but to go for a 60% margin. Instead, he fixed the election so that he won it by 98.2% of the vote. As a result, commentators around the world condemned it as being undemocratic even though the government of the United States praised it. The State Department claimed that it was evidence of "the evolution of orderly and effective democratic processes." The historian and Southeast Asia expert Bernard Fall wrote that, "There is not the slightest doubt that this plebiscite was only a share more fraudulent than most electoral tests under a dictatorship. In

[112] *The Pentagon Papers, Vol. 1*, pp. 247-248.

nearly all electoral areas, there were thousands more 'Yes' votes than voters."[113]

Despite evidence of rigged voting, Diem would have won anyway if the voting had been completely fair, because Bao Dai was living in France and not running a campaign. It was a one-man election. However, there had never been a real election in Vietnam before. Diem was not trying to create a new precedent of regular free and fair elections with his referendum, but to make a total political triumph over Bao Dai and transform the government of South Vietnam. Through the act of voting, the people participated in the creation of his new state. He called the new government of South Vietnam the Republic of Vietnam, but by a republic he did not mean a democratic republic, with free political parties and fair voting, but a state grounded around the ideals of personalism, with himself personifying them.[114]

Diem called it a different kind of democracy. He explained that democracy was not something created "by drafting and promulgating documents and regulations." Instead of being about civil liberties, it was about collective social and moral improvement. "Moral development remains the end of all rational activity," Diem said, "politics is only a means." "Democracy is primarily a state of mind, a

---

[113] Gibbons, p. 300.
[114] Chapman, pp. 151-152.

way of living that respects the human person, both with regard to ourselves and with regard to others," he continued, "more than any other form of government, democracy demands that we all display wisdom and virtue in our dealing with each other." That is why having the right moral leader was so critical.[115]

He used the referendum to try educate the people to what this was about. He claimed that he was running on the basic mandarin principles that he had a "mandate of heaven" to lead the nation. This was a Confucian notion, going back to thousands of years of Chinese tradition. The mandate of heaven gave leaders the responsibility to rule with strict moral and ethical standards. If they deviated from what was right, they then lost the "mandate of heaven," and society could suffer from wars and corruption as a result. It then became right for people to rebel against their leader to replace him.

Diem claimed that Bao Dai had lost that mandate. Going into the referendum, constant denunciations of Bao Dai appeared in newspapers, music, and posters, all over South Vietnam. Some slogans that appeared were, "Bao Dai, master keeper of gambling dens and brothels; being aware of vicious Bao Dai's preference for gambling, girls, wine, milk, and butter, those who vote for him will betray their country and despoil their people; to vote for

---

[115] Miller, pp. 140-141.

the revolutionary man Ngo Dinh Diem is to build a society of welfare and justice."

The contrast with the chaste and pious Ngo Dinh Diem was obvious for all. It was time to transfer the "mandate of heaven." "A sacred respect is due to the person of the sovereign," Diem wrote, "he is the mediator between the people and heaven as he celebrates the national cult." Diem's ideas were straight from the personalism of his brother Nhu and Father Mounier, who wrote that authority "taken politically is a vocation which the person receives from God (in the case of a Christian) or from his personality mission which rises out of his social function (in the case of a non-Christian)...Personalism is an effort and a technique for constantly selecting from all social ranks a spiritual elite that is capable of authority." Diem sought to mold his nation's governmental structures to this ideology.

Diem announced the creation of a new national assembly. People voted to elect candidates for it, but all candidates first had to have the approval of Diem before they could run. He insisted that the nation should have one national revolutionary movement, and one political party, to lead it, the Can Lao party controlled by his brother Nhu. He made all other parties illegal by declaring them to be illegal. He said they were either communists, or in league with communists, and, therefore, acting as terrorists against the state. He imprisoned tens of thousands of political opponents and even potential opposition soldiers in his army. Most were simply jailed for a few months, to undergo reeducation, and then released, but many were tortured and some were killed.[116]

All of this was made legal in a constitution passed by the assembly. It declared that "The President leads the nation." He had the authority to declare a state of emergency and suspend the laws of any part of the country at his whim. It stated that anyone who undermined "the republican form of government, the democratic regime, national freedom, independence, and unity" would be "deprived of all rights." An official at the U.S. embassy looked it over and said that its "dominant philosophy" was "its desire to maintain the present eminence of President Diem." Diem's Republic of Vietnam was a nationalist one-party police state, with power really resting in the armed forces, with Diem's authority over them. He pledged to use his power to improve the people and develop the nation in a "revolution."[117]

South Vietnam was not a colony, nor was it a communist state. It was an American ally in the Cold War of which money and development advisers flowed from the United States to Vietnam. A

[116] Chapman, pp. 154-171.
[117] Miller, p. 147.

lobby group called the American Friends of Vietnam formed to support the effort. It was headed by men, such as General John O'Daniel, who had just retired, and William Donovan, who had been the head of the OSS during World War II and had been the ambassador to Thailand, where he worked for the CIA just as much as he did for the State Department. Other members included wealthy publishers Henry Luce of Time and Life magazines and William Randolph Hearst, along with Arthur Schlesinger, Jr. Thirty-members of the House of Representatives were members of it and so were five senators, including Mike Mansfield and John Kennedy.

Now that the United States was no longer supporting French colonialism in Vietnam, but backing independent nationalism, Senator Kennedy was all for it. "Vietnam represents a proving ground of democracy in Asia. However, we may choose to ignore it or deprecate it, the rising prestige and influence of Communist China in Asia are unchallengeable facts. Vietnam represents the alternative to Communist dictatorship," Kennedy said, "the United States is directly responsible for this experiment - it is playing an important role in the laboratory where it is being conducted. We cannot afford to permit the experiment to fail."

What Kennedy believed was needed to succeed in Vietnam was to create "a political, economic and social revolution far superior to anything the Communists can offer - far more peaceful, far more democratic and far more locally controlled. Such a revolution will require much from the United States and much from Vietnam. We must supply capital to replace that drained by centuries of colonial exploitation; technicians to train those handicapped by deliberate policies of illiteracy; guidance to assist a nation taking those first feeble steps toward the complexities of a republican form of government."[118]

This was about America's role in the world as a global empire in battle with communism for the future of the Third World. Frances FitzGerald, whose father Desmond Fitzgerald, as the head of the CIA's Far Eastern Division, played a key role in the agency's aid programs to Diem, later wrote, "The idea that the mission of the United States was to build democracy around the world had become a convention of American politics in the 1950's. Among certain circles it was more or less assumed that democracy, that is electoral democracy combined with private ownership and civil liberties, was what the United States had to offer the Third World. Democracy provided not only the moral basis for American opposition to Communism, but the practical methods for making that opposition work. Whether American officials actually believed that

[118] Gibbons, pp. 301-304.

the Asians and Africans wanted or needed democracy - and many officials definitely did not - they saw lip service to it as a necessity to selling American overseas commitments to the American people. The Americans officials and scholars who backed Diem adhered to this convention precisely."[119]

Whether the Americans who saw Diem as a savior really believed that he was creating "democracy" or not, what is clear is that they all viewed him as a critical ally in a world they divided into two, with an us versus them mentality. Today, with the Cold War long over, American officials still see the world the same way. They see their mission to save people from chaos, which breeds instability and danger, by keeping nations in close alliance with the United States and the forces of international corporate capitalism. Those areas of the world seen as unstable they seek to control and improve through nation building exercises with foreign aid, covert action, and at times brute military force. It is empire. In the 1950's, men like John Kennedy wished to win the forces of nationalism, being unleashed by the collapse of colonialism, after World War II, on to the side of the United States through national development.

The American aid program to Vietnam was its biggest in the world outside of Europe and Korea.

---

[119] Gibbons, p. 312.

It spent close to $3.6 billion from 1950-1954 supporting the French there and then $2 billion helping Diem from 1955-1961. By 1961, there were 1,500 American government personnel in South Vietnam and 400 under government contract. The government also worked with groups like Michigan State University, the Brookings Institute, and the Ford Foundation to study and try to improve almost every element of the Saigon government down to the village level.[120]

Diem and his brothers believed whole heartily in bringing his people a "revolution" through nation building. The Viet Minh used land reform to build their state. Diem also engaged in a similar revolution in the countryside in his own way. In South Vietnam, in 1954, one quarter of one percent of the population owned forty percent of the rice growing land. Many peasants lived in starvation conditions and were hungry for land of their own. Instead of redistributing land, Diem moved people to previously unpopulated areas. By resettling people, he sought to build a "human wall" along South Vietnam's borders and "to mobilize the active participation and contribution of the people to the public projects of the government."[121]

The Diem government resettled one-hundred thousand of the northern refugees in one program

---

[120] Gibbons, p. 314.
[121] Miller, pp. 160-164.

it called the Cai San settlement, in an area which had previously been under the control of the Hoa Hao. Diem expected to move these people there t get them to immediately begin to farm as they began to arrive in January of 1956. He got them digging new canals and preparing fields. They needed the work done by spring to prepare for planting.

Diem expected the United States government to send him one hundred tractors to plow and harrow 30,000 hectares of land at Cai San, but they didn't get there in time for the rainy season. When they arrived, he found they had heavy steel wheels that got stuck in the mud with no caterpillar treads. As a result, only 5,000 hectares got seeded. The project turned into a disaster.

The settlers found that people still lived in the area. They thought they were going to be given title to the land they settled, but Diem's officials expected them to labor for them for a few years first. By the fall, some of them began to demonstrate. Diem deployed troops on them. A few Catholic priests that had gone with the settlers complained, so Diem made them subject to a corruption investigation.

Diem launched a new project called "The Land Development Program" to resettle more people. These people were natives and not refugees from the north. He created four separate settlement zones and moved 41,000 people into them. In a few years, 200,000 additional people were moved into these areas as part of this program. It also ran into problems. One American found that most of the settlement sites didn't have enough water for irrigation. One was placed ninety kilometers from the nearest town and the roads that led to it were impassable for months out of the year.

The US embassy told Diem to give the people "vigorous and continuing assistance" after he moved them, but the South Vietnamese President believed that they had to earn the right to own this land by showing their willingness to work for it with the government first. Only that way could they grow morally and learn personalism. He thought if they built the settlements with their own hands they would take pride in them.[122]

Before the war with France, most peasants gave up forty-percent of their crop to the French. During the war, the Viet Minh did away with those taxes. So, peasants had eight rent free years. Now Diem reinstated the tax. Settlers were being made to clear and irrigate the land and then pay for their titles. Many did not understand why they had to pay for the land. According to the Pentagon Papers, "since the immediate beneficiaries were more often than not Northerners, refugees, and Catholics, the programs acquired an aura of GVN favoritism, and deepened peasant alienation. In time there were

---

[122] Miller, pp. 167-177.

also rumors of corruption, with widespread allegations that the Diem family had enriched itself through the manipulation of the land transfers."

Diem's government seized nearly half a million acres of land. Some of it was rented out with the government acting as landlord. Some was given to army units and some was given to village councils who were allowed to sell it in auction. Most of the time, though, the people who showed up to the auction to bid on it were already farming the land and were paying an extra cost to protect all of the years of work they had put into it.[123]

Discontent increased among the peasantry and some of them trickled into the ranks of the remaining Viet Minh insurgents. In 1959, Diem tried a new land program to counter them. He proposed to build eighty new "prosperity and density centers" he called "agrovilles." He planned to place them strategically along key roads. Each one would have 2,000 to 3,000 people in them among 400 families with a system of walled community defenses, schools, public gardens, and even electricity. Each community would have as its center a grid of buildings that would spark an evolution from village living to modern living and make South Vietnam one of the most modern states in the Third World. But, the agrovilles turned into even a bigger failure than Diem's earlier resettlement programs.

---

[123] *The Pentagon Papers, Vol. 1*, pp. 309-310.

It was one thing for refugees to leave North Vietnam for good, but with this program Diem forced people, in the words of the Pentagon Papers, into these agrovilles to do "so unwillingly, for it often meant abandoning a cherished ancestral home, tombs, and developed gardens and fields for a strange and desolate place. The settler was expected to tear down his old house to obtain materials for the new." Many peasants abandoned the agrovilles and joined the Viet Minh. To Diem's eyes the agrovilles with their giant mounds and barbed wire looked like forts, but to the peasants they seemed to be prisons. Only 22 out of 88 of them even got completed and, according to Diem's intelligence organization, they became breeding grounds for the Viet Minh. He was trying to build a great nation. Diem thought that by protecting the people, and giving them modern amenities, they would become loyal devotees of his state, but they didn't. He was smart enough to realize what was happening, though, and stopped the agroville program.[124]

P.J. Honey, a British Foreign Office adviser toured the countryside, in 1959, and found that "for the overwhelming majority of the Vietnamese, heirs to experience of a century of French colonial rule, the government is a remote body which passes laws, collects taxes, demands labour corvees, takes away able bodied men for military

---

[124] *The Pentagon Papers, Vol. 1*, p. 313; Miller, p. 183.

service, and generally enriches itself at the expense of the poor peasant. Government is associated in the minds of the villagers with exactions, punishments, unpaid labour, and other unpleasant matters. There people are members of families and members of villages, and their loyalties to both are strong. But these loyalties do not extend beyond the village, nor has any past experience taught the peasants why they should. The idea that the peasants should assume any responsibility for the [extra-village] government themselves would be so alien to their thinking as to be comic."

The Viet Minh appealed to the peasants not as Marxists or Communist revolutionaries, but as conservative nationalists compatible with village traditionalism. At the end of the war with France, 60,000 Viet Minh were serving in units in South Vietnam. Most of them went back up to North Vietnam after the war, but the United States and government of South Vietnam estimated that somewhere between five and ten thousand stayed behind as a "cadre." Neither government knew a whole lot about what they were doing at the time, but they were eventually able to draw a picture of their activities from interrogating some taken prisoner over the years.

From a study of twenty-three of them, they found that only four of them had been engaged in military tasks after Geneva. Most spent their time preparing for a future uprising, by carefully recruiting in the villages. They felt that time was not right to strike militarily. One said that "from 1959 to 1960 the cadres who remained in the south had almost all been arrested. Only one or two cadres were left in every three to five villages. What was amazing was how one or two cadres started the movement so well. The explanation is not that these cadres were exceptionally gifted but the people they talked to were ready for rebellion. The people were like a mound of straw, ready to be ignited. If at that time the government in the South had been a good one, if it had not been dictatorial, if the agrarian reforms had worked, if it had established control at the village level, then launching the movement would have been difficult." [125]

Ngo Dinh Diem had in fact come close to completely destroying the Viet Minh in South Vietnam. He launched a program of propaganda and repression against them he called the Denounce the Communists Campaign that decimated them. It included nonstop rallies, parades, and indoctrination sessions throughout the country, even for the police and the army. "Personalism," Ed Lansdale explained, "became the official philosophy of the state" and "government employees were required to attend weekly sessions on its tenets." If the people could be shown the validity of personalism then

[125] *The Pentagon Papers, Vol. 1,* pp. 325-326, 329.

they would trust the government and understand what Diem was trying to accomplish for them.

As for Madame Nhu, she created the Women's Solidarity Movement, to help families of soldiers in the armed forces. They held blood drives, wrote letters to soldiers away from home, and delivered medicine to rural families. Most of the members were made up of upper-class wives trying to get favor with the Nhu family for their husband's government jobs. She then created Morality Laws that outlawed dancing, divorce, and prostitution. She banned the use of contraception, because "we are under populated," and then organized a paramilitary unit of all women trained at firing ranges. They marched in military dress in parades. She called her militia "my little darlings." Once she started to get involved in politics, Nhu and Diem began to pay attention to her. "Up until then they had not taken me seriously. But then they began to notice me," she later said. She told the American reporter Marguerite Higgins, "power is wonderful."

Ngo Dinh Nhu also created the SEPES, a special security service that spied on elements of his government to measure their loyalty. The SEPES successfully exposed some traitors in the government, but such measures led to in the words of the Pentagon Papers "bureaucratic overcentralization: Diem himself seems to have been particularly at fault in this instance, reserving for himself the power of decision in minute matters, and refusing to delegate authority to subordinates who might have relieved him of a crushing administrative burden. In part, this may have simply been inexperience in handling a large enterprise, but there seems to have been a deeper philosophical reason - a passion for perfection, a distrust of other men, a conviction that all subordinates required his paternalistic guidance. The result was an impairment of an administrative system already crippled by the absence of French civil servants. Subordinate officials, incapable of making decisions, fearful of making them, or forbidden to make them, passed upward even minute matters on paper to the brothers Ngo, glutting the communications of government, and imposing long delays on all, even important actions."

Diem announced that he signed Ordinance Number 6, which decried that all people deemed dangerous to the state should be placed in prison camps. Ordinance 47 then made being a communist a capital crime. Diem coined a phrase "Viet Cong" to lump together all who were Viet Minh and who willingly or unwillingly sympathized with them. The phrase caught on in the American press and in the imagination of all Americans. They heard it on TV.

Diem's government claimed to have rounded up 100,000 former Viet Minh and to have "entirely destroyed the predominant communist influence of the previous nine years." However, since there were only a small number of them in the country at the start of this campaign, he used it to not only stop them, but to also arrest all potential opponents of his regime. Inadvertently, he pushed non-communist religious groups, non-cooperative reporters, and unionists into alliance with the Viet Minh.[126]

Diem sent security agents into the countryside to implement this campaign. They placed colored placards outside of family huts to mark their loyalty to the state with a board listing the number and sex of their inhabitants. Those deemed loyal were given gold or white signs. Those suspect were forced to keep black signs outside beside their door. One of Diem's men confessed to an American that "during the resistance the communists had been the only ones in the village to fight against the French, so when we tried to explain that communists were evil people, the villagers just didn't listen to us." Diem's police state was mapping the villages to try to control them.

Diem's men would go into the villages and gather the people for what the Pentagon Papers described as "ceremonies similar to self-criticism sessions." In Saigon tens of thousands of people witnessed 2,000 people confess that they had been former Viet Minh cadres, but had now seen the

---

[126] Chapman, p. 183; Miller, pp. 133-135; *Pentagon Papers, Vol 1.*, pp. 300-301; Demery, p. 114, 125-127, 146.

light. In 1956, about 50,000 people were in jail for political crimes. P.J. Honey, who had been invited by Diem to tour the prisons, reported that on the basis of his talks with former inmates, "the consensus of the opinions expressed by these people is that the majority of the detainees are neither communists nor pro-communists."

By arresting so many people, the campaign did succeed in almost completely eliminating the Viet Minh in South Vietnam. In just over five years, their numbers shrank by ninety percent. By 1958, all of Diem's provinces were under firm government control and one year later in two of the country's provinces there were only six cadres. However, the indiscriminate repression alienated so many people that tens of thousands of them became ripe for Viet Minh activists. South Vietnam became a police state society in which the arrest and torture of the innocent became commonplace. Diem thought fear could serve as "the beginning of discipline" for the people. Strong government could build a strong state.

However, this was a much softer campaign than Mao and Stalin used to build their nation states up. It also was also nothing compared to the killings done by other dictators supported by the United States in places such as Indonesia, Guatemala, and El Salvador in the decades to come. A little torture here, and there, and jailing people for a few years at a time, was a far cry from mass murder, but it didn't win him any love of the people.[127]

The campaign's success forced North Vietnam to intensify its efforts in South Vietnam. Both the Soviet Union, and China, had told them to hold off, because they didn't want to risk a larger war. In 1957, the Soviet Union even proposed for both North Vietnam, and South Vietnam, to be granted diplomatic status in the United Nations. China and Russia pushed for political struggle instead of military struggle in Vietnam, believing that eventually Diem's regime might disintegrate on its own accord, but, by the late 1950's, members of North Vietnam's ruling Politburo committee became split on what to do.

On one hand, Vo Nguyen Giap wanted to focus on a "north first" strategy whose biggest priority was developing the nation of North Vietnam. He, and those of like mind, did not want to risk getting involved in a war in the south either. However, Le Duan, who was the most powerful Viet Minh leader in the south, argued that Diem was eliminating so many of his men, with his Denounce the Communists campaign, that they risked losing operational control of the Viet Minh. Le Duan went north and became a member of the Politburo and

[127] Miller, p. 197-200; *The Pentagon Papers, Vol. 1*, pp. 311-312.

eventually rose high enough in power to become the most powerful person in North Vietnam.[128]

Le Duan rose in influence, partly, because of an internal controversy inside the Politburo. Although North Vietnam's land reform campaign had won over the masses of the peasants, it also created huge disturbances in the countryside, just as Diem's did. In some parts of the country, forces had to be sent to stop demonstrations against its excesses that Ho Chi Minh had complained of a few years ago. Le Duan went to China and saw the living hell such land reform programs could create. Bodies were everywhere. A purge of the more extreme communist elements linked to China in North Vietnam's government took place and since Le Duan had been in the south, and not involved, he became a compromise candidate for leadership in the Politburo. On September 10, 1960, he became the General Secretary of the Communist Party in North Vietnam, a position that made him much more powerful than the aging Ho Chi Minh, who by then had become a figurehead in semi-retirement. Le Duan used his new position of power to lobby for intervention in the south.[129]

---

[128] Lien-Hang T. Nguyen, *Hanoi's War: An International History of the War for Peace in Vietnam* (United States: University of North Carolina Press, 2012), pp.42-43.
[129] Nguyen, pp. 29-35.

In 1960, North Vietnam formed the National Liberation Front to serve as the insurgent apparatus and voice of a new rebellion in South Vietnam. In late 1961, Le Duan sent 5,000 North Vietnamese soldiers into South Vietnam to foment rebellion. They joined up with 80,000 communist guerillas who mushroomed in size thanks to growing opposition towards Diem. They faced 280,000 of Diem's soldiers who would soon be aided and advised by over 15,000 military personnel sent by President Kennedy.[130]

American intelligence estimated that in one year the National Liberation Front forces grew in size to 300,000 Vietnamese. Although all North Vietnam had to do was send 5,000 men into South Vietnam to create this force, the first few years of Diem's rule marked a golden age for his government. William Colby, who helped advise him and would go on to become director of the Central Intelligence Agency in the 1970's, said "the main accomplishment" during this time "was truly Diem's, the result of his toughness in crisis times, his firm use of authority amid anarchy, his monastic devotion to his mission of non-communist nationalism and even his prickly refusal to accept counsels of caution and compromise when the situation appeared bleak. By 1958, not only had he put down his opponents, he was well launched on an extensive development program for South Vietnam.

[130] Nguyen, p.59.

Roads were reopened, schools proliferated in the countryside, a five-year DDT-spraying campaign was started to eliminate malaria, rice production began to climb, and light industry grew in the Saigon suburbs."

However, "there were in Diem's approach," Colby said, "flaws that would prove critical in time." Diem functioned "as a Mandarin administrator, a benevolent dictator, forcing his people into development for their own good, whatever they thought of it, authoritarian and undemocratic, using but complaining about the French-trained bureaucracy he employed to do so, believing that it could gradually be reformed and replaced by the graduates of American public-administration programs." He was doing the best he could do.[131]

Despite the fact that South Vietnam had become one of the largest recipients of American foreign aid during this time, the United States Congress as a whole paid very little attention to what was going on there. It is unlikely that most of the American people could have even pointed to it on a map. The events of the first few years of Diem's rule in Vietnam were being overshadowed in the American media by things such as the Suez Crisis, the launch of Sputnik, the failed Hungarian revolution, the U-2 shoot down, Elvis, Marilyn Monroe, the New York Yankees, the crisis in the Taiwan

---

[131] *The Pentagon Papers, Vol. 1*, p. 334; Gibbons, p. 332.

Straits, the nonexistent "bomber gap," and the equally ephemeral "missile gap." Most members of Congress simply deferred to a few of their colleagues, such as Senator Mike Mansfield, that they considered to be experts on Vietnam. Even the Senate Foreign Affairs Committee did not make Vietnam a high priority at the time.

John Newhouse, who handled Vietnam for the committee, claimed that "there was never any coherent point of view" on Vietnam in the foreign relations committee. Why? "It becomes a question of how much the committee is willing to absorb," he explained, "the key variable is the committee itself. If the committee wants to buckle down and get to the bottom of something, it can do that. In my five and a half years there I can count on the fingers of one hand the instances in which the committee wanted to get to the bottom of anything. That wasn't [Chairman] Fulbright's fault. He assumed, correctly, that the majority of his colleagues didn't have the time, or the attention span, or as in the case of a few members, they wanted to use their place on the Foreign Relations Committee mainly to impress people. It's very hard to get a congressional committee focused on anything for very long. If it's page one, and there's a lot of television, maybe. Otherwise, it's a sometime thing."[132]

[132] Gibbons, pp. 328-329.

By the time John Kennedy became president, it became clear to those that were paying attention that South Vietnam didn't seem to be working. Some men in his administration, though, believed that with their guidance and some tweaks here and there that the development strategy in South Vietnam could be made to work. If done right most of the people of Vietnam would come to be grateful. Of course there would always be some unruly elements, but they could be eliminated, or so they thought.

CHAPTER IV - THE IMPROVERS OF MAN

Many people inside the United States government, during the 1950's and 1960's, believed that they could use American power to make the world a better place. Walter Rostow was one of these men. He served as Assistant National Security Adviser to President John Kennedy and eventually became President Lyndon Johnson's chief National Security Adviser. During the 1950's, he was one of the leading advocates for using foreign aid to improve Third World nations and, in the 1960's, became the first civilian presidential advisor to advocate the use of mass bombing attacks in Vietnam to eliminate those unwilling to conform to Ngo Dinh Diem's regime.

Walt Rostow was one of the most well-known public intellectuals of his time, who tended to have empathy for the little guy and was a supporter of the black Civil Rights movement in the United States. He thought government action could help poor people and enable his country to lift up the world. Perhaps he sympathized with those living in poverty in the United States, because when he was a kid he was something of an outsider.

As a child, Rostow had a giant head on a small body and soda-pop glasses, which likely made him a target for bigger children to pick on. He skipped two grades in elementary school. One memory that stayed with him his whole life was the day a mean kid called his older brother Gene a "dirty Jew." Gene beat the boy to a pulp and then carefully looked after Walter. Both would move up in the highest circles of the American power elite together as they grew older.

Their father was born Victor Rostowsky in the Ukraine. He believed in socialism and fled Tsarist Russia to move to New York City around the turn of the 20th century. He changed his name from Rostowsky to Rostow to better fit in to America, got a job as a chemist, and spent much of his time encouraging his kids to read and taught them politics. Walter recalled that he grew up in a "socialist home" where "we were shaped by a particular tradition of Tolstoyan realism." His father taught him to hate Communist dictatorship, but at the same time to be fascinated by socialist theories. He named Gene Rostow after the World War I era socialist presidential candidate Eugene Debs and Walter after the poet Walt Whitman.[133]

Walter Rostow's grades impressed his teachers. He got accepted into Yale University where he

---

[133] David Milne, *America's Rasputin: Walt Rostow and the Vietnam* War (New York: Hill and Wang, 2008), pp. 14-22.

studied economics. There his biggest influence was a graduate student named Richard Bissell who ran an informal "black market" seminar. At the seminar was a fellow student named Max Millikan who later would become a leading economist at the Massachusetts Institute of Technology. In the 1950's, Bissell became one of the top officers of the Central Intelligence Agency, where he would serve as a deputy to director Allen Dulles. Bissell led the development of the U-2 spy plane for the CIA and was in charge of its disastrous Bay of Pigs invasion of Cuba. Millikan and Bissell served as leading confidants of Rostow and helped guide his career after he left college.

Walter Rostow studied Keynesian economics at Yale and came to the decision that one day he would single handedly destroy Marxism. He was "much impressed" by the writings of Karl Marx, but saw them as being harmful to the world. Rostow decided that he "would work on two problems. One was economic history and the other was Karl Marx. Marx raised some interesting questions but gave some bloody bad answers. I would do an answer one day to Marx's theory of history." If he could demolish Marx he could change the world. Being right could make him important. The world would see.[134]

---

[134] Ibid., pp.25-25.

Rostow won a prestigious Rhodes scholarship, which enabled him to spend two years studying at Oxford University in England. He loved it. "It was all new: the double-decker buses, the cars driving on the left side of the street, the distinctive trains - and the still more distinctive vowel sounds," he later said. One fellow scholarship student remembered Rostow at the time as someone "full of intellectual beans" who had "enormous confidence in his own ideas and views."

Rostow returned to Yale where he entered graduate school in the economics department. There he helped Richard Bissell run classes as his teaching assistant. His students were children of the American power elite. They included men, such as William and McGeorge Bundy, who would also go on to serve in the Kennedy and Johnson administrations. They joined the infamous Skull and Bones Yale fraternity and their father served as an Assistant to Secretary of War Henry Stimson. Rostow wasn't born into the rich upper crust like they were, but he had risen to their level on merit and brain power.[135]

Once World War II broke out, Rostow joined the precursor to the Central Intelligence Agency, the Office of Strategic Services. As an OSS officer

---

[135] Michael Swanson, *The War State: The Cold War Origins Of The Military-Industrial Complex And The Power Elite, 1945-1963* (South Carolina: CreateSpace, 2012), p. 210; Milne, pp. 27-31.

he worked in the Enemy Objectives Unit, where he analyzed the impact of Allied bombing on Germany. He looked over damage reports, picked out targets for bombing crews, and came up with the idea that if the bombers focused on German oil storage facilities they might be able to cripple their war efforts and bring them to their knees.

He had trouble getting anyone to pay attention to his idea, until finally a bombing mission destroyed a critical oil storage complex. It seemed to have a big impact on the German army. Walt Rostow felt vindicated, but remained frustrated with General Dwight Eisenhower, who was in charge of Allied forces, believing that he was extending the duration of the war by failing to take his findings seriously, by being too slow in increasing the bombing. It was a feeling that did not go away at the end of the war for him. Rostow later said that the costs of not listening to him "may have been high not only in human life foregone but also in terms of postwar diplomacy, for in the end, the location of Soviet and Western armies on VE-Day certainly played a role... in leading Stalin to conceive as realistic the creation of a Soviet empire in Eastern Europe."[136]

After World War II, Rostow landed in the Harvard economics department and then ended up

[136] Milne, pp. 32-33.

teaching at the Massachusetts Institute of Technology (MIT) thanks to the efforts of his old friend Max Millikan. Rostow became a devoted Cold Warrior, which made him a perfect for MIT. You see, Millikan had come to believe that the university could play a role in helping to win the Cold War. He helped it establish the Center for International Studies (CENIS), which served as a think tank to promote ideas to help the United States maintain its global dominance in the Cold War struggle.

Max Millikan placed Walt Rostow inside the CENIS as a key staff member and together the two worked to get the organization funding. The Ford and Rockefeller foundations chipped in and so did the Central Intelligence Agency. Some of the things the organization did is study economic trends in Asia and try to look for ways to subvert Soviet power in Eastern Europe. Its main purpose, though, became to lobby for an increase in foreign aid to Third World nations as a way to "modernize" them and draw them closer to not only the United States government, but also to the large corporate interests that helped to fund the CENIS and had investments in these nations. Since the CIA was also acting in many of these areas of the world too, its involvement with the CENIS represented a harmony of interests. Rostow later saw the main function of the group as to create "considerable propaganda activity conducted by political and academic figures: [constituting] books, articles, and letters to assorted editors; speeches and symposia; appearances before congressional committees, etc."

Walter Rostow wrote eight books and dozens of articles for scholarly publications on behalf of the CENIS and its beliefs, which he shared. Rostow believed that, with the end of colonialism, the Third World had become the place of East versus West conflict. In order to prevent, or displace, Soviet influence in Third World nations, Rostow promoted foreign aid as the way to win the new "protracted test between communist and non-communist methods of modernization in the developing world."

He was disturbed, however, that Presidents Harry Truman and Dwight Eisenhower did not seem enthusiastic about foreign aid spending. One of Eisenhower's main goals was to try to control government spending. As a result, he had little interest in foreign aid and pushed the idea of prioritizing nuclear weapons over conventional weapons in order to keep a lid on defense spending. This all annoyed Rostow. When Ike appeared to waffle in his eyes, during the Dien Bien Phu crisis, Rostow wrote a scathing article deploring the President for "refusing to involve American combat units" in Vietnam. Such views made him a leading "tough" hard-liner in the Cold War and gave him political inroads with hawkish Democrats.[137]

---

[137] Ibid., pp. 44-49.

He also became a well-known public intellectual with the publication of his book *The Stages of Economic Growth: A Non-Communist Manifesto* in 1960. He got a "Reflective Year Grant" from the Carnegie Corporation to take off work and write it. As he began to work on his book, he wrote his friend C.D. Jackson that his goal was to "uproot the bad works of that angry, passionate old man, Karl Marx" and replace them with his own. Jackson understood the importance of what he was doing, because he had served as head of the psychological warfare division of the OSS, during World War II, and as President's Eisenhower's key liaison man for the CIA and the Pentagon.

To help get his brain going and test his ideas Rostow presented a series of lectures on them at Cambridge University. He boasted to Jackson that what he was doing in his talks was putting "communism quite technically in its place for what it is: not the wave of the future, but a disease of the transitional process from a traditional society to a modern society; and I believe it will illuminate where we are and what we ought to be doing." What he was trying to demonstrate was how economic progress did not lead to a communist end game utopia, but to a corporate capitalist end point. If he could prove this, he would take Marx's place in the pantheon of intellectual history and change the world. He could improve man and he had the backing and friends to do it. Was Rostow in his element? Yes, because as he worked on the book he told former presidential candidate Aldai Stevenson, "it's been fun."[138]

Rostow argued in his book that human history contained a series of stages consisting of different forms of economic growth and power relationships between people. He saw the first stage consisting of traditional societies based primarily on farming, with fairly static economic growth rates in which the people's thoughts were "based on pre-Newtonian science and technology, and on pre-Newtonian attitudes toward the physical world."

He called the second stage "preconditions for take-off" in which people began to look for ways to use science to increase production in agriculture and in new industries. He claimed this stage occurred in Europe towards the end of the Middle Ages, with "the building of an effective centralized national state - on the basis of coalitions touched with a new nationalism, colonial power, or both."

After that stage, Rostow saw a "take-off" stage, which produced "the great watershed in the life of modern societies" in which "the old blocks and resistances to steady growth are finally overcome." Economic growth accelerates as technological innovation becomes a norm and people of old-fashioned values and primitive thinking are pushed aside by "the emergence to political power of a

---

[138] Ibid., pp. 59-60.

group prepared to regard the modernization of the economy as serious, high-order political business."

Most historians would call Rostow's "take-off" stage the industrial revolution, which took place around 1760 to 1820 in Great Britain, with a second industrial revolution taking place throughout Europe, Japan, and the United States from the 1860's to World War I with the growth of railroads, telegraph lines, and the steel and oil industries being the technological drivers of it. Walt Rostow argued that a new "drive to maturity" takes place for "some sixty years after take-off begins" in which innovation and higher growth permeates into various sectors of the economy as "some 10-20% of the national income is steadily invested, permitting output regularly to outstrip the increase in production."

Rostow claimed that, after this phase, all societies and nations entered a final end stage "age of high mass consumption." At this point, the people gain enough real income that they can transcend worrying about their basic needs for food, shelter, and clothing and enjoy living as a mass consumer man in an economy now able to focus on "durable consumers' goods and services."

After that, Rostow argued that people stop looking at "the further extension of modern technology as an overriding objective" and look to "allocate increased resources to social welfare and security." A new "welfare state" emerges as a result as the end point of human social and political history. In Rostow's view of 1950's America, the United States had achieved this final evolution of society, while Western Europe and Japan were moving into it, and the Soviets' were "engaged in an uneasy flirtation" with it, but still far behind.[139]

Rostow's theory actually shared a heavy similarity with the ideas of Karl Marx. That isn't too surprising, because he was obsessed with him. One reviewer of his book even called it "Marxism without Marx," because the idea that human history consisted of several stages of economic order in which man evolved through was central to Marx. To the Marxist, these evolutions were inevitable and could not be stopped.

The difference, though, is that Marx argued that society was still evolving and claimed it was heading towards a communist utopia endpoint in which private property would dissolve and the state would too. And he said there was nothing anyone could do to stop this process. Rostow simply used Marx's notion of human evolution via economic stages and replaced the communist end-point utopia with the United States. For Rostow, the United States represented the final political and economic

---

[139] Walt Rostow, *The Stages of Economic Growth: A Non-Communist Manifesto* (England: Cambridge University Press, 1991), pp. 4-11.

evolution that any society could reach and with its mix of dynamic corporate capitalism and state run welfare programs, guided by intellectuals working inside the government, it all meant that utopia already existed on earth. Or, perhaps you could say, it was as close to utopia as one could get.[140]

Ideas like Rostow's were commonplace in government and academia at the time. The United States found itself in a new position of superiority in terms of military power and economic might, after World War II, and faced a world in which the old colonial states held by Europe, of which Vietnam was just one, were becoming independent. Many members of the American power elite saw it as their role to "modernize" these new nations in order bring them into the orbit of the American empire.

The way to do it was to help American corporations build investments in these countries, get the American taxpayer to be willing to do his part to send foreign aid to them, and to destroy any elements of opposition inside of them. Rostow and Millikan sent a memo to CIA director Allen Dulles telling him that "in the short run communism must be contained militarily. In the long run we must rely on development, in partnership with others, of an environment in which societies which directly or indirectly menace ours will not evolve." American

---

[140] Milne, p. 64.

corporations could then make more profits, while at the same time the world could become home to many budding democracies, thereby becoming a more peaceful place. All other empires in world history exploited man. The American empire would improve him.[141]

The world modernization process, Rostow later explained to one of President Kennedy's advisers, would create "a new post-colonial relationship between northern and southern halves of the Free World... As the colonial ties are liquidated, new and most constructive relations can be built... a new partnership among free men - rich and poor alike." The United States needed to play a critical role in the evolution of these new nations by helping them jump quickly out of their traditional stage and into the take-off stage.[142]

Rostow warned that countries that went through his traditional phase of economic and social order into his "take-off" phase of industrial growth could fall into communism if the United States did not help them modernize. He claimed that the transition into "take-off" required a bit of centralization and growth in government, which had to be carefully guided, because such times

---

[141] Michael Latham, *Modernization as Ideology: American Social Science and "Nation Building" in the Kennedy Era* (North Carolina: The University of North Carolina Press, 2000), p. 55.
[142] Latham, p. 16.

bring with them momentous change. "It is in such a setting of political and social confusion, before the take-off is achieved and consolidated politically and socially as well as economically, that the seizure of power by Communist conspiracy is easiest; and it is in such a setting that a centralized dictatorship may supply an essential precondition for take-off and a sustained drive to maturity: an effective modern state organization," he wrote.

The way he saw it communism was "a disease of the transition." Therefore, in the world of Rostow, and friends of his with a like mind, more foreign aid and covert war against communist subversion was critical in order to modernize the Third World and keep it closely linked to the United States and out of the Soviet orbit. Communist agents were best excised from the body politic of developing countries throughout the world as one would remove cancerous tumors from a human body.[143]

Not everyone bought into Rostow's theories. The economist Kenneth Boulding went on to attack them in an article he titled "The Intellectual Framework of Bad Advice." He claimed that all Rostow had created were "empty taxonomical boxes" filled with phrases and slogans to explain the world and "merely introduced quantitative materials as a means of illustrating his preconceived

143 Rostow, pp. 162-163.

points." The economic historian Barry Supple argued that Rostow's book, *The Stages of Economic Growth*, was "less a theory than a language that gained its power to invade [the] discourse of development as it lost precision and specificity." Rostow's ideas became popular in certain circles, because they painted a positive picture for America's new role in the world. But, in the end, by positing that the evolution of mankind and society had reached an end point represented by 1950's America, Rostow's ideas were actually an egocentric rejection of logos – in short - a jumble of words of pretend reason that was an unreasonable rejection of the world as it really is.[144]

Some ignored the ideas. President Eisenhower and Secretary of State John Foster Dulles, for one thing, were very cool to the idea of using foreign aid as a key tool of policy. Eisenhower simply did not want to spend the money to do it. At the same time, Secretary of State Dulles was more interested in forming alliances with developing nations to keep them in the orbit of the American empire. He thought development was important, but loyalty was the real priority. However, Rostow's ideas caught on with many leaders of the Democratic Party.

Rostow supported Aldai Stevenson for president in 1956 against Eisenhower and got to know

[144] Milne, pp. 65-66.

many of the rising stars in the Democratic Party, including Senator John Kennedy. During the next few years, Democrats like Kennedy attacked the Eisenhower administration for being weak on defense and claimed that it was causing the United States to fall behind in the Cold War. Kennedy first got in contact with Rostow during the 1956 Democratic convention. He then wrote Eugene Rostow that he "had enjoyed and profited "from Walter's advice" on how to argue against Eisenhower's policies in regards to developing the Third World.[145]

Democrats like John Kennedy charged the Eisenhower administration with allowing the Soviets to leap ahead in nuclear technology, claiming that they now faced a "missile gap." It didn't exist, but it made for good headlines. Forces inside the defense industry and the military gave information to politicians and reporters that suggested that it did exist and they ran with it. It was a combination of profits, partisanship, and power driven by faulty intelligence and Cold War zealotry.[146]

Walt Rostow drafted several speeches for Kennedy and sent him letters full of ideas. In one speech he accused the Eisenhower administration of helping create an "economic gap" between rich nations and poor nations to be exploited by the Soviet Union. Foreign aid was the answer. Kennedy

---

[145] Ibid., p. 56.
[146] Swanson, pp. 187-195.

helped draft legislation that helped India get over $200 million in aid money.

As the 1960 Democratic primaries for president approached, John Kennedy gave Rostow a drive to the State Department one day and told him that he was planning to run for president. He joked that he might want to keep his head down now so he won't be seen "by his Republican friends," but Rostow told him not to worry, because "they know that I'm a Democrat." Rostow and Kennedy shared ideas with each other as the presidential election heated up.[147]

John Kennedy and Richard Nixon famously held the first televised debate in presidential history, which contrasted a telegenic Kennedy with an opponent bearing a five o'clock shadow. Kennedy beat Nixon by a narrow margin in the election, but it wasn't just television that helped him do it, but his message and youthful contrast to the Eisenhower administration. People wanted a change, inspiration, and a feeling of dynamism and the Democratic candidate provided that for them. Rostow lifted the phrase "The New Frontier" out of his book *The Stages of Economic Growth* and gave it to Kennedy to serve as his campaign slogan.[148]

At his nomination speech at the Democratic National Committee, Kennedy spoke of a nation in

[147] Milne, pp. 58-59.
[148] Rostow, p. 9.

crisis and in need of urgent change. "Courage, not complacency, is our need today; leadership, not salesmanship," he said, then asked, "are we equal to the challenge? Are we willing to match Russian sacrifice of the present for the future, or must we sacrifice our future in order to enjoy the present? That is the question of the New Frontier." "The New Frontier," he explained, "of which I speak, is not a set of promises - it is a set of challenges. It sums up not what I intend to offer the American people, but what I intend to ask of them. It holds out the promise of more sacrifice instead of more security. Beyond that frontier are uncharted areas of science and space, unsolved problems of peace and war, unconquered pockets of ignorance and prejudice, unanswered questions of poverty and surplus."[149]

Kennedy began his inaugural address by saying, "let the word go forth to friend and foe alike, that the torch has been passed to a new generation of Americans, born in this century, tempered by war, disciplined by a hard and bitter peace, proud of our ancient heritage, and unwilling to witness or permit the slow undoing of those human rights to which this nation has always been committed."

---

[149] K.A. Cuordileone, *Manhood and American Political Culture in the Cold War* (New York: Routledge, 2005), p. 172; Arthur Schlesinger, Jr., *A Thousand Days: John F. Kennedy In The White House* (New York: Fawcett Premier, 1965), p. 64.

In this speech he warned, "let every nation know, whether it wishes us well or ill, that we shall pay any price, bear any burden, meet any hardship, support any friend, oppose any foe to assure the survival and the success of liberty." "In the long history of the world," he said, "only a few generations have been granted the role of defending freedom in its hour of maximum danger. I do not shrink from this responsibility; I welcome it."

Kennedy also promised "to those new states whom we welcome to the ranks of the free, we pledge our word that one form of colonial control shall not have passed away merely to be replaced by a far more iron tyranny." The United States, he said, will assist those that "help themselves for whatever period is required, not because the Communists may be doing it, not because we seek their votes, but because it is right."

The American citizen was not to be a passive spectator in this battle for world freedom and a better life at home. "And so, my fellow Americans, ask not what your country can do for you; ask what you can do for your country," President Kennedy said. In this major speech, and during his campaign appearances, he declared himself to be a watchman for the free world who would awaken the contented masses to meet their common challenges. He spoke of the nation's obligations, its resolve, and called for people to become a part of the national endeavor against their communist competitors.[150]

John Kennedy's words resonated with an America at the height of the Cold War. He became president in what would soon be the darkest years of the Cold War, and two years before the Cuban Missile Crisis, in what would be the most dangerous days in the history of mankind. During his presidential campaign, he used a language of crisis and alarm that was commonplace in the United States in the decades that followed World War II.

Crisis became the dominant mode of thought during the Cold War. It led to what gonzo journalist Hunter S. Thompson called "fear and loathing." From Joseph McCarthy's campaign against Communist subversion, that was more imagined than real, to the "who lost China debate" during the Truman administration, and to all of the talk of "bomber gaps" and "missile gaps" the fear talk was everywhere. The spirit of the times showed up in Bert the Turtle film-strips shown to children teaching them to "duck and cover" to save themselves from atomic blasts, that could come at any moment, to episodes of the TV show *The Twilight Zone*. The fears of world war and doom justified the entire transformation of the United States from

---

[150] Daniel Rodgers, *Age of Fracture* (Cambridge: The Belknap of Harvard University Press, 2011), pp. 18-19; *John F. Kennedy Inaugural Address*, http://www.presidency.ucsb.edu/ws/?pid=8032, accessed 1/14/2015.

a continental republic into a global empire managed by a war state at home.

Anti-communism was the glue that held it all together. Political careers were built in the name of fighting communism. All decisions came to be justified as being a part of the struggle. Those who could create programs to help win the Cold War could find themselves granted new powers and importance. Allen Dulles learned this when he helped to create the CIA. Bureaucrats such as Walter Rostow rose up in private think tanks, and in government by positioning themselves as the smartest people to lead the battle.

Cold War ideology dominated the minds of men so much that it became something few questioned anymore. A constant vigilance and ready for instant war permeated society. People no longer thought about this as something new and unusual, because it became a part of everyday life. And it required a certain denial of reality, because one could go crazy if one worried about the dangers of nuclear war all of the time. The need for denial also hid the reality of empire from people and made the erosion of liberty and freedom at home that came with it easy to accept, and for some to even welcome.

Big war states require big governments, which in time requires all to sacrifice for. By 1953, three fourths of the entire federal budget of the United

States became earmarked to national security programs. Defense spending came to equal eighteen percent of the nation's entire gross national product and a full one-third of the country's business activities. President Eisenhower called this the military-industrial complex. Just about everything the government did became justified as part of the Cold War confrontation. Even building highways and funding college scholarships was justified as necessary for defense. War ideology dominated American life.

The imperial premises of the war state were codified in national security strategy document NSC-68 signed by Harry Truman. It dictated that "order" in the world be a new objective for the United States to not only wish for, but to actively strive for. The document said that from now on every nation in the world should be considered friend or foe in the struggle against communism. This meant that nations that tried to proclaim themselves neutral should be turned to friend lest they align themselves with the communists. CIA backed overthrows of elected leaders in places such as Iran and Guatemala were one result. And the logic led to Kennedy's approval of the CIA's failed Bay of Pigs invasion of Castro's Cuba.[151]

However, John Kennedy's view of the world was a little more nuanced than much of his tough

[151] Swanson, pp. 85-91.

campaign rhetoric suggested. Kennedy also said, in his inaugural address as president, that the United States should "not fear to negotiate." "To those nations who would make themselves our adversary, we offer not a pledge but a request: that both sides begin anew the quest for peace, before the dark powers of destruction unleashed by science engulf all humanity in planned or accidental self-destruction," he said.[152]

President Kennedy didn't see the world in the pure binary terms of us versus them that his predecessors did, especially people like Secretary of State John Foster Dulles. He argued that colonialism was dying out and third world nationalism was taking its place as shown by people such as Gamal Nasser in Egypt and a wave of new nation states and leaders that emerged in Africa in the place of colonial governments. Kennedy did not believe that the United States could oppose nationalist forces and succeed. He carried out personal one on one diplomacy with leaders of the Third World in letters and in personal meetings to engage with them. When some of them formed a "Non-Aligned Movement" to proclaim independence from both the Soviet Union and the United States he did not turn away

[152] *John F. Kennedy Inaugural Address*, http://www.presidency.ucsb.edu/ws/?pid=8032, accessed 1/14/2015.

from them or try to punish them as Dulles would have.

Undersecretary of State George Ball later explained President Kennedy's thinking by saying, "postwar diplomacy had rested largely on the assumption that the United States... was a status quo power, while the Soviet Union was essentially a revolutionary power, and that the United States would benefit by encouraging stability; the Soviet Union by exploiting turbulence... The Kennedy Doctrine challenged this approach... If America failed to encourage the young revolutionaries in the new countries, they would inevitably turn toward the Soviet Union.... America should, therefore, stop trying to sustain traditional societies and ally itself with the side of revolution."

This strategy fit in with modernization theories, such as those popularized by Walt Rostow in his book *The Stages of Economic Growth*. Kennedy created such programs as the Peace Corps to send Americans overseas to build new relations with people in the new post-colonial nation states and sent foreign aid to them. He formed the Alliance of Progress to implement foreign aid programs to Latin American countries in hopes that the assistance would help develop and diversify their economies.

In 1953, there were only four independent nation states on the African continent and by the time

Kennedy became President there were twenty-three more. In Senator Frank Church's view, Kennedy was "the first American president to take a personal interest in African affairs. He understood the importance of the collapse of colonialism on that continent, the emergence of the independent governments, and the need for the United States to establish good relations with these governments." This was no surprise to African leaders, because as a Senator President Kennedy had denounced French colonialism in Algeria, even in the face of criticism from the Eastern Establishment journal Foreign Affairs. "African chiefs of state had a feeling of great esteem, I can even say, great admiration, for President Kennedy," said Leopold Senghor, who served as president of Senegal from 1960 to 1980.

This was a big break from the past. President Eisenhower met on average with one head of state from Africa a year while Kennedy met on average one a month. But it went further than just personal meetings. Ben Bella of Algeria took a trip to Washington, D.C. to meet with Kennedy and then went to meet Fidel Castro in Cuba. "I was treated worse than the devil in all the newspaper offices of America," Bella remembers, because of his plans to meet with Castro.

However, when he met President Kennedy, "he gave me the impression of a courageous and honest man, but he seemed to be subjected to endless pressure and to be, to an extraordinary degree, the prisoner of a system. I finally took my leave of Kennedy," Bella said, "with personal feelings of sympathy and respect towards him." When Bella went to his plane, though, he feared that the CIA, without Kennedy's knowledge, might blow it up at the airport or attack it on its way to Cuba.[153]

Asia also represented new possibilities and challenges for John Kennedy. Kennedy long had an interest in Vietnam dating back to when he visited it during its war with France in 1951. However, he did not fully support the French war effort, because he saw colonialism as something with little future. When he came back home, he said, "There is no broad support of the native Vietnam Government among the people of that area. To check the southern drive of communism makes sense but not only through the reliance on the force of arms. The task is rather to build strong native non-Communist sentiment within these areas and rely on them as a spearhead of defense. To do this apart from and in defiance of innately nationalistic aims spells foredoomed failure."

---

[153] Philip Muehlenbeck, *Betting on the Africans: John F. Kennedy's Courting of African Nationalist Leaders* (England: Oxford University Press, 2014), pp. xiv, 51, 132, 225; for an overview of Kennedy's policies to the third world also see Robert Rakove, *Kennedy, Johnson, and the Nonaligned World* (England: Cambridge University Press, 2014).

This logic led him to oppose direct US military intervention in Vietnam, when elements inside the Eisenhower administration lobbied for such a move during the siege at Dien Bien Phu, and to support Ngo Dinh Diem as an anti-communist force of nationalism afterwards. Kennedy joined the American Friends of Vietnam in 1955, which acted as lobby for Diem. In a speech for the group, he explained that he saw Diem's regime as "a proving ground of democracy in Asia" and said that "the United States is directly responsible for this experiment - it is playing an important role in the laboratory where it is being conducted. We cannot afford to permit that experiment to fail."

Kennedy explained that he saw South Vietnam as a "new state" born out of colonialism and threatened by communism. He argued that "what we must offer them is a revolution - a political, economic, and social revolution far superior to anything the communists can offer - far more peaceful, far more democratic, and far more locally controlled. Such a revolution will require much from the United States and much from Vietnam." The aid required, Kennedy said, money, people to spread literacy, and "military assistance to rebuild the new Vietnamese Army, which every day faces the growing peril of Vietminh armies across the border."[154]

As president, Kennedy expanded the American effort in Vietnam by increasing the number of advisers there and the amount of money sent to Diem's government, but he resisted multiple calls by his advisors and the Joint Chiefs of Staff to send combat troops to the country. However, he did not really spend a lot of his time on Vietnam, until the final months of his presidency when turmoil in the country increased to the point of crisis. Most of his time as president when it came to foreign affairs was taken up by relations with the Soviet Union, which were marked at first by an increase in tensions over Berlin, the dangerous Cuban Missile Crisis, and then a move towards détente by both Khrushchev and Kennedy that culminated in the signing of a Test Ban Treaty outlawing the detonation of atomic weapons in the atmosphere or underwater, and hopes for more diplomatic moves that ended with Kennedy's death in Dallas, Texas, on November 22, 1963.

Vietnam was also overshadowed by one crisis after another, such as those involving Laos, Cuba, and the Congo in Africa. My previous book, *The*

---

[154] William Gibbons, *The U.S. government and the Vietnam War: Executive and legislative roles and relationships, Volume II* (New Jersey: Princeton University Press, 1986), pp. 4-6.

War State, goes in depth into the Bay of Pigs invasion, the Cuban Missile Crisis, and Kennedy's dealings with Khrushchev so these are topics I am not going to go into detail in this book. This book is about the Vietnam War.

However, there was one thing about the Bay of Pigs invasion that was important for Kennedy and Vietnam. It had a big impact on his decision making. The operation was such a complete disaster that it caused him to distrust the advice of the Joint Chiefs of Staff and people in the Central Intelligence Agency. He took the Bay of Pigs invasion plans at face value and afterwards would not take advice from his advisors and leaders of the war state bureaucracy without question ever again.

When John F. Kennedy first became president, the members of the Joint Chiefs of Staff and the leaders of the CIA were people he inherited from President Eisenhower. After the Bay of Pigs invasion, he relied more on a few of his closest and most trusted advisors for advice than on them. He appointed General Maxwell Taylor to be his personal military adviser and go between for him and the Joint Chiefs of Staff and had Ted Sorenson, who had worked with him as his trusted top assistant in the Senate for years, take on a role in foreign affairs. At key moments, he had his brother Robert Kennedy, who was the Attorney General, play a key role in foreign affairs too. He also put more faith and trust in Robert McNamara, who he had brought into his administration as Secretary of Defense.

McNamara became particularly close to the Kennedy family to the point of spending social time with them outside work hours. Robert Kennedy held regular social seminars at Hickory Hill, an elegant white Georgian mansion situated on five and a half acres of land in McLean, Virginia. It had served as the Civil War headquarters of General George McClellan and was later owned by Supreme Court Justice Robert Jackson. The seminars gathered around a nightly lecture. The subjects ranged from Isaiah Berlin and Al Capp to foreign affairs. McNamara attended regularly. Arthur Schlesinger organized them.[155]

Jacqueline Kennedy went to most of them. At one seminar Walt Rostow gave a lecture. "Jack was out of town," Mrs. Kennedy said, "and making a speech somewhere, and he called me up, and I was called out of the room, and he said, 'what's the seminar?' And I said, 'It's Walt Rostow, talking about underdeveloped countries.' ...And he said - so loudly, I had to put my hand over the receiver - 'Jesus Christ! You mean all those people are - Walt Rostow's got all those people trapped in there, listening to him?' Because he really thought Walt Rostow went on and on, and was hard to listen to.

---

[155] Arthur Schlesinger, Jr., *Robert Kennedy And His Times* (New York: Ballantine Books, 1978), pp. 162, 638-639.

He said, 'I'm glad I'm not at that seminar.' But he liked him. He never said anything mean about him."[156]

Robert McNamara was only forty-four years old when he accepted Kennedy's request to become Secretary of Defense. Before that he had had risen to the CEO position of the Ford Motor Company. He served during World War II as a lieutenant colonel involved in the logistical planning for the B-29 bombing campaign against Japan. He was a determined activist and originator of programs, using statistical analysis to make budgeting decisions in the defense department. He brought people in from the RAND Corporation to the Pentagon to engage in "cost effectiveness" and "system analysis" studies.

This often rubbed up against the interests of the individual members of the Joint Chiefs of Staff, who represented the different branches of the armed forces and often looked after their own parochial budget demands instead of the whole. They also tended to be much older and possessed hands on experience going back to World War II. The civilians in the Kennedy administration often looked at them as tradition bound when they were looking

[156] Caroline Kennedy and Michael Beschloss, *Jacqueline Kennedy: Historic Conversations on Life with John F. Kennedy* (New York: Hyperion, 2011), pp. 315-316.

to make new innovations, while the chiefs looked at them as unseasoned youngsters.

General Lyman Lemnitzer, who served as Chairman of the Joint Chiefs of Staff, had a career going back to 1942, when he served as the Plans and Operations Officer for the North African invasion during World War II. He then served as the Deputy Chief of Staff to British General Harold Alexander in the Mediterranean theater and then commanded an infantry division during the Korean War. A few years later, he became the Chief of Staff of the Army and then was promoted to the Chairmanship by President Eisenhower.

Admiral Arleigh Burke sat on the Joint Chiefs of Staff as Chief of Naval Operations when the Kennedy presidency began. He led a fleet of destroyers in the Pacific during World War II and then took command of a carrier task force. In Joint Chiefs of Staff deliberations he was always very articulate and ready to defend navy programs. George Anderson succeeded him in July of 1961. Anderson had been an aide to Admiral Radford when he drew up the plans for Operation Vulture during the siege at Dien Bien Phu.

General George Decker served as Chief of Staff for the Army on the Joint Chiefs of Staff. He spent the final years of World War II as head of the Sixth Army in the Pacific theater. He then became comptroller of the army and head of the United Nations command of Korea after the Korean War. General Earl Wheeler would take his place in 1962. At the same time General David Shoup represented the Marine Corps in Joint Chiefs of Staff meetings as its Commandant, a position he had held since 1959. Shoup had won the Medal of Honor in Tawara during World War II.

Finally, General Thomas White of the Air Force served on the Joint Chiefs of Staff until he retired in June of 1961. Then Vice-Chief-of Staff General Curtis LeMay succeeded him. LeMay had a reputation for being outspoken and aggressive as the commander of the bombing forces that destroyed Japan during World War II and then as the organizer of the 1948 Berlin airlift. After the war he single handily created the Strategic Air Command and led its future efforts. General LeMay was blunt to the point of being crude, which made him a popular figure with some, but at times led to acrimony with the other members of the Joint Chiefs of Staff. He enjoyed riling people up sometimes even blowing cigar smoke in people's faces to do it.[157]

All of these men had vast military experience. General LeMay, however, had more political power outside the military world than the other chiefs did

---

[157] Walter Poole, *History of the Joint Chiefs of Staff: The Joint Chiefs of Staff and National Policy: Volume VIII, 1961-1964* (Washington, D.C.,: Office of the Joint History Office of the Chairman of the Joint Chiefs of Staff, 2011), pp. 2-3.

thanks to the fact that, as the Kennedy administration began, twenty-seven percent of the defense budget was going to his strategic nuclear forces. This meant huge profits for the defense companies building and servicing them and connections with Congressmen in whose districts the companies operated in. It also led to struggles between LeMay and McNamara over budget priorities.[158]

General LeMay claimed that McNamara could give an "impressive performance," but often with "what he called facts and figures and so forth that may or may not have been correct." Curtis LeMay came to believe that "everyone that came in with the Kennedy administration is the most egotistical people that I ever saw in my life. They had no faith in the military, they had no respect for the military at all. They felt that the Harvard Business School method of solving problems would solve any problem in the world. They were capable of doing it; they were better than all the rest of us; otherwise they wouldn't have gotten their superior education, as they saw it. And the fact that they had entitled them to govern the rest of us, and we shouldn't question their decisions."[159]

As the words of a volume published by the Office of Joint History of the Office of the Chairman

---

[158] Steven Rearden, *Council of War: A History Of The Joint Chiefs Of Staff, 1942- 1991* (Washington, D.C.,: National Defense University Press, 2012), p 250.
[159] Swanson, pp. 254-255.

of the Joint Chiefs of Staff summed it up, after the failed invasion of Cuba at the Bay of Pigs, "President Kennedy's doubts about the Chief's competence were matched by their doubts about his determination to do whatever might be necessary to prevail. In a setting where war in some place and at some level seemed more likely than not, the Chiefs could see only one solution for Cuba: invade the island and oust Castro. Arms control, in this climate seemed to them pointless, and even dangerous, superior military strength was what communist leaders understood. The limited test ban treaty of 1963 was an anomaly, which they endorsed only with important qualifications."[160]

As a body the Joint Chiefs of Staff met three times a week. They were not responsible for the day to day running of the service branches. That's what the Vice-Chiefs did. The Joint Chiefs of Staff oversaw about four hundred staff officers who turned out war planning and position papers that were used to set the agenda for the meetings of the chiefs. All the bureaucratic paper work served as a cover for fierce infighting among the services over budgets and force levels. Most issues were routine, but often their disagreements were watered down into positions added together in a mishmash joint paper.

---

[160] Poole, p. 297.

The way this process worked is that a staff officer would prepare a position on "flimsy" paper. It was then given a review by individual action officers and printed on buff paper. It then received a joint staff review and published on green paper with dissenting opinions attached. If that paper was then important enough it was passed on to the Joint Chiefs of Staff for them to issue a final opinion on it. If they approved it the paper was then printed as a final "red-striped" decision paper. This whole process took about three weeks from start to finish and over 15,000 items went through it every year.[161]

As Marine Commandant David Shoup and his assistant Colonel James Donovan explained it, "the service planners are a most influential group in the military establishment. These largely nameless and obscure officers are predominantly eager, hard-working, and ambitious young lieutenant colonels, Navy commanders, colonels, and captains, who have been carefully selected for duty on the top staffs. They are qualified by attendance and distinguished performance at the service and joint schools. They are capable staff-paper writers, articulate briefing officers, and professionally well informed. They have demonstrated their loyalty to

[161] Jack Schulimson, *History of the Joint Chiefs of Staff, The Joint Chiefs of Staff and the War in Vietnam, 1960-1968, Part I.* (Washington, D.C.,: Office of the Joint History Office of the Chairman of the Joint Chiefs of Staff, 2011), pp. 4-6.

their services' 'party line.' The planners are the key schemers and military doctrinaires... Theoretically they are divorced from their service loyalties and biases while serving on the Joint Staff. But each officer understands that his parent service keeps an eye on his performance and expects him to faithfully represent his service's doctrine and to protect its functions, roles, and missions in all phases of joint planning."

According to Colonel Donovan, "there is nothing outside of Congress' legislative bill production which compares to the paper ritual of the Joint Chiefs and the service staffs in the creation of national-level defense plans, programs, and policies. In this process the top generals and the various civilian appointees in the Office of the Secretary of Defense tend to become captives of these 'Indians' - the planners - who do the research, write the papers, learn the details, and have the answers. The vast number of projects and problems which occupy the efforts of the top military staffs are frequently so complex, technical, or extensive that they have to be reduced to simplified briefings in order to be digested and even understood by the busy service chiefs and the Pentagon civilians. In the process, opinions tend to become facts and what commences as objective analysis crystallizes into policies and positions. The recommendations of the middle-level staff officers go forward to the highest echelons of the defense establishment because the top leaders either don't fully understand the problems or have no other ideas and information."

"It is in this arena of staff planners on the joint staffs," Donovan writes, "where the results of careerism, parochialism, and interservice rivalry become dominant factors affecting the ideological values of the military profession, the purposes of many defense programs, the aggressive nature of contingency planning - and the militarism of the defense establishment. Officers in staff planning assignments have only a few years to make their marks as high-level staff officers. They work hard to satisfy their chiefs to foster their services doctrines and to establish a reputation as loyal defenders of their respective organizations." They make sure that their respective branch of the service gets its proper role and recognition in operations planning and budgeting.[162]

Bureaucracies that were similar, but not as large or complex, existed in all departments of the federal government, including the Department of State and the Central Intelligence Agency. While individual presidents came and went, the men in the bureaucracies stayed and existed as a "permanent government." This type of system rarely produced grand well thought out decisions and strate-

---

[162] James Donovan and David Shoup, *Militarism USA* (New York: Scribners, 1970) pp. 75-77.

gies, but instead resulted in ad hoc decision making. Policies then, and today, rarely change in one grand sweep, but instead do so slowly as modifications to existing policies.[163]

Roger Hilsman, who served in the Department of State during the Kennedy years, wrote, "Officialdom, whether civil or military, is hardly neutral. It speaks, and inevitably it speaks as an advocate. The Army battles for ground forces, the Air Force for bombers; the 'Europe faction' for policy benefiting NATO, and the 'African faction' for anticolonialist policies unsettling to our relations with Europe. All of these many interests, organizations, and institutions inside and outside government - are joined in a struggle over the goals of governmental policy and over the means by which these goals shall be achieved. Instead of unity there is conflict. Instead of majestic progression, there are erratic zigs and zags. Instead of clarity and decisiveness, there are tangle and turmoil, instead of order, confusion."

The American news media tends to focus on partisanship and personalities in its reporting of American politics, while political scientists engage in polling and study voting trends. However, real power politics happens inside of government and is rarely reported about on the television news. "Abusive rivalries arise between the government agencies engaged in making policy," Hilsman wrote,

---

[163] Swanson, pp. 245-247.

"and even within a single agency different factions battle, each seeking allies in other agencies, and among the press."[164]

The best of presidents stay above all of this and put themselves in a position to look after the interests of the nation as a whole. For a president who wants to make a foreign policy decision of his own the permanent government war state is more of a political actor to be reckoned with than the voting public is. President Eisenhower dealt with this system by holding frequent, long, and formal National Security Council meetings in which the position papers of the bureaucracy were brought to him for a final decision.

President Kennedy wanted to make sure that he was not simply approving the decisions of others, so he streamlined this process. He held less frequent National Security Council meetings and dealt more with an "inner circle" of advisers. He reduced the number of people serving on his National Security Staff and gave them greater individual power. He eliminated the Planning Board and the Operations Coordinating Board that gave the Joint Chiefs of Staff a direct access to the White House. The chiefs closed their office of special assistant for national security affairs that they had in the White House and conducted National Security Council

---

[164] Roger Hilsman, *To Move A Nation* (New York: A Delta Book, 1964), p. 8.

business through a small liaison office next to the Old Executive Office Building.

For the most part, Robert McNamara and General Maxwell Taylor handled the Joint Chiefs of Staff for Kennedy, so they played a diminished role in White House policy making. President Kennedy acted almost as if he were his own Secretary of State, communicating directly with world leaders himself through letters and personal one on one meetings. On issues that he had a great interest in he tried to position people he held in great trust into key positions inside of the bureaucracy that could act as his eyes and ears that had similar policy objectives as he had. "His actions showed that he was reading people's memos, and he called up 'little' men on the phone, all of which created an excitement that the bureaucracy had not known for many years," Hilsman wrote.[165]

President John Kennedy appointed McGeorge Bundy to be his national security adviser. His brother, William Bundy, also joined the administration working for McNamara in the defense department. At one point, Kennedy had considered Arthur Schlesinger for national security adviser, but instead he chose McGeorge Bundy, who, looking back later, thought the president was looking for someone he both felt comfortable with and

[165] Rearden, pp. 212-213; Hislman, p.568.

would be more "acceptable to what was then called the establishment."[166]

John Kennedy let Walter Rostow know that he wanted him to have a key foreign affairs position too in his administration as he put it together. Kennedy had considered Arkansas Senator William Fulbright as Secretary of State, but his segregationist civil rights positions in the South made that impossible. So, he turned to Dean Rusk, who had served as Assistant Secretary of State for Far Eastern Affairs during the Truman administration. He had a reputation for being a noncontroversial manager of bureaucracy. He was heading the Rockefeller Foundation when Kennedy asked him to join his cabinet, which gave him the right Eastern Establishment credentials as a bonus.

He told Rusk to consider Rostow to take a position as head of the State Department policy planning staff. Rusk asked Rostow to draft a position paper on how the United States could defend its interests without resorting to the use of nuclear weapons. The Kennedy administration wanted to move away from the Eisenhower and Dulles doctrine of "massive retaliation" and towards a policy of "flexible response," a term coined by General Maxwell Taylor to describe limited wars that the United States was more likely to engage in. Rostow came back with a well thought out paper that said

---

[166] Swanson, pp. 210-211.

that "limited war" was something the country had to be prepared for, but he also said that there was one scenario in which "limited war might be consistent with the use of nuclear weapons." That is if there was a breakout in Asia "by Chinese communist forces on a large scale over the southern and especially southeastern boundaries of the country." If China put troops into Vietnam he thought the United States would have to reply with atomic weapons.

Rusk had a tough meeting with Rostow and let him know that he didn't want him on his staff and gave the job to George McGhee instead. In a fit of anger Rostow told Rusk, "McGhee is a fine man... but he is the last man in the world to do a planning job. Planning is not his cup of tea." Rostow thought Rusk didn't understand who he was dealing with, because he had a limited picture "of me as a professor who wrote books, who could perhaps contribute speeches, but he had no sense that I had operated seriously in government."

After the meeting, Rostow met with Kennedy in a hotel suite ten days before he became president. Rostow remembered that Kennedy came out of the bathroom "without affection and stark naked. This was a man comfortable with human beings and human situations." He put on a robe and the two talked. Kennedy told Rostow that he could work as McGhee's assistant, but Rostow told him he would never serve under a man like him. Kennedy promised to think of something better.

A few days later, Kennedy asked Rostow to be his deputy special assistant for national security affairs. Rostow immediately accepted. He would officially work directly under McGeorge Bundy. Rostow once had Bundy as a student. Although Bundy was officially Rostow's boss, the two divided the world up together. Bundy focused most of his energy on relations with the Soviet Union and Europe, while Rostow took responsibility for most of the work concerning Asia.

Bundy tended to act as a secretary who organized the views of others and presented them to Kennedy, while Rostow tended to create ideas of his own and advocate for them. But one of his old colleagues from MIT, Lucian Pye, worried when he read the newspaper story about Rostow's appointment. Pye began a class telling his students about the news - "you know, you don't quite sleep so well any more when you know some of the people going to Washington."[167]

The first big thing Rostow and Kennedy dealt with was not Vietnam, but neighboring Laos. Vietnam wasn't hardly even on the radar as the final days of President Eisenhower's administration came to a close. Kennedy and a few of his advisors held a meeting with President Eisenhower. They

---

[167] Milne, pp. 71-73.

didn't say a word about Vietnam. It just wasn't a concern. Instead, they talked about Cuba and Laos. Eisenhower said Kennedy might have to put troops in Laos, because the country was on the verge of collapse.

"What about China?" Kennedy asked him. Would China invade Laos if the United States put troops there like they intervened during the Korean War? Would the Soviets respond by moving on Berlin?

"It's a high-stakes poker game," Eisenhower replied, "there's no easy solution." It was a game that would put Walter Rostow right in the thick of the action and would have a big influence on Kennedy's decision before the year was over to make more of a commitment to help Diem in South Vietnam. According to the Pentagon Papers, "the fact was that our stake in Vietnam had increased because of what had been happening in Laos." What happened in Laos included the presentation of proposals to President Kennedy that could have led to nuclear warfare if he had implemented them.[168]

---

[168] Swanson, pp. 201-203; *The Pentagon Papers*, Gravel Edition, Volume II (Boston: Beacon Press, 1971), p. 51.

CHAPTER V - THE PRIZE OF SOUTH-EAST ASIA

Only a few weeks after John Kennedy became president, he organized a task force on Laos that included Walt Rostow, Assistant Secretary of State for the Far East J. Graham Parsons, who had been an ambassador to Laos for a few years during the Eisenhower administration, Dean Rusk, and Kennedy's new Assistant Secretary of Defense for International Security Affairs, Paul Nitze. Laos did not have a strong government and was home to several armed factions. Communist Pathet Lao forces allied with North Vietnam and China inside the country were making inroads.[169]

On March 20, 1961, Kennedy held a meeting with Rostow and his Laos advisers. Also present at the meeting were other men close to the President including McGeorge Bundy, Arthur Schlesinger, Jr., and Ted Sorenson. CIA Director Allen Dulles,

---

[169] William Gibbons, *The U.S. government and the Vietnam War: Executive and legislative roles and relationships, Volume II* (New Jersey: Princeton University Press, 1986), pp. 4-6.

Secretary of Defense Robert McNamara, and Admiral Arleigh Burke were also in attendance. So was Roger Hilsman who was serving as the Director of the Bureau of Research and Intelligence of the State Department. Rostow argued that the United States should send troops into neighboring Thailand where they could be stationed to be deployed into Laos at any moment.

His idea was not to engage in combat with these troops, but to use them as a potential bargaining chip. Rostow believed that they could deter the Pathet Lao and be used to force negotiations with them. Admiral Burke said that the Joint Chiefs opposed this idea. He said that they did not want to send troops to the mainland of Asia and predicted that if the President sent troops to Thailand that the Chinese or the North Vietnamese would simply pour troops into Laos to stiffen the Pathet Lao.

In Burke's view, that would mean a potential war with China. The only way they could win is if they sent 60,000 troops into Laos and backed them with air cover and even nuclear weapons. The way he saw it they should go all the way or stay out.

The Joint Chiefs did not want a repeat of what happened in Korea and did not want a massive land war in Asia to ever happen again. "Most students of international politics," Roger Hilsman later explained, "think of the Korean War as a success - an overt aggression was stopped and the

Communists brought to discipline their ambitions by a limited use of force which confined the war and prevented its spiraling to engulf the whole world. But to many of the higher-ranking American military, the Korean War was a frustrating humiliation. The American army had been fought to a standstill by Asians, and by Asians whose arms and equipment were somewhat primitive by American standards. Air power, though freely used on the supply lines between the Yalu and the thirty-eight parallel, had not succeeded in stopping the flow of men and equipment. The significance to the military of the limitations and restrictions put on a wider use of force - principally, bombing China north of the Yalu - was probably as much a rationalization as a frustration. But attitudes formed and hardened, and by 1961, it was a shibboleth among the Joint Chiefs of Staff that the United States ought never again to fight a limited war on the ground in Asia."

At the end of the meeting, Kennedy decided not to send troops to Thailand, but to instead put an alert on a task force in Okinawa that was trained for fighting in Asia. He ordered a fleet of Navy ships to sail to the Gulf of Siam and readied a Marine unit stationed in Japan. He then got on national television and declared to the American people, and to the world, that a superpower confrontation in Laos was now at hand. He had a map of Laos sitting behind him and said that he was seeking the goal of a "truly neutral Laos" and that if communist attacks continued to thwart neutrality they would have to "consider their response." "The security of all of Southeast Asia will be endangered if Laos loses its neutral independence. Its own safety runs with the safety of us all - in real neutrality observed by all," he declared, "I know that every American will want his country to honor its obligations to the point that freedom and security of the free world and ourselves may be achieved."[170]

Laos was a tiny landlocked nation full of mountains, a dense jungle that airplane pilots couldn't even see through, and was so primitive that it didn't even have a single railroad in it and only a handful of roads. Before World War II, only a dozen people in Laos had a college degree and in the 1950's most government officials had the equivalent of a United States junior high school education. How did this nation become so important that Americans were watching Kennedy on their

---

[170] Document 35, *Foreign Relations of the United States, 1961-1963. Laos Crisis: Volume XXIV,* U.S. Department of State; https://history.state.gov/historicaldocuments/frus1961-63v24/d35, accessed 1/14/2015.; Arthur Schlesinger, Jr., *A Thousand Days: John F. Kennedy In The White House* (New York: Fawcett Premier, 1965), pp. 310-311; Roger Hilsman, *To Move A Nation* (New York: A Delta Book, 1964), pp. 127-131.

television sets tell them that it was now the center of a Cold War crisis?[171]

Laos was a new nation established by the 1954 Geneva Conference, which ended the war between France and the Vietnamese communists. The conference not only created North and South Vietnam, but also granted independence to Laos, which had also been a part of French-Indochina. The nation had a population of about two million people and was bordered on the east by the two Vietnams, to the South by Thailand, and to the North by China. It was totally landlocked and stuck in the middle of all of these countries, some of which were antagonistic to one another. Historically, it existed for centuries as a neutral kingdom surrounded by larger powers. President Eisenhower had approved a CIA nation building operation in Laos and the United States was funding its entire military budget.

The Geneva agreements ordered all foreign combat units including French and Vietnamese out of Laos and recognized the sovereignty of the Western leaning Royal Laotian Government over the country. In the northern provinces next to Vietnam, though, the communist Pathet Lao forces controlled large amounts of territory. The Geneva agreement didn't allow combat troops from France,

---

[171] William Rust, *Before The Quagmire: American Intervention In Laos, 1964-1961* (Kentucky: University Press of Kentucky, 2012), p. 6.

but allowed for 1,500 French military personnel to remain in order to train the forces of the Royal Government. [172]

The American State Department sent Charles Yost to serve as a minister in Laos in 1954 and then as ambassador in 1955. When he arrived the entire US government operation consisted of a small "legation" office, which was a detachment of the US embassy in Saigon. The embassy in Laos was two simple rooms in the Laotian capital of Vientiane overlooking the Mekong River. A few hundred yards down the waterway was a slaughterhouse that dumped animal parts into the river. The smell reached the embassy. Heat and poor sanitation gave the reputation for this as being "the most difficult post in the entire Foreign Service." Undersecretary of State Walter Bedell Smith told Yost that "there's not any point in our sending a lot of stuff up to you there, because the whole place is going down the drain very shortly."

One of the first things Yost did in Laos was to speak with Prince Souvanna Phouma, who was serving on behalf of the Royal Family as the nation's Prime Minister. He told Yost that his goal was to unite his country by trying to stay out of the Cold War conflicts. He argued that no real Laotian could be a communist and that what he wanted to do was split off members of the Pathet Lao from

[172] Ibid., p.8.

the North Vietnamese communists that were supporting them. His half-brother Prince Souphanouvong was the public leader of the Pathet Lao, so he had reason to do think he could do this, but Yost found the idea dangerous and so did most people in Washington.[173]

After eighteen months in Laos, Yost lost twenty pounds. He caught dysentery and went home. As he left, he sent a cable to Washington about the future of Laos. He noted that ninety-percent of the nation's people lived self-sufficiently in remote areas with little contact with the government. He doubted that the nation would be able to "exist indefinitely as a wholly independent nation" and that the United States was sending it subsidies that amounted "to five times national revenues."

He thought its best hope would be some sort of partition, but that the worst thing the United States could do would be to force it to take a "military posture which the Lao government would consider rash and provocative," because it would damage relations "seriously and perhaps fatally." His immediate superiors liked his paper, but his advice was essentially ignored by President Eisenhower and John Foster Dulles, who wanted Laos as an ally and not a neutral nation. Yost was replaced by Graham Parsons.

---

[173] Ibid, pp. 14-18.

In a National Security meeting, CIA Director Allen Dulles declared that if the Royal Laotian Government talked with the Pathet Lao it "would result in substantial gains for the communists." He advised doing everything possible to build up government military forces as a counterforce. The CIA opened up a station in Laos ran by Milton Clark and two other men. One American embassy staffer noted that "they had their own airline. All of their cars were marked specifically. They had separate nice housing. They stood out, not like a sore thumb, but like a sore hand." CIA case officer Stuart Methven said," we operated in the open, because there was little cover, no place to hide, no secret that wouldn't come out, no 'plausible denial.'" Case officers in his situation spent most of their time talking with government and military officials and giving them money. Such relationships were termed "assets" in CIA spy parlance. [174]

The Joint Chiefs of Staff in turn opened up a Programs Evaluation Office (PEO) in Laos with twenty-two military personnel. To avoid breaking the Geneva agreement they wore plain clothes. Their communication cables went straight to the commander of the US forces in the Pacific with copies sent to the Pentagon and the Laos ambassador. The PEO was commanded by Brigadier General Rothwell Brown, who had served as an advisor to Chiang Kai-shek in Manchuria during World

---

[174] Ibid, pp. 42, 48.

War II and then worked in counterinsurgency operations during the Korean War.

Brown believed that the United States was going down the "blundering path to final defeat" in Asia "for it is in the East that the final struggle will occur between our Christian-industrial-technological civilization and the explosion of teeming millions who, like lemmings on route to the sea, may burst their present boundaries and attempt to inundate the world." He saw Laos in crisis, but was disturbed that "the nature and characteristics of the Lao people make evaluation of morale, as Americans understand it, almost impossible. Their attitude is friendly, however, it is nearly impossible to implant a sense of urgency or desire for hard work or the accomplishment of projects on schedule."

The United States sent $40 million per year in military aid to Laos and roughly $10 million in development assistance. Brown found that "by American standards corruption is high." A great number of the foreign aid dollars were funneled to the Royal Laos Government Treasury through the US Commodity Import Program. The RLG gave the US dollars to local importers in return for Lao currency bills, called kip. The importers were "often key government officials," according to a PEO report, or people who needed a government license to operate. The government claimed that 35 kip equaled one US dollar, but the kip was really worth a fraction of that value outside of Laos.

What this meant is that importers were able to buy goods by using currency that they purchased from the Laos government at a third of their true value and then sell goods they bought with the kip to people in Laos at a giant multiple to the value they paid for them. A US government report concluded that this led to "gross misuse of US aid funds" and that "the RLG bureaucracy had neither the will, leadership, [nor] discipline to play the system straight." The United States created the United States Operations Mission (USOM) to oversee this aid program and American contractors operating in Laos, but rumors of corruption in the mission grew. Ambassador Parsons said that one USOM director was so stupid that "to put it charitably, had to have been prematurely senile." But others thought he was the perfect fit for the job and in a sense he was.[175]

The corruption hit the front pages of the Wall Street Journal in an article titled "Living It Up in Laos." Reporter Igor Oganesoff found that Laotian elites connected to the government were "ecstatically drowning in American aid." He explained that "a Laotian trader can buy 100,000 kip in the free money market for $1,000. He then applies for an import license for, say, $1,000 worth of building

[175] Ibid, pp. 61-65.

cement, but puts up only 35,000 kip to get the $1,000 from the government at the official rate. This leaves him 65,000 kip before he has even moved the goods."

Actual nation building projects were jokes used to simply blow money. Oganesoff claimed that "representatives still blush over the $27,000 tilapia project. Local ponds were stocked with these imported fish. Then it developed that, while the local populace didn't like their taste, the other fish in the ponds did, and quickly gobbled up the entire supply." Even worse was the construction of a 150 mile road from the capital of Vientiane to Luang Prabang, which when completed quickly became unusable due to monsoon rains that washed away entire sections of it and caused landslides. "No new roads are contemplated" wrote Oganesoff, while "meanwhile, back in the countryside, the rank and file of the Laotians, a handsome dark people, live much as they have always lived, oblivious to U.S. help."

The article was reprinted in Reader's Digest, the largest circulating magazine in the United States at the time. Congressmen denounced the corruption and the House Foreign Affairs Committee opened up an investigation into it. Ambassador Parsons was forced to appear and explain that while there were "things to be corrected... we have been trying to correct them." Some Congressmen gave him a tough time, but the head of the committee declared that "it is encouraging that there is no sign of fraud, malfeasance, or gross misadministration on the part of U.S. officials." So the aid program continued.

However, one former aid worker told his story. Joel Halpern joined the USOM program fresh out of Columbia's Ph.D. program armed with an anthropology degree and his wife, a fellow anthropologist who also joined the aid program. "The airport, if you can call it that, is an expanse of red dust outside of town," they recalled, "off to one side is a shack. I don't mean a wooden building, but a one storey-dilapidated hut with box-like appendages built out from it. This is Vattay, Aerodrome de Vientiane, capital du royaume Lao." A jeep came from the USOM to pick them up when they arrived. "Welcome to Laos, rectum of the universe," the driver greeted them.

They found that the Americans working for the USOM had isolated themselves from the people of Laos. The USOM compound was walled off with barbed wire and so was a "separate embassy compound made up of prefabricated aluminum houses." The Americans spent almost all of their time either in one of the compounds or going quickly from one to another. "It is possible, I think, to spend two years - the normal tour of duty - in Laos without ever really coming into contact with the people," Halpern reported home, "this is made possible by the grouping of the American colonies."

He traveled into villages inspecting them and coming up with ideas to help the people. When Halpern sent them to the USOM, though, they acted "as if we didn't exist." The projects he was involved in were "one shot affairs." He told the USOM that Lao farmers could use farming tools. The USOM in turn sent thousands of shovels and axes to one town, but when Halpern came to witness their delivery he found a "stream of men, women, and in some cases children" come to get them. They had no idea what to do with them. He noticed that they "wore wrist watches and other signs of city life" and realized that they weren't really farmers. He figured it was a game of the RLG.

Halpern wrote a letter to his parents reporting that "the situation is quite fouled up." He found that almost all of the aide simply stayed in the capital where all the government elites lived. What he saw as a result was "an air-conditioned nightclub plus many other types of luxury consumer goods. Building is going on like crazy with absolutely no planning." Bars and clubs sprung up in town, but there was no sewage system put in place. Sidewalks didn't exist. Garbage and human waste were covered by wooden planks, so you could walk over them without getting your feet dirty.

Halpern came to conclude that the people of Laos didn't have "a definite will.... for development." It was "a recreation and ceremonially oriented society." He noted that "one time a car failed to meet a visiting UNESCO delegation and the governor explained that it was engaged in transporting people to a boun [festival]," which was "more important."

After eight months, he wanted to get out of there. He wrote a letter to the head supervisor in Washington, D.C., telling him that "I have now completed one-third of my tour in Laos and have done exactly nothing in community development." Washington rebuked him for complaining. “Your little sonny boy has a conscience and I feel I should be attempting to do the job that is costing Uncle Sam $10,000 a year to do," he wrote his parents.

Ambassador Parsons got the US government to donate three fire engines to Laos. But when they arrived, he found that "for the Lao, fire engines were good - bright, shiny, mobile - and the impressive jet streams of water they produced were fun." The embassy put on a contest to see which of the three Lao fire companies could put out a fire the fastest. "No one had ever seen the Lao, normally expert at conserving human energy, move so rapidly," Parsons wrote. After the contest, though, the fire companies vanished and the fire engines were then used to deliver water to officials. When a house caught on fire no one came to help. He came to conclude that "the local people are extremely lethargic and dealing with them is overly taxing to one's patience."

The foreign aid program to Laos made nation building modernization theory look like a crazy pipe-dream. The theories sounded exciting, but didn't translate into reality. Not in Laos, where eighty-percent of the population existed off of subsistence farming and never even used the Lao currency. They simply bartered. Ninety-percent of them couldn't read. Parsons saw it as existing in the "fourteenth century" with the people completely oblivious to the Cold War struggle of good and evil.

There was "no more obvious vacuum of power, no greater vulnerability, could be imagined," he reported and complained of "the frail and incompetent human material with which we had to work" to build a nation. He knew Secretary of State John Foster Dulles wanted him to make it a "bastion of freedom," but "it would be difficult to make Laos into a flea flicker." He explained in a report sent back to Washington that the people of Laos "wished only to be left alone" and were "the least warlike, most passive of all the components of the Indo-China peninsula."[176]

Scholars who have looked back at the history of Southeast East Asia have argued that it was natural for the people of Laos to want to be neutral in the Cold War confrontation. Laos was the Switzerland

---

[176] Seth Jacobs: *The Universe Unraveling: American Foreign Policy In Cold War* Laos (Ithaca: Cornell University Press, 2012), pp. 83-119.

of Asia, full of mountains rising to the heavens, and surrounded by historic enemies. For centuries kingdoms in Laos had always been wary of China and Vietnam and had always played their neighbors off one another. In the Cold War, neutrality was the only way Laotian nationalists could keep their nation independent and at peace without becoming a virtual colony to a foreign power, but President Eisenhower and the two Dulles brothers didn't see it that way.[177]

Prime Minister Souvanna Phouma told Parsons that he was accepting an invitation by Chinese Foreign Minister Chou En-Lai to visit their capital in Peking. He explained that he couldn't refuse and make a "gratuitous affront to a big neighbor" that "little Laos [could] not afford." The State Department in Washington thought he was "dangerously wobbly." Souvanna told Parsons that he "would occasionally have to maneuver and do things which might appear incomprehensible" to Americans.

He began talking with Pathet Lao leader Souphanouvong. They worked on a deal to bring in Pathet Lao leaders into his cabinet in return for restoring government control to several northern provinces. Souvanna told Parsons that these men were not communists.

Assistant Secretary of State Walter Robertson informed John Foster Dulles that "this settlement

[177] Ibid, p. 18.

is clearly of the dangerous type we have been trying to prevent." Admiral Felix Stump, the Commander-in-Chief of the US Forces in the Pacific, sent a cable to Admiral Arleigh Burke and PEO commander Brown saying it was time for a "take-over in Laos by strong anti-Communist leader."

As ambassador Parsons wrapped up his tour in Laos, on January 15, 1958, Souvanna Phouma traveled to Washington, D.C., to try to smooth things over. He told the Americans that, even though the Pathet Lao received support from North Vietnam, the people in Laos were "neither by temperament, civilization, nor social traditions predisposed to communism." They were simple farmers and without a "dissatisfied peasantry or urban proletariat" he didn't see how Marxist-Leninism could thrive in Laos.

Secretary of State John Foster Dulles met with Souvanna. He told him that he accepted that the prime minister had an "intimate knowledge of the situation in Laos" and told him that the US government and he, himself personally, had a global "experience in the way international Communism operates, in the subtlety of its means and the disguising of its purposes until it is too late." Dulles handed him a paper detailing how communists subverted governments in Eastern Europe after World War II. "It might provide useful ideas of the kind of thing the Prime Minister and his associates should be on guard against," he said.

Souvanna replied by saying that he "did not misunderstand the Communist danger." He said, just as you feel like you need to remind me about the dangers of communism, I need to tell you about my country. It lost territory due to French rule and needs to be reunified. He claimed that only a few hundred of the Pathet Lao were really communists and it was more of a tribal army than anything else. As for the lessons of Europe, he claimed that the reasons why Romania, Hungary, and Czechoslovakia went red were not because of subversion, but because Stalin's Red Army occupied them. A better comparison to Laos is Finland where the Red Army withdrew from after the war and is now free and independent.

Dulles replied by saying that "Finlandization" was only one exception and if there are only a hundred communists in the Pathet Lao it didn't matter. "They always preferred to operate from a minority position," he lectured him, "Stalin, in his discussions of Leninism, had stated the revolutionary party must always remain a minority, because only a minority could be highly trained, disciplined, and efficient. A majority group became incompetent and the slave of mass opinion."[178]

The two talked for over an hour past one another. After Souvanna left, the CIA went into action. It created a program called "Booster Shot"

---

[178] Rust, pp. 46-47, 77.

that pumped in $500,000 worth of supplies into rural military forces and friendly villages. Rufus Philips, who answered to Colonel Edward Lansdale, stationed in Saigon, ran it. He worked under USCOM cover and was head of CIA pacification programs in Laos. The CIA also sent a new station chief to Laos named Henry Hecksher. He had been involved in Operation PB success, the CIA backed overthrow of the government of Guatemala, in 1954. Parsons later described the "Booster Shot" operation as the sky "raining supplies" from Air Force planes onto pro-CIA military forces.

Hecksher described his mission as "keeping the Pathet Lao from taking over the Lao Government either through subversion, the elections, or a combination of both." He found younger Lao army officers who wanted to rise up in the system in disgust with the "Francophile gerontocracy." Hecksher organized meetings with them and held seminars in which, according to CIA officer Methven, he spent hours "lashing out at communism and corruption, extolling freedom and democracy. He told his audience that they were tomorrow's leaders and should start thinking about what they could do for their country."

CIA agent Rufus Phillips acted as a bag man for Hecksher. They would get CIA money and transform one dollar into 85 kip and buy supplies in Thailand, which they would then bring back into

Laos. But this made things an adventure for Phillips, because the Lao currency had no large denominations, so he had to pile boxes full of money into his Nissan jeep, "with as much money as it could hold." He gave extra cash to Lieutenant Colonel Oudeone Sananikone. They stored the supplies they got from Thailand in a building and delivered them by air drop to forces in friendly villages for "Booster Shot."

They created the Committee for the Defense of National Interests (CDNI) as a political front led by military officers. It isn't clear exactly what happened, but within a few months Souvanna was forced to resign as prime minister after the CDNI announced a boycott of his government. PEO chief Brown later said that the CIA overthrew him. John Gunther Dean, who later was ambassador to Cambodia and Thailand claimed, "Henry Hecksher was committed to opposing the neutralist Prime Minister and perhaps bring about his downfall. That is what happened in 1958."[179]

The result was a murky revolving door of coups and chaos in Laos over the next few years, serving as the catalyst for sporadic off and on civil wars between government forces, the Pathet Lao, and armed neutralists third forces all in battles with one another interrupted by attempts to form coalition governments. Eventually, things in the United

---

[179] Rust, pp.82-86, 94-98.

States mission also broke down with the ambassador and CIA station chief in open conflict with one another, by 1959, over which faction to back in Laos. By 1960, things had disintegrated so much in the country that the State Department and its Laos country team, the CIA, and the Pentagon each had their own distinct view of what to do in Laos, which were only resolved after months of conflict with one another. The US government employees in Laos learned to follow their own institutional directives and had less and less to do with representatives of other government agencies in the country. United States foreign policy in Laos became a disaster.[180]

By the end of 1959, the US ambassador in Laos was sending telegrams back home saying that "the chances are far better than even that this country will go down the drain" and that they needed to "consider cutting our losses," instead of "having Laos go down in history as a US defeat or, conversely, risk[ing] all-out war over [the] wrong place at [the wrong] time." As for the CIA, it put the bulk of its support behind a figure in the CDNI, Colonel Phoumi Nosavan, and with the full backing of the Eisenhower administration and the CIA, he seized power in a coup in 1960. CIA operative John Hasey who served as his case officer, described Phoumi as an insecure "complex character" full of ambition

---

[180] Ibid, pp. 115-116.

and wild mood swings. He operated like a gangster, but President Eisenhower's Secretary of Defense said he was "our boy."

The US ambassador said of Phoumi that royalist politicians he talked too "distrusted his ruthlessness, his cleverness, and his driving ambition." The ambassador cabled the State Department that he did not approve of a coup, and later said that he was "overruled" by unnamed coup "proponents" in Washington. To help Phoumi get in power, the Eisenhower administration had suspended aid to Laos. Once Phoumi took over, the North Vietnamese sent two companies into Laos to aid the Pathet Lao and plenty of supplies and weapons for them too in reaction. The American PEO then expanded from 25 men to 515 men by the end of 1959.[181]

However, on August 9, 1960, another military officer on the payroll of the PEO acted on his own and took over the capital of Vientiane. He was supposed to be under the command of Phoumi, but waited till Phoumi and the RLG cabinet were out of town for a week and took over in the space of three hours. The Americans and Phoumi had no idea what this man was up to. Not a shot was fired. He simply came in with his army unit and took over warehouses full of weapons and walked into the capital building.

---

[181] Rust, pp. 102, 132; Jacobs, pp. 135, 139, 142, 147.

His name was Kong Le. He was only twenty-six years old, five feet tall, and weighed one hundred pounds, but he declared that "I am tired of seeing Lao fight Lao." He wanted Laos neutral and out of the Cold War and invited Souvanna to come back and rule as Prime Minister again. Kong Le got on the radio and rallied the people of Laos by saying, "we are disgusted with this civil war. It is made by a handful of people for foreign money" and it was time for "a policy of genuine neutrality" and closed by saying "I suggest that everyone now clap and cheer!" Crowds thronged to him.

He took the CIA in Laos completely by surprise. Colonel Edward Lansdale saw that as a huge failure, because Kong Le "had spent the night before his coup with a group of American friends, and there wasn't a damn one of them that knew that he was going to have a coup in the morning. This type of thing I just found inconceivable. People get nervous and sort of absent-minded about what's happening at the time when they're planning an action like that the next morning, and somebody there among the Americans should have been sensitive" and "gotten some feeling on it." The cultural barriers for Americans in Laos were staggering.

The CIA reported that Kong Le's talks were "disjointed and rambling. He stared into space and appeared to be mentally deranged." For him to abandon the Cold War struggle had to mean that he was crazy. In Washington, Undersecretary of

State Douglas Dillon said that it was obvious that he was "dangerously immature and irrational." Kong Le told the current Ambassador to Laos, Winthrop Brown, that "I have fought for many years, and I have killed many men, and I have never seen a foreigner die." Decades later he explained that he had been scared to do what he did, but he gained confidence after he saw an omen. The day before his coup it was raining lightly and he saw a frog swallow a snake. If it could do that he could stop the evils afflicting his country too.[182]

At an emergency National Security meeting, CIA Director Allen Dulles told President Eisenhower that Kong Le was a "Castro communist-type individual." He said "it would be almost a miracle if we can hold on there and expressed the view that the cards were stacked against us," but they had a chance. At a second meeting, Dulles said that there was a difference of views on what to do in Laos among the Americans there and among Laotian elites, but "we were in a better position in Washington to know what was going on in Laos than the Laotians were themselves."

---

[182] Rust, p. 177; Jacobs, pp. 154-157; Saowapha Viravong, "The colonel from Savannakhet," http://asiapacific.anu.edu.au/newmandala/, accessed 1/14/2015; Edward Lansdale, Oral History Interview JFK #1, 7/11/1970, JFK Library, https://www.jfklibrary.org/sites/default/files/archives/JFKOH/Lansdale%2C%20Edward/JFKOH-EL-01/JFKOH-EL-01-TR.pdf, accessed 9/11/2019.

Dulles explained that "Phoumi wished to send troops against Vientiane and that we had strongly urged him not to do so. He could not do much at the moment anyway because his troops were scattered around the country. He had sent some troops down the Mekong River. It was our hope that he would not attack Vientiane; he did not have the necessary forces there. It would be difficult to get them in overland and he had only one C–47. He had had three C–47's but two were out of commission. He had appealed to us for more."

According to notes of the meeting, Defense Secretary "Gates asked why we hoped that Phoumi would not attack Vientiane. He pointed out that Vientiane was being held by one man (Kong Le) and 800 people. He thought that the sooner we knocked off Kong Le the better. In response Mr. Dulles pointed out that the Lao are not much given to fighting. Mr. Dillon said that it was State's feeling that our first objective should be to get rid of Kong Le. The more we hear of him, the more he sounds like a very bad actor." Army Chief of Staff General Lyman Lemnitzer thought that "Phoumi should be brought to Vientiane as rapidly as possible."

The Joint Chiefs of Staff let the State Department know that they recommended "aggressive support of General Phoumi" and thought it was time to "liquidate Kong Le coup group." Air Force Chief of Staff General Curtis LeMay didn't see "what was wrong with telling Phoumi we will give him everything he wants." Winthrop Brown, the current Ambassador to Laos, thought it might be time to back away from Phoumi and move to neutralism. That suggestion made some in the Pentagon label him "that communist ambassador."

Souvanna came back to Laos as Prime Minister. The United States once again cut off aid to his government and sent arms to Phoumi. Brown thought they were making a mistake, claiming that Souvanna was the "only rallying point left" in Laos and Phoumi wouldn't fix anything. He didn't think he would be able to "reunite the country" and even if he did it would only be "precariously by force."[183]

The result was a round of civil war. The Pentagon and CIA encouraged Phoumi to fight, but his forces scattered in retreat after confronting Kong Le's men ninety-miles outside of the capital. Admiral Felt reported to the Joint Chiefs of Staff that Phoumi had personally fled in "fear for his personal safety."

---

[183] Document 359, *Foreign Relations of the United States, 1961-1963. Laos Crisis: Volume XXIV,* U.S. Department of State; https://history.state.gov/historicaldocuments/frus1958-60v16/d359, accessed 1/14/2015; Document 373, *Foreign Relations of the United States, 1961-1963. Laos Crisis: Volume XXIV,* U.S. Department of State, https://history.state.gov/historicaldocuments/frus1958-60v16/d373, accessed 1/14/2015; Jacobs, pp. 159-163.

At a Pentagon meeting with the State Department, Admiral Burke said they had no choice but to keep supporting him, because he was "still the only anti-communist with a force in being. We have to use the assets we have." John Steeves, a representative from the State Department said of "Phoumi, we always knew, was either stupid, inept, corrupt - he was a bastard, but he was our bastard. We must stick with the anti-communist group no matter how bad they were. Try to reform, try to control them, but you couldn't stop paying the troops. You couldn't stop aiding the country. All you could do was put up with their nonsense as best you could and try to control them."[184]

As the situation descended into even further chaos in Laos, it became harder to tell what was really happening there. Admiral Felt reported that they were relying on intelligence information "subject to distortion" from Phoumi. As the final months of President Eisenhower's term as president approached, he seemed to lose interest in Laos and his administration had no clear plan of action. John Steeves of the State Department approached the President in the Rose Garden and told him maybe they should just try to bribe Souvanna. Steeves thought Eisenhower just "couldn't care less" and had "abysmal ignorance," like all of them did at the time, of what was happening in Laos. Eisenhower told his aids that he couldn't

---

[184] Rust, pp. 209-210.

think of doing anything "beyond what is now being done" in Laos.

President Eisenhower had a history of being forceful on foreign policy issues, but in the final months in office he took a few steps back. He had tried to bring an air of peace with the Soviet Union by organizing a summit in May of 1960 that got ruined by the shoot down of an American U-2 plane over Russia. During the 1960 presidential campaign, Republican Richard Nixon indirectly distanced himself from Eisenhower, while John Kennedy attacked him for being weak and claiming that he allowed a dangerous "missile gap" to grow. The day after the election, Eisenhower told his son "all I've been trying to do for eight years has gone down the drain." He had tried to control defense spending and the arms race and now both threatened to accelerate. At his last National Security Council meeting Eisenhower wondered, "Can free government overcome the many demands made by special interests and the indulgence of selfish motives?" In his last act as president, he warned the nation of the power of the "military-industrial complex" in his farewell address. Privately, he expressed the fear of "heavy spending leading in the direction of authoritarian government."[185]

---

[185] Rust, pp. 217-28; Michael Swanson, *The War State: The Cold War Origins of the Military-Industrial Complex and the Power Elite, 1945-1963* (South Carolina: CreateSpace, 2011), pp. 192-195.

President Kennedy would try to control the American war state. He came into office after a few months of back and forth battles brought Phoumi forces in control of the Laotian capital. Souvanna fled to Cambodia, while Kong Le formed an alliance with the Pathet Lao and fought back after receiving aid from Soviet parachute drops. Kong Le and the Pathet Lao were sitting in the Plain of Jars region of Laos gaining strength.

Phoumi launched an offensive against them, outnumbering them 60,000 to 18,000. Despite the assistance of American PEO officers on the ground with them, and some American air support, Phoumi's attack failed. Kennedy was told that they collapsed "without much fight" due to "some unobserved artillery fire, which fell in the area and scared them to death." Admiral Felt had been advised that Phoumi was now "rather desperate" and could not be talked into another offensive. This was the situation when President Kennedy met with his Laos task force on March 21, 1961, and discussed the possibility of American intervention in Laos.[186]

According to Arthur Schlesinger, Kennedy told him that he thought the effort to make Laos into a

---

[186] Jack Schulimson, *History of the Joint Chiefs of Staff, The Joint Chiefs of Staff and the War in Vietnam, 1960-1968, Part I.* (Washington, D.C.,: Office of the Joint History Office of the Chairman of the Joint Chiefs of Staff, 2011), pp. 121-126; Jacobs, p. 244.

"pro-western redoubt had been ridiculous and that neutralization was the correct policy," but now "American prestige was deeply involved." "We cannot and will not accept any visible humiliation over Laos," Kennedy said to him.[187]

Kennedy wanted to get first-hand information on what was happening in Laos, so he summoned Ambassador Brown to Washington to meet with him as soon as could. The Ambassador didn't know what to expect. Walt Rostow told him not to worry, because the President is "a wonderful listener."[188]

As soon as Brown entered the oval office, Kennedy asked him, "what kind of people are these people - Souvanna, Souphanouvong and Phoumi and the king and Kong Le?" Brown started to answer by saying, "Well, sir, the policy is -" and Kennedy quickly cut him off. He didn't want to hear the State Department line.

"I said, what do you think - YOU - the ambassador," the President said.

Brown told him what he really thought. He said that Phoumi was "overrated" and a "poor politician," who was not even "all that good of a general. He told him the king was a "total zero," who actually "cried several times when he talked to me." He told Kennedy that Kong Le was a "patriot, not a

[187] Schlesinger, pp. 307-308.
[188] Jacobs, pp. 243-244.

communist" and that in the end Souvanna was the "one person in Laos who could be a unifying force."

Ambassador Brown advocated supporting neutralist forces in Laos and not the course of action that had been pushed by the CIA and Pentagon for the past few years only to lead to failure. Brown said of the meeting, "I had the feeling that I could say anything I wanted and it would be like the confessional." He told him Phoumi's army was led by men who couldn't even "lead a platoon around a corner."

In the end, Brown said that he thought most of the people in Laos didn't have a care about the Cold War or communism "to the extent that there were thinking Laotians about these problems" and "there weren't too many of them." He thought that they felt that "if they could establish a neutral position... all these problems would go away and they would be left alone to be peaceful."

Kennedy listened closely and then stood up and told Brown that the meeting had to end due to time. Brown had spoken with the President for a complete hour. He left thinking that his words had a big impact on the President who placed a high value on getting the opinions of those right on the spot.[189]

---

[189] Ibid, pp. 242-244.

Just as Kennedy authorized some minor military moves and gave his speech to the American people on television in regards to Laos on March 23, 1961, he also made moves for negotiation. He met personally with the Prime Minister of England Harold MacMillan, who told Kennedy that they needed to push for a cease-fire in Laos and that he was wary of any military intervention there. Laos made the British uneasy and the UK ambassador to Laos feared that the United States "might feel impelled [to] take some military action which would lead to escalation and World War III." Kennedy told him that he "was not all anxious to undertake a military operation in Laos." Contacts were made and on April 1, 1961, Soviet Premier Khrushchev said he would like to see an international conference on Laos.[190]

The month of April was critical for Laos, but it has been overshadowed in history by the disastrous Bay of Pigs Operation that occurred in that month too. Kennedy took public responsibility for the failed invasion of Cuba, but privately he believed that the CIA and the Joint Chiefs of Staff failed in their planning of it and had given him miserable recommendations for it. The operation pitted 1,500 CIA backed Cuban exiles against an army of 20,000 well trained Castro forces and a potential

---

[190] Gibbons, pp. 22-23; William Rust, *So Much To Lose: John F. Kennedy And American Policy In Laos* (Kentucky: University Press of Kentucky, 2014), p. 21.

reserve force of 200,000 more men. Against such odds, and on their own, all they could do was surrender.

Kennedy told Ben Bradlee of The Washington Post, "The first advice I'm going to give my successor is to watch the generals and to avoid feeling that just because they were military men their opinions on military matters were worth a damn." Kennedy's mistake was approving the invasion. "All my life I've known better than to depend on the experts. How could I have been so stupid to let them go ahead?" he lamented to his aide Kenneth O'Donnell.

Robert Kennedy thought that "if he hadn't gone ahead with it, everybody would have said it showed that he had no courage." The President, though, in particular lost confidence in Joint Chiefs of Staff Chairman General Lyman Lemnitzer in the middle of the invasion. One evening, during the Bay of Pigs operation, he held a meeting that included Lemnitzer. When it was over Robert Kennedy called Admiral Burke and told him, "The President was going to rely upon you to advise him on this situation. He needs advice... the rest of the people in the room weren't helpful." Twenty-minutes later the President called Burke and repeated his brother's message.

Admiral Burke told his aide, "What do you do? He is bypassing Lemnitzer, the Chairman, the

SecDef, SecNav, CIA, and the whole works and putting me in charge of the operation. That is a helluva thing." Kennedy eventually appointed former Army Chief of Staff Maxwell Taylor to act as his personal adviser on military affairs. He eventually became Chairman of the Joint Chiefs of Staff, but the situation in Laos got more intense first. What the Bay of Pigs did is make Kennedy more skeptical of the advice they gave to him from then on in regards to Laos.[191]

On April 5, 1961, Phoumi launched another offensive against Kong Le and the Pathet Lao forces at the Plain of Jars. It quickly collapsed. Phoumi forces ended "with evacuation of the troops after little actual fighting." A garrison was left "completely uncontrolled." The Pathet Lao and Kong Le turned the tables and pushed back against Phoumi. They took Thakhek, a provincial capital town on the Mekong River. The Joint Chiefs were informed that Phoumi's forces there were now "demoralized" and were now "an ineffective fighting force." A cease fire was supposed to be in the works, but Phoumi was on the verge of being destroyed.[192]

On April 26, 1961, Ambassador Brown cabled back and said that if the Pathet Lao continued their advance they would end up taking all of the major

---

[191] Schulimson, pp. 1, 74-75; Swanson, pp. 242-243.
[192] Rust, *So Much To Lose*, pp. 23-25.

cities in Laos. "Muong Sai has fallen. MAAG representatives report Siho forces north of Nam Lik have bad morale and likely dissolve if struck hard. They have received some artillery fire. Their dissolution would leave clear way open to Vientiane," he wrote. The ambassador didn't think there was any way to stop them if they continued except a major air campaign and possible intervention with American ground troops. His cable caused immediate alarm in Washington. Under Secretary of State Chester Bowles sent a memo to the White House saying that he now faced two options. He had to decide whether "to intervene militarily in Laos" or "accept a political solution which will lead to a Souvanna government" that "would turn us out of Laos and in time convert Laos into a Communist puppet."[193]

Bundy received the memo and instead of just forwarding it on to the President talked to him personally about it. They set an emergency meeting that afternoon with McNamara, Nitze, Rostow, and Admiral Burke. Bundy had Bowles come to the meeting.

Kennedy read the alarming cables from Laos to open the meeting and noted that China is now saying that there will not be a cease fire in Laos until the United States withdrew all of its advisors and

---

[193] Document 61, *Foreign Relations of the United States, 1961-1963. Laos Crisis: Volume XXIV,* U.S. Department of State; https://history.state.gov/historicaldocuments/frus1961-63v24/d61,accessed 1/14/2015.

equipment first. After some back and forth discussion, a general consensus was reached, with the exception of Admiral Burke, that a conflict should be avoided. "The President was confronted with general agreement among his advisers that such a conflict would be unjustified, even if the loss of Laos must be accepted. As to whether an intervention in Vientiane would provoke strong military response, there was some uncertainty, but on balance it seemed wise to avoid a test if possible. At the same time the possibility of a strong American response is the only card left to be played in pressing for a cease-fire, and accordingly the President explicitly refused to decide against intervention at this time," read notes taken from the meeting.

After this meeting, Kennedy ordered an increase in readiness for the United States military forces in the area and in the Pacific. Admiral Felt was ordered to move "naval forces into Gulf of Siam and into the South China Sea." Also put on alert were SEATO Plan 5 units "earmarked for air movement into Laos." The Joint Chiefs of Staff directed the US Pacific Command (CINCPAC) that the first alert steps of SEATO Plan 5 were now in effect.

SEATO Plan 5 was a set of military plans drawn up by the Joint Staff of the Joint Chiefs of Staff for intervention in Southeast Asia. It consisted of a series of escalatory steps ranging from the simple movement of forces all of the way up to the use of nuclear weapons against China. If the plans were followed to the letter they meant that if the capital of Laos were to fall the United States would send troops into Southern Laos, South Vietnam, and Thailand and prepare to begin air strikes against North Vietnam and China. In the cable to Admiral Felt of CINCPAC the Joint Chiefs of Staff informed him that there is a "reluctance to use nuclear weapons initially and that decision remained with the President."[194]

On the morning of April 27, 1961, Secretary of Defense Robert McNamara held a meeting with the Joint Chiefs of Staff and asked them a series of questions. He wanted to know if they thought they should intervene in Laos. Admiral Burke and General Thomas White of the Air Force said yes. Generals Decker of the Army and Shoup of the Marines said no, claiming that China and North Vietnam would react just as strongly to a small-scale US deployment in Laos as they would to a full-blown intervention. They also said you can expect American troops to die of tropical diseases in the jungle.

Kennedy held a National Security Council meeting at 10:00 in the morning with thirty-three people. It was one of the most unusual national security meetings ever held by a president of the

---

[194] Schulimson, pp. 76-77; Document 62, *Foreign Relations of the United States, 1961-1963. Laos Crisis: Volume XXIV,* U.S. Department of State, https://history.state.gov/historicaldocuments/frus1961-63v24/d62,accessed 1/14/2015

United States, because it went outside the national security bureaucracy and included Vice-President Johnson and representatives throughout the administration from the Treasury Department and even FBI Director J. Edgar Hoover. The nation was on the edge of war and he wanted men outside of the national security state complex to know what was going on and what was being recommended. This is why so many people were at the meeting.

Walter Rostow, as head of Kennedy's Laos task force, recommended a limited troop deployment of a few thousand men in Thailand as a bargaining chip. W. Averell Harriman, who was now acting as the chief State Department negotiator on the Laos crisis, agreed. Admiral Burke, and other members of the Joint Chiefs of Staff, said that if there is going to be a show of force there should be enough to take on a military offensive. They proposed sending in 120,000-140,000 men into Laos with the authority to use tactical nuclear weapons. General Shoup of the Marine Corps did not agree.

According to Kennedy aide Ted Sorenson, the military representatives disagreed with each other on what to do, but "the majority appeared to favor the landing of American troops in Thailand, South Vietnam and the government-held portions of the Laotian panhandle. If that did not produce a cease-fire, they recommended an air attack on Pathet Lao positions and tactical nuclear weapons on the ground. If the North Vietnamese or Chinese then moved in, their homelands would be bombed. If massive Red troops were then mobilized nuclear bombings would be threatened and, if necessary, carried out."

David Bell, then Director of the Bureau Budget, attended the meeting and was appalled. "To us outsiders," he said," that is to say to those of us who weren't part of the Pentagon-State Department complex, this was a shocking meeting, because at least two of the Joint Chiefs were extremely belligerent, as we saw it, and were ready to go in and bomb the daylights out of them or land troops or whatever." He thought "there was a predisposition" of "some members of the military leadership to go shooting off into the Southeast Asian jungles on what at that time was plainly no substantial provocation. It seemed to most of us to have been simply a militaristic adventure, not at all justified in terms of American foreign policy interests."[195]

According to Arthur Schlesinger, the Pentagon was developing a "standard line" for Southeast Asia. They had "unrelenting opposition to limited intervention except on the impossible condition that the President agree in advance on every fur-

---

[195] Document 63, *Foreign Relations of the United States, 1961-1963. Laos Crisis: Volume XXIV,* U.S. Department of State, https://history.state.gov/historicaldocuments/frus1961-63v24/d63, accessed 1/14/2015; Gibbons, pp. 26-27; Schulimson, p. 128.

ther step they deemed sequential, including, on occasion nuclear bombing of Hanoi and even Peking. At one National Security Council meeting General Lemnitzer outlined the process by which each American action would provoke a Chinese counteraction, provoking in turn an even more drastic American response. He concluded: 'if we are given the right to use nuclear weapons we can guarantee victory.'" China had no nuclear weapons of its own. "The Chiefs had their own way of reacting to the Cuban fiasco," Schlesinger wrote, "it soon began to look to the White House as if they were taking care to build a record which would permit them to say that, whatever the President did, he acted against their advice."[196]

President Kennedy held a meeting later that day with Congressional leaders. The President and Admiral Burke briefed them on the situation. Kennedy said that the capital of Laos could fall within forty-eight hours and if it does he'd have to decide whether to send troops to Laos. Burke told them that he supported US military intervention, because without it "all Southeast Asia will be lost." He said they all "must be prepared for [a] tough, long, and hard war, which may well involve war with China."[197]

---

[196] Schlesinger, p. 316.
[197] Document 65, *Foreign Relations of the United States, 1961-1963. Laos Crisis: Volume XXIV,* U.S. Department of

At Kennedy's request, after Admiral Burke spoke, McNamara noted that it is the "opinion of the Joint Chiefs of Staff that if United States forces became engaged and the North Vietnamese or Chinese communists came to the aid of the Pathet Lao, we would not be able to win by conventional weapons alone. But even that scenario assumed that our landing would be unopposed." The United States would not be able to get forces into landlocked Laos fast enough by air to prevent a possible bloodbath if enemy forces attacked them in mass.

Kennedy said that "the communist could put into Laos five men to our one." Bowles then said that the Chinese "stated they would enter Laos if we did." Kennedy then asked the congressmen what they thought.

Senator Richard Russell said that this Laos was "an incredible fantasy." He thought America can only fight "where we have an ally that will fight for himself." He told Kennedy "we should get our people out of Laos and write the country off."

That talk upset Admiral Burke, so he invoked the domino theory. "If we don't help the Laotians now," he said, 'the [South] Vietnamese will give up, the Thais will find an accommodation with the communists, and it will only be a matter of time

---

State, https://history.state.gov/historicaldocuments/frus1961-63v24/d65, accessed 1/14/2015.

until the gradual erosion of all Southeast Asia takes place."

Russell said he did not advocate surrendering all of Southeast Asia, but just Laos. If you want to put in troops "let's put our troops in Thailand and South Vietnam and take our stand there," he said.

Senator Dirksen agreed with Russell, saying of the people of Laos, "they do not want to kill each other and there seems to be no fighting heart present."

Burke replied by saying "no one wants to fight," but if we don't fight in Laos, then "where do we fight - in India? Iran? Or where? With respect to the fighting qualities of the Lao, it takes a long time to train troops, and we have not had that time."

Senator Mansfield said that he been "thinking about Laos for a long time" and that "the worst possible mistake we could make would be to intervene there." He said that "hundreds of millions of dollars have been spent and we have nothing in return."

Bowles, while making notes of the meeting for Secretary State Dean Rusk, wrote that all of the Congressmen were against intervening in Laos no matter what the "consequences to our position" in Southeast Asia might be. Kennedy told the congressmen to keep this talk confidential, because all they had for a bargaining chip was "the threat of

US intervention and the uncertainty of the other side in this regard."

Undersecretary of State Alexis Johnson came away from the meeting thinking that it was the "turning point on Laos." Kennedy didn't say it, but "it was quite clear in the minds of all of us that, whatever happened, we were not going to militarily intervene." McGeorge Bundy considered it "an operational rejection to the domino theory."[198]

As soon as the meeting was over, Admiral Burke approached President Kennedy, who quickly brushed him off, telling him that there was no point in further discussion. The admiral handed him a one page memo, which predicted that giving up Laos would mean losing all of Southeast Asia to China, and left. What Kennedy had done with this meeting was demonstrate that there was zero political support for American military intervention in Laos. If he wanted to do so, he could now tell the Joint Chiefs of Staff that he didn't have the political backing in Congress to be able to go down the SEATO 5 roadmap.[199]

Nevertheless, the wheels for intervention continued to roll at a tense National Security Council meeting on April 29. At this meeting, members of the Joint Chiefs of Staff called for intervention again. Admiral Burke talked about sending troops

---

[198] Jacobs, pp. 236-240; Schulimson, p. 78.
[199] Schulimson, p. 129.

to the capital of Laos. "The situation had deteriorated quite a bit, but he still thought it possible to go in. War is dangerous, he said. If pushed we could retreat across the river, reinforce from Udorn and go back and fight," notes of the meeting read.

Robert McNamara pointed out that this would be a tough mission, because there was only one little air strip in Laos. "It would be easy for the enemy to deny us the airfield as we would need thirty-six sorties a day to get US troops into Vientiane," he said. This could leave American forces pinned down.

McGeorge Bundy mused that "if we took this action we would be doing something which most countries would not appreciate."

According to notes of the meeting, "The Attorney General asked where would be the best place to stand and fight in Southeast Asia, where to draw the line. Mr. McNamara said he thought we would take a stand in Thailand and South Viet-Nam."

Army Chief of Staff General Decker "thought that there was no good place to fight in Southeast Asia but we must hold as much as we can of Viet-Nam, Cambodia and Laos." Retreat from Laos made no sense to him as you would just have to fight elsewhere.

Deputy Assistant Secretary of State John Steeves argued that if we can't hold in Laos we won't be able to hold any of Southeast Asia. "If we decided that this was untenable then we were writing the first chapter in the defeat of Southeast Asia," he said.

Burke said, "each time you give ground it is harder to stand next time. If we give up Laos we would have to put US forces into Viet-Nam and Thailand. We would have to throw enough in to win—perhaps the works. It would be easier to hold now than later. The thing to do was to land now and hold as much as we can and make clear that we were not going to be pushed out of Southeast Asia. We were fighting for the rest of Asia."

According to General Decker, "Thai and US troops might be placed together in Vientiane and, if they could not hold, be removed by helicopter. Even if they were defeated they would be defeated together and this would be better than sitting back and doing nothing."

Decker thought any forces sent to Laos would have a tough time, because "all the advantage we have in heavy equipment would be lost in the difficult terrain of Laos where we would be at the mercy of the guerrillas." So we had to face the facts "we cannot win a conventional war in Southeast Asia; if we go in, we should go in to win, and that means bombing Hanoi, China, and maybe even using nuclear bombs," he said.

President Kennedy said, "we would look sillier than we do now if we got troops in there and then backed down." Therefore, sending a few troops meant looking at the big question, "whether we are ready to go the distance?"

Secretary of State Dean Rusk said, "We would want to get the United Nations mixed up in this."

According to meeting notes, "General LeMay did not believe that it would be possible to get a cease-fire without military action. He admitted that he did not know what US policy is in Laos. He knew what the President had said but he also pointed out that the military had been unable to back up the President's statements. He then enumerated a number of possibilities: 1) do nothing and lose Laos; 2) use B–26's and slow up the enemy; 3) use more sophisticated bombers and stop supplies and then perhaps Phoumi's forces could be brought up to where they could fight; 4) implement Plan 5, backing up troops with air. General LeMay did not think the Chinese would escalate but believed on the contrary that a cease-fire could then be brought about. He added that he believed we should go to work on China itself and let Chiang take Hainan Island. He thought Chiang had a good air force."

Steeves said that they were now facing history. This was the destiny of Asia. He said that he "felt that the prize to be focused on was Southeast Asia."

“The question to be faced," he thought, "was whether we could afford to lose Southeast Asia."

Rusk said that Harriman and officials were working on a cease fire and "if a cease-fire is not brought about quickly, then it would be necessary to get the UN to come in with the SEATO forces committed in a Plan 5 action."

Admiral Burke and McNamara agreed that it would take about two weeks to see what the UN would do. But "only the United States could pull its own chestnuts out of the fire," concluded Burke.

It was a question of who would rule Asia. Bowles said that "the main question to be faced was the fact that we were going to have to fight the Chinese anyway in 2, 3, 5, or 10 years and that it was just a question of where, when, and how. He thought that a major war would be difficult to avoid."

Air Force General LeMay agreed, saying, "in that case, we should fight soon since the Chinese would have nuclear weapons within one or two years."

Secretary of State Dean Rusk ended the meeting saying that he would like his team in the State Department to consider the matter. No final decisions were made at the meeting.[200]

The next morning Secretary of State Rusk sent the President a memo saying that they were on two tracks for Laos. Track one was an attempt at a cease-fire, which if successful would lead to some split government in Laos or a division of the country. Track two was military intervention.

Senator Michael Mansfield sent Kennedy a private letter saying that the United States needed to look at reality in Laos. He recommended Kennedy "get out of the center of this thing and into a position more commensurate with our limited interests, our practical capabilities, and our political realities at home." He predicted that if Kennedy sent the military into Laos people will cheer at first, but "as soon as the first significant casualty lists are published" people would be asking "what are we doing in Laos?" in "Kennedy's War."

The senator recommended cutting the losses on Laos and focusing on Vietnam where they had "the

---

[200] Document 67, *Foreign Relations of the United States, 1961-1963. Laos Crisis: Volume XXIV,* U.S. Department of State, https://history.state.gov/historicaldocuments/frus1961-63v24/d67, accessed 1/14/2015.

greatest potential in leadership, human capacities, and resources."[201]

Robert McNamara and his deputy Roswell Gilpatric circulated a position paper that listed the pros and cons of going to war in Laos and advocated intervening if no cease-fire was achieved quickly. "We must be prepared for the worst," it said. McNamara asked the Service Chiefs and the Service Secretaries to submit in writing their views on Laos.

Some of the members of the Joint Chiefs of Staff thought that the Secretary of Defense was "perhaps subconsciously" now assuming the role of JCS Chairman by leading discussions and soliciting written opinions. However, their individual responses showed no clear consensus. Admiral Burke wanted to put troops into Thailand and South Vietnam in forty-eight hours and then into areas of Laos still held by Phoumi.

Marine Commandant David Shoup recommended sending troops only to Thailand and South Vietnam and then making an ultimatum for a cease-fire. However, he said he favored a non-interventionist course first.

[201] Gibbons, pp. 31-33.

Army General Decker advocated to be ready for "direct intervention," but said the decision was a political decision to be made by the President.

General Thomas White of the Air Force said that it was true that Laos and the Asia mainland were "a most unfavorable area" for a land war and therefore only token land forces should be sent, because anything more would be a "maldeployment." However, if there was no cease-fire in forty-eight hours then aircraft should strike the Pathet Lao in Laos and then bomb Hanoi, which would probably cause the ultimate conflict with China.

White was ready for that, because, as he wrote, "I believe that war with China is inevitable if we take decisive action in Southeast Asia and I would seize the initiative."[202]

After sending these papers to McNamara, the Joint Chiefs of Staff attended a National Security Council meeting with the President. Kennedy asked Burke to outline the military options. According to notes of Theodore Sorensen, Kennedy said this all "looked very different from the operation originally envisioned; and the closer [the President] looked,

---

[202] Walter Poole, *History of the Joint Chiefs of Staff: The Joint Chiefs of Staff and National Policy: Volume VIII, 1961-1964* (Washington, D.C.,: Office of the Joint History Office of the Chairman of the Joint Chiefs of Staff, 2011), pp. 130-131; Schulimson, p. 82.

the less justifiable and definable those answers became."

He wanted them to tell him, "Once in, how and when do we get out?" After the meeting, Kennedy saw Schlesinger and told him, "if it hadn't been for Cuba, we might be about to intervene in Laos." He waved some papers from General Lemnitzer and said, "I might have taken this advice seriously."

Later that day news came from Laos that the Pathet Lao's advance had run out of steam. They called for a cease-fire on the radio and within a few days they signed a formal one with Phoumi. The drive to war in Laos stopped. "In retrospect, the Laos crisis of 1961 seems in some ways a dress rehearsal for the Cuban missile crisis of 1962," Schlesinger later wrote, because "it was marked by a restraint of manner, toughness of intention, and care to leave the adversary a way of escape without loss of face."[203]

At a meeting Kennedy had with his advisors, a few days later, "most agreed the chance for salvaging anything out of the cease-fire and coalition government was slim indeed." The group discussed ways to reassure Thailand and South Vietnam and decided to send Vice-President Lyndon Johnson to visit them. "The decision to compromise in Laos made it essential to convey by word and deed that the US would stand firm in South Vietnam and in

[203] Schulimson, pp. 82-83; Schlesinger, p. 317.

the rest of Southeast Asia," later wrote William Bundy, who was in the State Department at the time.[204]

President Kennedy campaigned as a man who would prosecute the Cold War with vigor. After the Bay of Pigs disaster, and what some in the Pentagon saw as a failure to go all of the way in Laos, it was just as important, perhaps more important, for Kennedy to reassure the war state bureaucracy as it was to show strength to potential adversaries. As soon as the shooting stopped in Laos, members of the Joint Staff of the Joint Chiefs of Staff drafted new plans on what to do if the cease fire fell through. The Joint Chiefs of Staff approved new contingency plans for the President to sign that would give them a guarantee that the "United States is thereby prepared and committed to succeed... regardless of the extent of possible communist escalation." It stated that such a statement "was an unequivocal fundamental to US military action."

This document ultimately didn't reach President Kennedy, but it is doubtful that he would have signed it, because it would have meant limiting the presidential power to decide whether the United States should go to war or not, and even how, and placing it into the hands of the Joint Chiefs of Staff

[204] Gibbons, pp. 33, 41.

by pledging to guarantee carrying out their contingency plans in advance. On May 14, Admiral Felt officially ended the alert status for US naval forces in the South China Sea and Gulf of Siam. Four days later, he told the fleet that if needed, "with good luck and sufficient time before the [next] 'flap' we can pick up the pieces... [and be] ready to jump again in an orderly fashion."[205]

Admiral Burke wrote a memo to Secretary of Defense McNamara telling him that it was the opinion of the Joint Chiefs of Staff that "US forces should be deployed immediately to South Vietnam; such action should be taken primarily to prevent the Vietnamese from being subjected to the same situation as presently exists in Laos, which would then require deployment of US forces into an already existing combat situation." "I believe that we are facing a repetition of the unhappy sequence of events in Laos... which can only lead to the loss of Vietnam," complained General Lemnitzer. The Joint Chiefs of Staff as a body then claimed to McNamara that "credibility in the US deterrent is waning. The challenge has been made in Southeast Asia."[206]

President Kennedy had created a task force for South Vietnam as he entered the White House, just as he had for Laos. However, it took up very little of

---

[205] Schulimson, pp. 84-87; Poole, p.132.
[206] Schulimson, p. 89;

his time as nothing much seemed to be happening there and everyone's energy was focused on Laos and Cuba. He soon got a report from the Vietnam task force in what was in the words of the Pentagon Papers in "an atmosphere wholly dominated by Laos" and with a desire "in developing a new program that would offset the impact of Laos."[207]

Walt Rostow and Robert McNamara would soon follow the lead of the Joint Chiefs of Staff in asking Kennedy to send combat troops to South Vietnam. The implications of the events of the past few weeks were pretty clear to Arthur Schlesinger. He believed that President Kennedy had "made a de facto deal with the national security establishment: if it went along with neutralization in Laos, he would do something for resistance in South Vietnam."[208]

---

[207] *The Pentagon Papers*, pp. 33, 39.
[208] Arthur Schlesinger, Jr., *Robert Kennedy And His Times* (USA: Ballantine Books, 1978), p. 758.

CHAPTER VI - A DRIVE FOR ACTION

According to the Pentagon Papers, "in the summer of 1959, it was hard to find an American official worried about Vietnam. This was not because things were going well. They were not. A National Intelligence Estimate published in August portrayed Diem as unpopular, his economy developing less rapidly than its rival in the North, and his government under pressure from guerrillas encouraged and supported from the North. Nonetheless, the NIE suggested no crisis then or for the foreseeable future." When it came to the view from Washington, Vietnam was just one area of the world. There was a new formal counterinsurgency plan being developed for Vietnam for most of 1959 and 1960, but it took eight months before it even reached the White House on January 28, 1961, just days after Kennedy became president.[209]

This program offered Diem enough money and supplies to increase his army by 20,000 men at the cost of a forty-two million dollar increase of what

---

[209] *The Pentagon Papers, Gravel Edition, Volume II* (Boston: Beacon Press, 1971), pp. 17-19.

was then a $220 million US aid program. Ngo Dinh Diem's strategy was to use his army to maintain military outposts throughout South Vietnam and to concentrate the population into fortified villages along main roads where they could learn personalism. He called this building "lines of strength." His forces would then make periodic sweeps between the outposts in order to demonstrate "nominal" control of the countryside.

The United States Military Assistance Advisory Group (MAAG), headed by Lieutenant General Lionel McGarr, disagreed with Diem and tried to get him to approve of a "net and spear" concept. The Americans wanted Diem to order small units to go into the jungles beyond pacified areas and try to find the enemy and "net" him. They would then call in reserves who would serve as the "spear" to attempt to destroy the enemy units instead of "tying up most of his forces defending fixed installations with periodic uneventful sweeps through the hinterland." Such tactics, though, made Diem uneasy, because they would mean casualties for his forces and it wasn't clear to him if it was even a realistic strategy. He depended on the loyalty of his army for his very survival and if he led it to defeats and deaths he could be overthrown. Diem's attitude annoyed the US Ambassador to Vietnam Eldridge Dubrow.[210]

---

[210] Ibid. pp. 23-26.

Colonel Edward Lansdale became the Assistant to the Secretary of Defense for Special Operations. He answered directly to the Joint Chiefs of Staff and Secretary of Defense Robert McNamara, as the head of covert operations for the Pentagon. He took a trip to South Vietnam and found that "President Diem feels that Americans have attacked him almost as viciously as the Communists, and he has withdrawn into a shell for self-protection. We have to show him by deeds, not words alone, that we are his friend."

In a written report, he advised replacing the ambassador, actually he in essence was lobbying to replace the ambassador with himself, by arguing that "if the next American official to talk to President Diem would have the good sense to see him as a human being who has been through a lot of hell for years - and not as an opponent to be beaten to his knees - we would start regaining our influence with him in a healthy way. Whatever else we might think of him, he has been unselfish in devoting his life to his country and has little in personal belongings to show for it."

Lansdale's report shook President Kennedy up. After he read it, he told Walt Rostow, "this is the worst one we've got, isn't it? You know, Eisenhower never mentioned it. He talked at length about Laos, but never uttered the word Vietnam." Lansdale's report opened with a dire warning that "the free Vietnamese and their government, probably will be able to do no more than postpone eventual defeat - unless they find a Vietnamese way of mobilizing their total resources and then utilizing them with spirit." He suggested treating South Vietnam as a "combat area of the cold war, as an area requiring special treatment."

When Lansdale arrived back home he went to meet McNamara at the Pentagon. Lansdale recalled that:

> "I had a lot of Viet Cong weapons, punji stakes, and so on, that I'd collected in Vietnam to get the Special Forces to start a Fort Bragg museum of guerrilla weapons. They still had Vietnamese mud on them, rusty, and dirty. They were picked up from the battlefield. So, I tucked all of these under my arm and went to his office. He had told me on the phone that I had five minutes to give him a briefing on Vietnam. I went in and he was sitting at his desk, and I put all of these dirty weapons down - crude looking, and including those big spikes that they had as punji stakes dried with blood and mud on them - I put them on this beautiful mahogany desk - I just dumped them on that. I said, 'The enemy in Vietnam used these weapons - and they were just using them just a little bit ago before I got them. The enemy are barefoot or wear sandals.

> They wear black pajamas, usually, with tatters or holes in them. I don't think you'd recognize them as soldiers, but they think of themselves that way. The people that are fighting them, on our side, are being supplied with weapons and uniforms and good shoes, and all of the best that we have; and we're training them. Yet, the enemy's licking our side,' I said. 'Always keep in mind about Vietnam that the struggle goes far beyond the material things of life. It doesn't take weapons and uniforms and lots of food to win. It takes something else, ideas, and ideals, and these guys are using that something else. Let's at least learn that lesson.' Somehow I found him very hard to talk to. Watching his face as I talked, I got the feeling that he didn't understand me."[211]

McNamara didn't get Lansdale's point and didn't want to take the time to try to figure it out either. He had a simple reason. Although "I knew of only one Pentagon officer with counterinsurgency experience in the region - Col. Edward Lansdale, who had served as an adviser to Ramon Magsaysay in the Philippines and Diem in South Vietnam,"

---

[211] William Gibbons, *The U.S. government and the Vietnam War: Executive and legislative roles and relationships, Volume II* (New Jersey: Princeton University Press, 1986), p. 11-13

McNamara later wrote, he "was relatively junior and lacked broad geopolitical expertise."[212]

According to Roger Hilsman, President Kennedy had "all but decided to send Lansdale himself as the new American ambassador, but the suggestion raised a storm in the Pentagon, where Lansdale was viewed as an officer who, through his service with CIA, had become too 'political.' Since there was, of course, a certain amount of truth in the charge, McNamara was persuaded and Lansdale was put aside."

Lansdale later was told that Secretary of State Dean Rusk had threatened to resign if he were to become the ambassador to South Vietnam. So, Kennedy decided to send Frederick Nolting to South Vietnam instead. Nolting was "a career foreign service officer from an old Virginia family. Nolting was a big, soft-spoken man who was so comfortable to be with that almost everyone used his nickname, Fritz. He was ideal for the job of restoring good relations with Diem and attempting to influence him towards concessions that would bring his regime wider support from within Vietnam and make it politically easier for the United States to give him the aid he requested," wrote Roger Hilsman. As for Colonel Lansdale, Kennedy eventually put him in charge of covert operations

[212] Robert McNamara, *In Retrospect: The Tragedy And Lessons Of Vietnam* (New York: Time Books, 1995), p. 32.

against Fidel Castro's Cuba in a program called Operation Mongoose, while McNamara's office got him a promotion to general.[213]

Kennedy approved the counterinsurgency program for South Vietnam, in a decision which in the words of the Pentagon Papers, "was apparently seen as a routine action." The President, though, was very interested in counterinsurgency. Soviet Premier Nikita Khrushchev gave a speech in response to Kennedy's inaugural address, in which he pledged to support "war of liberation or popular uprisings," which would begin as "uprisings of colonial peoples against their oppressors" and then develop into "guerilla wars".

Kennedy gave copies of the Khrushchev speech to his top aides and read it time and again in his office, and even alone. He would read it aloud to people and ask for them to comment. The President always listened to other people's opinions, but for Kennedy this was what the real battle for the Third World in the Cold War was really about, not nuclear warfare, and winning that battle meant harnessing the forces of nationalism against those of

---

[213] John Newman, *JFK And Vietnam* (New York: Warner Books, 1992), p. 40; Roger Hilsman, *To Move A Nation* (New York: A Delta Book, 1964), pp. 419-420; Roswell Gilpatric interview, JFKOH-RLG-01, JFK Library, 5/5/1970.

the communists. He quickly made counterinsurgency his own personal project.[214]

The Pentagon, however, had little interest in fighting guerilla battles, because the American military was not really designed for it. "The army had fallen into the hands of organization generals after the departure of Ridgway, Taylor, and Gavin who looked on the counterinsurgency business as a faddish distraction from the main responsibility of training for conventional assault," explained Arthur Schlesinger, "the professionals, infatuated with the newest technology and eager to strike major blows, deeply disliked the thought of reversion to crude weapons, amateur tactics, hard life and marginal effects of guerilla warfare."

Guerilla warfare was exactly the type of warfare Walt Rostow had been interested in for years. Kennedy had Rostow look into what the Pentagon was doing. He found that they only had a thousand men serving in the special forces at Fort Bragg. The President then "instructed the Special Warfare Center at Fort Bragg to expand its mission, which had hitherto been largely the training of cadres for action behind the lines in case of a third world war, in order to confront the existing challenge of guerrilla warfare in the jungles and hills of underdeveloped countries. Over the opposition of the Army

[214] Pentagon Paper, p. 27; Gibbons, p. 16.

bureaucracy, which abhorred separate elite commands on principle, he reinstated the SF green beret as the symbol of the new force," wrote Schlesinger.[215]

Kennedy appointed Major General William Yarborough to run the school and created a special counterinsurgency task force that included Walt Rostow, Robert Kennedy, Maxwell Taylor, and Richard Bissell. Rostow viewed this as part of the modernization process. He went to Fort Bragg and delivered a speech to special forces, telling them that they were shock troops in the most important conflict in human history. The communist enemies "are scavengers of the modernization process," while "communism is best understood as a disease of the transition to modernization," he said. The excise of communists through their extermination was the logical implication. Rostow saw guerilla warfare as a new type of conflict that consisted of the "sending of men and arms across international boundaries and the direction of guerilla war from outside a sovereign nation" through aggressive conspiracy, which required "action against those whom aggression is mounted" to "seek out and engage the ultimate source of aggression they confront." Roger Hilsman, who had real life experience fighting guerilla style warfare in Burma during World War II, emerged as the State Department

[215] Arthur Schlesinger, Jr., *A Thousand Days* (New York: Fawcett Premier, 1965), pp. 318-319.

expert on the topic and got the personal ear of Kennedy.[216]

Rostow urged Kennedy to organize for an "effective counter-offensive" in South Vietnam. It was really the only American ally engaged in a guerilla war, so it could be seen as a test case. "We must somehow bring to bear our unexploited counter-guerrilla assets on the Viet-Nam problem; our armed helicopters; other Research and Development possibilities; our Special Forces units. It is somehow wrong to be developing these capabilities but not applying them in a crucial active theater," Rostow wrote Kennedy in a memo.[217]

Rostow was on Kennedy's Vietnam Task Force, along with Desmond Fitzgerald, Ed Lansdale, Paul Nitze, and General Charles Bonesteel III, representing the Joint Chiefs of Staff. It was headed by McNamara's deputy Roswell Gilpatric. Years later, after Vietnam turned into a disaster, Gilpatric said, "we took all of these masses of suggestions that came in from all of these people, Lansdale and others, who had been out there and we talked them over and threw them around at various sessions we had at State and Defense, and came up with this whole package of different measures. I think we bought that whole line and then put it forward as

---

[216] David Milne, *America's Rasputin: Walt Rostow and the Vietnam War* (New York: Hill and Wang, 2008), p. 257, Hilsman, p. 422.
[217] Gibbons, p. 34.

our own with much more assurance than I would ever do again. I think we were kidding ourselves into thinking that we were making well-informed decisions."[218]

They were making recommendations on Vietnam in the context of the Laos crisis and the views of some of the Joint Chiefs of Staff on the need to flex American power in Southeast Asia in face of the rise of China. General Lemnitzer was angry. While touring Asia he sent a cable to the Pentagon about the "unhappy sequence of events in Laos" that "can only mean the loss of Vietnam" unless they acted. "Does the U.S. intend to take the necessary military action now to defeat the Viet Cong threat or do we intend to quibble for weeks and months over details of general policy," he wanted to know, "while Vietnam slowly but surely goes down the drain of Communism as North Vietnam and a large portion of Laos have gone to date?"

Admiral Burke wired Admiral Felt that they only needed to send a few troops to Vietnam to get something big going. "Where there are no U.S. troops in place, there is no will to send them when the going gets tough," he wrote, and with a few units in Vietnam a decision to later reinforce them "is more easily taken." He explained that "we have

[218] Ibid, p. 36.

missed the boat in Laos by not having [a] foot in [the] door."[219]

On May 4, Roswell Gilpatric chaired a meeting of the Vietnam Task Force. The group discussed the cease fire situation in Laos and what it meant for sending troops to Vietnam. He noted that a US Marine brigade could be sent to Vietnam on twelve hours of notice and then reinforced by "Army forces in Hawaii over a somewhat longer period of time as requirements demanded."

Walt Rostow remarked that, with this troops issue, "it was essential that we have a maximum degree of clarity both as to the types of US troops which were required in Viet-Nam and as to the precise missions which they would be expected to fulfill." Rostow said there were three "alternative rationales" they could use to recommend sending American troops to Vietnam:

1. A step-up in our previous activities directed against the insurgency movement by involving additional training forces, etc.

2. Provision of sufficient force to act as a trip wire and

3. Sufficient forces to meet an anticipated ChiCom invasion.

---

[219] Newman, pp. 57-58.

Rostow argued, in regards to the first rational involving counterinsurgency, it would only take a few hundred additional personnel to help train and advise the South Vietnamese army and that was a "different matter from putting in US combat units." Gilpatric then asked General Bonesteel what plans the Joint Chiefs of Staff had for sending troops to Vietnam.

The General said that they "had made an assessment in terms of the Laotian situation, but not specifically" for Vietnam. He then said that he did not think it were possible to stop the infiltration of communists and supplies into South Vietnam across the 1,500 mile wide border of Laos. The US Ambassador to Thailand, Kenneth Young, who was in the meeting, questioned why then should the United States "pour hundreds of millions into Viet-Nam if we can't choke off the problem?" General Bonesteel said that it would take "very sizeable force commitments" in Vietnam and that what the Joint Chiefs really wanted was a clear "statement of the real national intent as possible in order to give clear policy guidance concerning the commitment of forces."[220]

After this meeting, Gilpatric sent a request to the Joint Chiefs of Staff asking them for their views

---

[220] Jack Schulimson, *History of the Joint Chiefs of Staff, The Joint Chiefs of Staff and the War in Vietnam, 1960-1968, Part I.* (Washington, D.C.,: Office of the Joint History Office of the Chairman of the Joint Chiefs of Staff, 2011), pp. 91-93.

on troops in South Vietnam. With the help of their planning staff, they replied as a body recommending that troops be sent immediately, "assuming the political decision is to hold Southeast Asia outside the communist sphere." In this decision, they believed that "South Vietnam should not be considered in isolation," but in conjunction with "their overall rclationship to the security of Southeast Asia." Such troops would "provide visible deterrent to potential North Vietnam and/or Chinese Communist action" and "provide a nucleus for support of any additional U.S. or SEATO military operation in Southeast Asia; and indicate the firmness of our intent to all Asian nations." The troops would "assist in training the Vietnamese forces," but in the geopolitical picture would enable the United States to maintain its dominant power position in Southeast Asia and block China.

The chiefs recommended contacting President Diem to encourage him "to request that the United States fulfill its SEATO obligation, in view of the new threat now posed by the Laotian situation, by the immediate deployment of appropriate US forces to South Vietnam."

Upon receiving the input of the Joint Chiefs of Staff, the Vietnam Task force completed a report and submitted it for presidential approval. It recommended sending enough assistance to Diem to enable him to increase the size of his army from

170,000 to 200,000 men and recommended sending 400 US special forces personnel to help in training purposes along with two full US combat battle groups to Vietnam for a "limited war mission in South Vietnam." These troops "would place the Sino-Soviet Bloc in the position of risking direct intervention in a situation where US forces were already in place, accepting the consequences of such action. This is in direct contrast to the current situation in Laos." At this point, "come what may, the US intends to win this battle," the report said.

Kennedy held a National Security Council meeting on May 11, 1961, to discuss this Task Force Report. In the end, he approved the deployment of a 400 man special forces team to South Vietnam and more assistance to Diem, but he rejected the combat troop request by tabling it for further study. Roger Hilsman believed that Kennedy preferred advisers over combat troops, as "a token to keep the military quiet." According to the Pentagon Papers, "in the context of the time, the commitments Kennedy actually made seem like a near-minimal response which avoided any real deepening of our stake in Vietnam."[221]

At the same time that Kennedy was holding this meeting, Vice-President Lyndon Johnson was in

---

[221] Gibbons, pp. 38-40; *Howard Jones, Death Of A Generation: How The Assassinations Of Diem And JFK Prolonged The Vietnam War* (New York: Oxford University Press, 2003), pp. 48, 51.

South Vietnam, along with his wife Lady Bird and Kennedy's sister and brother in-law, Jean and Stephen Smith. At first LBJ didn't want to go. "I don't want to embarrass you by getting my head blown off in Saigon," Johnson told him. He was scared.[222]

But Kennedy forced Johnson to go. The Vice-President was attending a labor function in New York when he heard an announcement on the radio saying that he was going to South Vietnam. He didn't like to be bossed like that, so he went back to the White House and told Kennedy he was not going to go.

Air Force Colonel Howard Burris, who served as the Vice-President's personal military aide, recalls that "I was sitting there against the wall in the NSC meeting listening to all this screaming taking place. Kennedy said he wanted Johnson to go and Johnson just refused. Kennedy said, 'you're going tonight and the Foreign Service and Bundy will brief you.'"

Johnson left the room, and then "went out and just got stoned," Burris said, "he came back and went to sleep on his couch and finally let the Foreign Service guys in. I think one or two were Assistant Secretaries." One of them was the Assistant Secretary of State for Public Affairs, Carl Rowan. Rowan remembers Johnson telling him as soon he got in the room that "I want you State Department

[222] Jones, pp. 60-61.

folks to know that I think you're a bunch of little puppy dogs, leaking on every hydrant."

Johnson was angry about the news leak of the trip on the radio and blamed the Under Secretary of State. "I sat there in astonishment," Rowan said, "absolutely certain that the leak came not from Chester Bowles, but from the President of the United States."

"We got on the plane that night," Burris said, "and there was this briefing book with all the inputs from the various agencies and so forth." He handed it to Johnson, who threw it back at him, saying, "Howard, if you give me any of this State Department crap again I'll throw you off this plane." Rowan said that LBJ was drinking excessively and the more drinks he drank the more mean he got, "in ways I found hard to believe." When he was sober, though, he spoke about wanting to help lift nations and poor people up with more feeling "than any individual I ever knew in my life." The Vice-President was a complex man, Rowan noticed that throughout the entire trip Johnson "talked over and over about the fact that he had not been born rich like the Kennedys" and had not gone to Harvard or Yale, but to some "little crappy Texas college." "Johnson had one of the greatest inferiority complexes I ever saw in a high-level public official," Rowan later wrote.[223]

---

[223] Newman, pp. 67-69.

After the party's plane landed in Saigon, they were met by a delegation of South Vietnamese officials and their wives. Lyndon Johnson saw Madame Nhu and made a bee line for her to shake her hand. The Americans then went to a dinner hosted by Ambassador Nolting on the rooftop of the Caravelle Hotel. Kennedy had his family members on the trip to impress Diem on how important the United States considered him and his nation to be.[224]

LBJ met with Diem the next morning at 8:00 AM. Minutes before the meeting, Johnson received a cable from CINCPAC labeled "OPERATIONAL IMMEDIATE" from the Joint Chiefs of Staff sent only to him and General Lionel McGarr in Saigon. Not even Ambassador Nolting knew of it. The message contained a transcript of the Joint Chief's recommendations to McNamara for troops and their desire that Diem "be encouraged to ask for combat troops." It also said that McNamara knew of the requests, but had "not as yet" approved them.

When Johnson met with Diem, he first presented him with a letter from President Kennedy that said, "We are ready to join with you in an intensified effort to win the struggle against Com-

[224] Monique Demery, *Finding The Dragon Lady: The Mystery Of Vietnam's Madame Nhu* (New York: Public Affairs, 2013), p. 124.

munism and to further the social and economic advancement of Vietnam" in a "joint campaign." Kennedy's letter did not mention combat troops or even a defense treaty, but contained a promise to increase aid. Diem read it closely and told Johnson that he had problems financing his 20,000 increase in his army and needed more money. Johnson promised that the United States could send him helicopters and equipment for the army for free. The Vice-President saw that Diem was "tickled as hell" with that suggestion. The two talked for a few hours and Johnson suggested to Diem that he write a "letter of reply" to Kennedy with a list of things he needed from the United States. He said nothing about combat troops to Diem, as the Joint Chiefs wanted him to do.[225]

Ambassador Nolting, Johnson, and the Kennedy family members then went to an official luncheon in Diem's palace with his family. Vice-President Johnson found that his chair was seated next to Madame Nhu's, so he waited for her to sit down before he took his seat. As they ate, he made her promise to visit him at his ranch in Texas. She laughed and nervously covered her mouth with a napkin and told him that she will come "when you become President." In front of his wife and everyone at the dinner, Johnson then grabbed her hand and pulled her away from the table. They went out

[225] Gibbons, p. 42; Newman, pp. 69-70.

to the balcony and Johnson asked her to "show me the sights" of Saigon.[226]

Johnson had been in a bad mood, but now he was pumped up. Just a few hours before he called Carl Rowan a "dummy" and told him that he was going to take the next plane back to Washington if things went sour. Now suddenly, during the lunch, Rowan received a phone call from LBJ. The Vice-President told him that he wanted to make up and talk to reporters. He had Rowan round up a bunch of them and come to LBJ's room. "There followed the only press conference that, to my knowledge, a senior American official held in his skivvies," said Rowan.

In the afternoon, Johnson decided to go on to the streets of Saigon and plunged into the crowds. He praised Diem as the "Churchill of Asia." An American reporter thought that it was as if Johnson "were endorsing county sheriffs in a Texas election campaign." He made love to the people by shaking their hands and kissing babies.

After another state dinner, Johnson again met in private with Diem. Diem told him that he wanted more men, because of Laos. Instead of an increase of 20,000, he wanted to increase his army by 100,000. Johnson responded by asking him why 150,000 men could not deal with only 10,000 Viet Cong? Then Johnson asked Diem what would he

[226] Demry, p. 125.

think about asking for US combat troops? Diem said that he didn't want any American combat troops in South Vietnam unless there was an "open invasion," but he would accept more US training personnel. Diem was a great leader, who by his example was the living embodiment of personalism, and had no interest in turning himself and his nation into a total dependent of a foreign power. Diem told Kenneth Young, the American ambassador to Thailand, who was with Johnson on this trip, to "be extremely careful about such a proposal" and that all Americans must "exercise tact and restraint in Vietnam in this critical and delicate period."[227]

As Johnson left South Vietnam, he knew he would have to write an official report about Vietnam and Diem. Diem first sent a cable immediately to President Kennedy telling him that "he was deeply gratified by this gracious gesture by your distinguished Vice-President, particularly as we have not become accustomed to being asked for our own views as to our needs." One of Kennedy's aides wrote in the margins next to this sentence the word "touche!" Diem said he would give an estimate of his needs in about a week.[228]

Lyndon Johnson stopped in Bermuda, before going to Washington, D.C., and spent three entire

---

[227] Newman, pp. 69-73; *Pentagon Papers*, p. 55; Schulimson, p. 96.
[228] Newman, p. 77.

days in isolation writing his report of his trip with the assistance of his aide Colonel Burris. LBJ was trying to craft a report that would please both the Joint Chiefs of Staff and President Kennedy. It was tough, because "after a lot of backing and filling and changing directions totally," Burris remembers," the recommendation that was going to the press was do not get bogged down, Mr. President, in a land war in Southeast Asia." Yet, Johnson had supported the Chiefs when they wanted to intervene directly in Laos and they now wanted to send combat troops to South Vietnam.

Johnson seemed to be more concerned about Washington politics than the real situation in Vietnam. "I don't think he had a really deep perception and comprehension of what the whole scene was about," said Burris. In the end, Johnson decided to write in his report that the situation in Vietnam and Southeast Asia was now serious after Laos, but that this was not the time for combat troops yet.[229]

In his report to the President, Johnson said that "there is no mistaking the deep - and long lasting - impact of recent developments in Laos. Country to country, the degree differs but Laos has created doubt and concern about intentions of the United States throughout Southeast Asia." LBJ said that

---

[229] Ibid, pp. 89-92.

his visit helped buck up the confidence of the leaders of these nations, but "if these men I saw at your request were bankers, I would know - without bothering to ask - that there would be no further extensions of my note."

In Johnson's opinion, "the battle against Communism must be joined in Southeast Asia with strength and determination to achieve success there - or the United States, inevitably, must surrender the Pacific and take up our defenses on our own shores." In the end, "we must decide whether to help these countries to the best of our ability or throw in the towel in the area and pull back to our defenses to San Francisco and a 'Fortress America' concept."

However, Johnson found that "Asian leaders - at this time - do not want American troops involved in Southeast Asia other than on training missions. American combat troop involvement is only not required, it is not desirable. Possibly Americans - fail to appreciate fully the subtlety that recently - colonial people would not look with favor upon governments which invited or accepted the return this soon of Western troops."

"In Vietnam," Johnson wrote, "Diem is a complex figure beset by many problems. He has admirable qualities, but he is remote from the people, is surrounded by persons less admirable and capable than he. The country can be saved - if we move quickly and wisely. We must decide whether to support Diem - or let Vietnam fall. "

LBJ advocated sending more aid and support to Diem in a "major effort in support of the forces of freedom in the area or throw in the towel. This decision must be made in full realization of the very heavy and continuing costs involved in terms of money, of effort, and of United States prestige. It must be made with the full knowledge that at some point we may be faced with the further decision of whether to commit major United States forces to the area or cut our losses and withdraw should those efforts fail. We must remain master in the decision."[230]

President Kennedy sent 400 special forces advisors to South Vietnam and military and economic aid to Diem also. He also got professor Eugene Staley of the Stanford Research Institute to head the US Special Financial group to oversee the economic aid package going to South Vietnam. The professor went to visit Diem and made his own report.

Staley's group recommended a "Joint Action Program" to create 100 new agrovilles or strategic hamlets and enough assistance to Diem to help him increase his army to 200,000 men. It argued that the long run success of the military aspects of the program would depend upon the success of

[230] *Pentagon Papers*, pp. 56-59.

"emergency" economic and social planning that would improve the living conditions of the people of Vietnam enough in order to achieve a "breakthrough." "Our joint efforts," the report concluded, "must surpass the critical threshold of the enemy's resistance, thereby putting an end to his destructive attacks, and at the same time, we must make a decisive impact on the economic, social, and ideological front."[231]

Although Kennedy approved these recommendations, a drive for war planning continued inside the government. At the time, the general public had no clue to how important Vietnam was becoming inside the imagination of men leading the American war state. One reason why is that Congress had completely stopped paying any attention to it. For the rest of the year, during two key Foreign Relations Committee executive sessions with Secretary of State Dean Rusk, there was not even a single mention of Vietnam or Southeast Asia. There was a foreign aid bill that mentioned money going to these regions in passing and one single hearing on Laos on August 16, 1961, for the rest of the year. However, a working committee headed by Walt Rostow and General Maxwell Taylor engaged in deep war planning. Also planning with them were National Security Council staffers Robert Komer,

[231] Gibbons, p. 51.

Roswell Gilpatric representing the Secretary of Defense, and Deputy Under Secretary of State U. Alexis Johnson.[232]

On June 20, 1961, Rostow sent a paper to President Kennedy and U. Alexis Johnson titled "The Present Situation in Southeast Asia." He said that what he wanted was to get Washington, D.C., "to consider more explicitly the military and political links between Laos and the Viet-Nam problems." He thought it would be time to see if they "take the initiative fairly soon to raise the question of aggression against Viet-Nam in some international forum." "Here, as you know," Rostow wrote, "I favor designing and looking hard at an air-sea (iron-bomb) counter-guerilla war, with as many SEATO friends as will play, along with continued vigorous efforts within Diem's boundaries. But if that more ambitious course should be rejected, we would have still strengthened our position before the world, should it be necessary for us sharply to increase our assistance to Diem inside South Viet-Nam. And, at the minimum, this seems likely."

Rostow wrote to Dean Rusk that he thought it was now time to "free our hands and our consciences for whatever we have to do." Bombing could fix everything. He wanted to revise Pentagon SEATO Plan 5 so that it would immediately strike at North Vietnam. He told Rusk that the United

---

[232] Ibid, p. 53.

States now needed to be prepared for three levels of action.

The first consisted of "a sharp increase in the number of Americans in South Viet-Nam for training and support purposes." The second was "a counter-guerrilla operation in the north, possibly using American air and naval strength to impose about the same level of damage and inconvenience that the Viet Cong are imposing in the South." And finally "if the Vietminh cross their border substantially, a limited military operation in the north; e.g., capture and holding of the port of Haiphong."[233]

At the same time, General Taylor sent a request to the Joint Chiefs of Staff to develop a Southeast Asia contingency plan that would focus on the following three objectives:

"1. The securing of the Laotian panhandle and part of the Mekong Valley;

2. The launching of offensive air and guerrilla operations from the panhandle; and

3. The application of military pressure against North Vietnam."

He insisted that the plans must rely mainly on American airpower and restrict American combat troops to logistical support. Instead, most of the

---

[233] Ibid, p. 55.

ground troops should be "indigenous" troops of South Vietnamese, Laotians, and Thais. American infantry troops should be used "to provide immediate protection to US air and supply bases, and the Special Force trainers needed to support the guerilla and anti-guerilla effort." In effect, Taylor wanted to send American combat troops into Laos and the Mekong Valley to create a regional staging base of operations to begin a striking operation against North Vietnam.[234]

On July 18, 1962, Rostow, Taylor, and U. Alexis Johnson met together to discuss the "inter-connection between various elements of policy in Southeast Asia." They agreed on the need "of using evidence of North Viet-Nam aggression as a foundation for more aggressive limited military action against North Viet-Nam." Undersecretary Johnson said that he would get the State Department to "collect and examine the persuasiveness of the evidence" coming in and to examine "the best diplomatic forum or series of forums in which the issue might be raised."

U. Alexis Johnson had one of his staffers prepare a paper titled "Contingency Information Program" for their use. It said that "before we could use force or publicly announce our decision to use force American public opinion would have to be conditioned to support such action. The Congress

[234] Schulimson, pp. 101-102.

would have to be fully informed and convinced of the necessity for such action."

In order to do this they "should float perspective articles through selected newspaper columns such as those of Messrs. Alsop, Drummond, Childs, Reston, etc. While these would reach one audience, a broader exposition for a different audience should be made through Sunday newspaper supplements such as the American Weekly, Parade, The New York Times Magazine, and if time permits through the Saturday Evening Post and movie newsreels which have a claimed audience of 40 million weekly."

It would be "profitable for later exploitation to place some profile articles on Gen. Maxwell Taylor as an expert on limited warfare." "The Senate, or some of its key members, should be taken into confidence of the Executive early in the process and they should be told why alternative courses of action are unacceptable. We should induce some senators to make public speeches on the seriousness of the situation, etc."

The report noted, though, that "if by this time public opinion has not begun to call for positive action, we should begin to withdraw to a fall-back position; we should prepare now the terrain to which we might be obliged to withdrawal." As for the content of the messages "to be sent to the public by these means, the paper recommended that the public and Congress be told about the history of Communist aggression and subversion in Vietnam, as well as the consequences of Communist control of Laos, and that 'the domino theory' should be fully explained."[235]

National Security Staffer Robert Komer sent Rostow a memo to assist him. He titled it "Are We Pushing Hard Enough in South Vietnam?" He argued that even though the Staley group "crash" program is beginning, "we do not yet have things turned around in Vietnam." He worried that, after Kennedy approved their program, "the agencies tend to slip back toward business as usual with only the White House providing the nod."

In Komer's view, "we should regard this as a wartime situation in which the sky's the limit." "What do we lose if such an initiate fails," Komer asked, "are we any worse off than before? Our prestige may have become a little more heavily engaged, but what else? And the risk involved if we fail to prevent the Viet Cong threat from developing into a full-fledged civil war is clearly overriding." "After Laos," it was clear that "we cannot afford to go less than all-out in cleaning up South Vietnam."

On July 27, 1961, Taylor and Rostow sent President Kennedy a memo saying that his choices were

[235] Gibbons, pp. 55-57.

"to disengage from the area as gracefully as possible; to find as soon as possible a convenient political pretext and attack with American military force the regional source of aggression in Hanoi; or to build as much indigenous military, political, and economic strength as we can in the area, in order to contain the thrust from Hanoi while preparing to intervene with U.S. military force if the Chinese Communists come in or the situation otherwise gets out of hand." [236]

The next day, Rostow, Taylor, and U. Alexis Johnson met with President Kennedy and his senior advisors, including Dean Rusk, McGeorge Bundy, George Ball, and John Steeves, the Deputy Assistant Secretary of State for Far East Affairs, to discuss their Vietnam planning. U. Alexis Johnson started the meeting by saying that he was skeptical that anything good was going to come out of diplomatic negotiations for Laos, so what was needed was to "introduce a new element." Therefore, he said, there have been "working discussions in US government" for "the creation of a plan to take and hold the southern part of Laos with the combined forces of the Royal Laotian Government, Thailand, Vietnam and the United States." If the North Vietnamese intervened in response then the United States could bomb the North Vietnamese port city of Haiphong and its capital city of Hanoi.

---

[236] Ibid., pp. 57-59.

President Kennedy interrupted Johnson with some pointed questions. He said he doubted that bombing the cities would make the North Vietnamese back down if things came to that. He also said that he saw no evidence that any workable and realistic plan to take and hold the ground in southern Laos had ever been developed. What is more, if they went into North Vietnam he questioned "whether it would be easy to hold what had been taken in a single attack."

U. Alexis Johnson responded by saying that Taylor was working with the Joint Chiefs of Staff and General Lemnitzer to make it work. Kennedy said he saw this same thing in April when "optimistic estimates were invariably proven false in the event" for Laos. He wanted to see more "realism and accuracy" in planning and made note of "the reluctance of the American people and of many distinguished military leaders to see any direct involvement of U.S. troops in that part of the world."

Undersecretary Johnson countered by saying that with "a proper plan, with outside support, and above all with a clear and open American commitment, the results would be different from anything that happened before."

President Kennedy still remained skeptical, saying that he recently met with Charles De Gaulle of

France who told him "of painful French experience... of the difficulty of fighting in this part of the world."

Undersecretary Johnson then made it plain that he understood that "no decision was being sought at this meeting, but that it would be most helpful in planning if it could be understood that the President would at some future time have a willingness to decide to intervene if the situation seemed to him to require it."

Kennedy then said that he "believed that the negotiations in Geneva" for Laos "should be pressed forward, that we should not get ourselves badly separated from the British, that the American people were not eager to get into Laos, that nothing would be worse than an unsuccessful intervention in this area, and that he did not yet have confidence in the military practicability of the proposal, which had been put before him, though he was eager to have it studied more carefully."

President Kennedy then again repeated the necessity for a "more accurate assessment of the situation in the future." In exasperation, he said it was his "hope that someone well known to him could go out and look at the situation directly," implying that General Taylor should go to Vietnam. The General said that he needed "to look first at the problem itself to make clear what facts need to be checked." He seemed to want to let the Joint Staff planners do more work first. The Indians were busy.[237]

From meetings like this, U. Alexis Johnson came to conclude that President Kennedy did not like to think about the big strategic end game. “He liked to deal in hard realities,” Johnson said, “the immediate, specific issue that required decision at the time... without trying to look too far ahead.” Assistant Secretary of State Harlan Cleveland complained that “the President would ask a very specific question about some little piece of the jigsaw puzzle but he gave no sense of having a view of the whole puzzle.” President Kennedy simply did not want to box himself in meetings like this with all of his advisors at once.[238]

Rostow sent another memo to Kennedy telling him that "your decision here is not easy. It involves making uncertain commitment in cold blood. It is not unlike Truman's commitment on Greece and Turkey in March 1947; for in truth, Southeast Asia is in as uncertain shape as Southeast Europe at that time. But - like Truman's commitment - it has the

---

[237] Gibbons, p. 60; Schulimson, pp. 102-104; Document 109, *Foreign Relations of the United States, 1961-1963. Vietnam: Volume I, 1961, U.S. Department of State*; https://history.state.gov/historicaldocuments/frus1961-63v01/d109 , accessed 5/12/2015.

[238] Frank Jones, *Blowtorch: Robert Komer, Vietnam, and American Cold War* Strategy (Annapolis: Naval Institute Press, 2013),p. 33.

potentiality of rallying the forces in the area, mobilizing the will and strength sufficient to fend off the Communist threat, and minimizing the chance that U.S. troops will have to fight in a situation which has further deteriorated."

In private, Averell Harriman told President Kennedy that he opposed making a troop commitment for Southeast Asia and opposed the calls to "bomb Hanoi." Kennedy jokingly told him that he thought of Rostow as the "Air Marshal" for his zest for bombing.[239]

Rostow also wrote a memo to Robert Kennedy, which said, "I deeply believe that the way to save Southeast Asia and to minimize the chance of deep U.S. military involvement there is for the President to make a bold decision very soon."[240]

On August 24, 1961, a top-level meeting in Secretary of State Dean Rusk's office on Southeast Asia was held. At it a draft proposed plan of action consisting mainly of Rostow's ideas was attacked by Secretary of State Robert McNamara and Averell Harriman, who was in charge of the Laos negotiations, for being inconsistent with Kennedy's desire to go for a negotiated settlement before beginning military action. Rusk threw his weight in opposition to Rostow's plans, while General Taylor

[239] Jones, p. 77.
[240] Gibbons, p. 63.

and Steeves tried to defend them, but failed to convince Rusk and McNamara. Although Rostow's ideas were crushed for the moment, he did not leave the meeting diminished. He was riding a wave of a drive for action that had not subsided. Dean Rusk could never ruin him. According to Roger Hilsman, Rusk was trying to steer the State Department away from any controversy in regards to Vietnam, seeing it essentially as a problem for the Defense Department and the Pentagon.[241]

McGeorge Bundy came to "the feeling that Dean Rusk is a very careful fellow; he doesn't let his guard down." He thought he was good at summarizing the views of others, "but if you want to be sure what he thinks, that's going to be a little harder, and that's not going to be the first card he plays." Nicholas Katzenbach, who served as assistant Attorney General for Robert Kennedy and then under Rusk during the Johnson administration, said that Rusk "did not like to take positions. That made it awfully difficult for him to advise the President, because he had to know what the President thought before he advised him."[242]

The situation in South Vietnam was not improving. By mid-August, a National Intelligence Estimate concluded that about 12,000 Viet Cong

---

[241] Gibbons, p. 64; Hilsman, p. 421.

[242] Andrew Preston, *The War Council; McGeorge Bundy, The NSC, And Vietnam* (Cambridge: Harvard University Press, 2006), pp.44-45.

guerillas were in South Vietnam. General McGarr reported of an "enhanced sense of urgency and offensive spirit now present within" Diem's army and government, but the number of guerillas did not shrink and the problems weren't a secret. Reporter Theodore White discovered that "the situation gets worse almost week by week... The guerillas now control almost all the southern delta - so much so that I could find no American who would drive me outside Saigon in his car even by day without military envoy."[243]

In September, the Vietcong mounted an offensive that tripled the tempo of their attacks. For the first time a number of VC overran a provincial capital fifty-five miles north of Saigon in a region that bordered a long-time Communist stronghold. They took over the town and held a "people's trial" that ended with the beheading of the province chief and his assistant. It was a gruesome and troubling affair and by the end of the month US intelligence estimated that the VC had grown in strength to 17,000 men. However, US intelligence estimated that 80-90% of the VC had been locally recruited and that there was little evidence at all that they relied on external supplies. Almost all of their weapons were of U.S. or French origin left over from the French war or had been captured from Diem's forces. Standard counterinsurgency doctrine called

---

[243] Schulimson, p. 107.

for a ten-to-one ratio in fighting guerillas, so Diem's army was being stretched to its limit.

Brigadier General William H Craig, who was one of six top planning deputies to the Director of the Joint Staff, went on a fact finding trip to Thailand, Laos, and South Vietnam for General Lemnitzer and found that the "enemy may be accepting stalemate for time being within Laos and giving priority to stepping up offensive action against South Vietnam." He believed there to be a "build-up of Pathet-Lao-Viet-Minh forces in Southern Laos and the beginnings of additional pressure on Central Vietnam from that area." "The future of the US in Southeast Asia is at stake. It may be too late unless we act now one way or another," he concluded.[244]

The main purpose in Craig's trip was to help the Joint Staff of the Joint Chiefs of Staff bring Vietnam plans to the table. General Lemnitzer forwarded a planning memo to Robert McNamara of the "consequences and effectiveness of certain United States courses of action against North Vietnam." The planners argued that "a large proportion of the support for communist aggression in all of Southeast Asia passes through North Vietnam." They said that the United States could "substantially cut the flow of communist military support

244 Schulimson, pp. 109-110; Gibbons, pp. 65, 77; Jones, p. 84; Newman, p. 116.

passing through North Vietnam, if and when it is decided to commit United States forces openly to this operation." They accepted the fact that such measures "would probably generate Communist Chinese overt countermeasures" and were studying ways to respond to anything they may do.

As General H. Craig, and the Joint Staff, completed their studies, Walt Rostow reported to President Kennedy on September 15, 1961, on their work. He told Kennedy that the Joint Chiefs wanted "the implementation of SEATO Plan 5 now - or if that is not possible, the execution of preparatory measures such as laying the command and logistic base and moving closer to Laos the foreign troops who would take part." General Craig added a written report in which he said that Ambassador Nolting agreed that there was a need now for "positive action in Laos." He also said he met with Diem, who reported that he was ready for a US brigade or division to serve as "school troops" and was fully ready for American combat troops "when the balloon goes up." Rostow did not pass on Craig's report on his discussion with Diem to Kennedy.[245]

On October 3, 1961, a regular "Tuesday morning" planning luncheon group of senior foreign policy administration figures met to discuss Vietnam. At the lunch were Walt Rostow, U. Alexis Johnson, Paul Nitze, and William and McGeorge Bundy. The

---

[245] Schulimson, pp.109-111.

group came to all agree that events in South Vietnam were now going badly and that "a major change of course" was needed. According to McGeorge Bundy's notes, this "triggered" Walt Rostow into formally recommending the deployment of SEATO troops "under urgent JCS consideration." Rostow wanted to put a 25,000 man force along the South Vietnamese and Laotian border.

A few people in the Kennedy administration were not happy with this idea. Two days after this meeting, Under Secretary of State Chester Bowles sent a memo containing his own analysis to Secretary of State Dean Rusk. He said that a direct military response in South Vietnam would foolishly place "our prestige and power in a remote area under the most adverse circumstances." Bowles said that they should instead search for an alternative besides "diplomatic humiliation" and a "major military operation." He advocated as a solution a diplomatic overture to Russia for the creation of a neutral band of nations that would include Laos, Cambodia, Thailand, Malaya, and South Vietnam. The memo received "a relatively negative reaction" in the State Department and Dean Rusk did not want to put his name to such an initiative much less be viewed as pushing for it.

According to Roger Hilsman, President Kennedy saw it "as a farseeing expression of the ultimate goal for Southeast Asia toward which we should work, but it's time had not come yet. I think he would have said that our policy should lead toward the goal of a neutral Southeast Asia and avoid getting the United States prestige so thoroughly pinned to 'victory' in Vietnam as to preclude that goal, but that until Communist ambitions had been blunted against the realities of native resistance from within Southeast Asia we could not do much more than continue to support that resistance."[246]

On October 9, 1961, Secretary of Defense Robert McNamara and Deputy Assistant William Bundy met with the Joint Chiefs of Staff to talk about Vietnam. Admiral George Anderson Jr. was at the meeting as the new Chief of Naval Operations, having relieved Admiral Burke who went into retirement. Bundy told the Chiefs that political reasons were laying behind recommendations to place US forces in Vietnam. Admiral Anderson said that the Chiefs recognized that and wanted troops sent there "as long as... when actually in Vietnam they NOT be put on [the] border." They did not think Rostow's border proposals were feasible. McNamara said he wanted a "positive recommendation" then. "If we cannot get into Laos, we should get into South Vietnam," Admiral Anderson responded.

After this meeting, General Lemnitzer sent McNamara a written reply to his requests. The Chiefs said that they needed to act, because "the

---

[246] Schulimson, pp. 113-114, Hilsman, pp. 423-424.

time is past where actions short of intervention by outside forces could reverse the rapidly worsening situation." It said that Rostow's border plan would not work, because it would mean spreading out the forces to such an extent that they would become vulnerable to piecemeal attacks and would not be able to seal off the border to the extent necessary to stop infiltration anyway. Allied SEATO forces would also be forced into poor defensive positions. The paper also said that putting forces directly along the demilitarized zone between North and South Vietnam would not stop the infiltration of supplies and guerillas into South Vietnam, as they were coming from Laos and could only serve to threaten North Vietnam, "thus promoting the possibility of communist harassment and destruction of friendly combat and logistic forces concentrated near the parallel, if not escalation." "What is needed is not the spreading out of our forces throughout Southeast Asia, but rather a concentrated effort in Laos where a firm stand can be taken," the paper said.

This position paper of the Joint Chiefs of Staff argued that one should not just look at South Vietnam as one hot spot, but instead look at it only in the context with its relationship to Southeast Asia and American power. To not look at Laos or at least a substantial part of it was "militarily unsound." In their view, the best program was one which would confront the Communists directly in Laos with some version of SEATO Plan 5. They recognized that this probably was ruled out due to political considerations, so they were willing to accept the deployment of an initial 20,000 US combat troops centered on Pleiku in the central highlands of South Vietnam near Laos to form a base of action as a first step.[247]

The paper called for a will for ultimate victory starting with attacks on North Vietnam. It noted that North Vietnam could invade South Vietnam in response and if they did it would be necessary to bring in up to 129,000 American combat troops. If China then came into the game then consideration would have to be given "whether to attack selected targets in North China with conventional weapons and whether to initiate use of nuclear weapons against targets in direct support of Chinese operations in Laos."[248]

Deputy Secretary of State U. Alexis Johnson received a copy of Rostow's proposals, and the position paper that the chiefs had sent to McNamara, and prepared a talking paper that tried to incorporate both views. He titled it the "Concept of Intervention in South Vietnam." According to the Pentagon Papers, "it was pretty clear that the main idea

---

[247] Schulimson, pp. 114-115; *Pentagon Papers,* pp. 73-74; Newman, pp. 119-120.
[248] Gibbons, p. 68.

was to get some American combat troops into Vietnam, with the nominal excuse for doing so quite secondary."[249]

William Bundy wrote an interesting memo to his boss Robert McNamara in response. Most memos available in the historical record were formal staff papers written for an audience. Pushing for policies and strategies that created consensus could raise one's stature inside the bureaucracy. At the same time, trying to get people to go along with an unpopular idea or one they were not ready for could mean banishment from the circles of power. Chester Bowles would learn that lesson the hard way. What makes this Bundy memo interesting is that it was written only for his boss, so it presents a totally candid picture of one man's thoughts to another of how effective intervention could be in South Vietnam. He wrote:

> "An early and hard-hitting operation has a good chance (70% would be my guess) of arresting things and giving Diem a chance to do better and clean up. Even if we follow up hard, on the lines the JCS are working out after yesterday's meeting, however, the chances are not much better that we will in fact be able to clean up the situation. It all depends on Diem's effectiveness, which is very problematical. The 30% chance is that

[249] Schulimson, pp. 116.

we would wind up like the French in 1954; white men can't win this kind of fight.

On a 70-30 basis, I would myself favor going in. But if we let, say, a month go by before we move, the odds will slide (both short-term shock effect and long-term chance) down to 60-40, 50-50 and so on. Laos under a Souvanna Phouma deal is more likely than not to go sour, and with more and more things difficult in South Viet-Nam, which again underscores the element of time."[250]

In effect, at this moment, President Kennedy faced tremendous pressure in a call for intervention in Southeast Asia. The first call took place in April and May for Laos. This time Vietnam became the focal point for a drive for action, and, instead of the Joint Chiefs being the main engine for intervention, now they had the support of the bulk of the President's national security advisors. Some such as Walt Rostow and U. Alexis Johnson were in fact ambitiously leading the way. Kennedy had expressed repeated misgivings about sending combat troops to Asia, but never firmly said no, so planning inside the war state bureaucracy continued in that direction and forced him to a decision at a morning National Security Council meeting on October 11, 1961.[251]

---

[250] *Pentagon Papers*, p. 79.
[251] Newman, p. 12.

U. Alexis Johnson's "Concept for Intervention in South Vietnam" was used as a talking memo for this meeting. Undersecretary Johnson presented several proposals that needed a presidential decision. One asked whether the United States should explore with its allies for SEATO Plan 5 intervention in Laos. The second item was whether "to send to South Viet-Nam a very high-level military figure to explore with country team, Diem, and CINCPAC, as well as on the ground feasibility and desirability, of the proposed plan for SEATO intervention in South Viet-Nam. Such a person could also make recommendations for additional immediate action short of intervention which might be taken in the present situation."[252]

The President did not approve of gathering allies for SEATO Plan 5, but approved an item of allowing the Air Force to send a "Jungle Jim" squadron to South Vietnam to begin bombing attacks against Vietcong strong holds. These "Jungle Jims" were a detachment of the 4400th Combat Crew Training Squadron code named "Farm Gate" and consisted of a dozen T-28 fighter bombers and B-26's. All were propeller planes. In order to remain in accordance with Geneva Conventions prohibiting introducing bombers into Indochina, they were designated "Reconnaissance Bombers." Robert McNamara authorized them to engage in bombing runs as long as a South Vietnamese crewmember

[252] Schulimson, pp. 116-117.

was on board. On missions such men sat in the back seat as "trainees."[253]

These "Jungle Jims" actually represented General Curtis LeMay's attempt to get the Air Force involved in counterinsurgency and special forces operations. He considered this combat group to be an elite unit that could be a counterpoint to the Green Berets. He had them wear Australian-style bush hats and special patches on their uniforms to make them stand out. LeMay would not be left out of the action.[254]

Finally, Kennedy decided to send General Taylor and Walt Rostow together to head a fact-finding mission to South Vietnam, with Ed Lansdale and William Jorden of the Department of State to join them. In his memo of this meeting, Deputy Secretary of Defense Roswell Gilpatric made a note for himself that the mission's goal was to examine "the plan for military intervention." They also were to look at the possibility of an alternative plan of placing a small force in Da Nang or a southern port "for the purpose of establishing a US presence in Vietnam." General Lemnitzer cabled General McGarr, in South Vietnam, that Taylor was coming to review the "feasibility and desirability from a political and military standpoint of US intervention in Vietnam." They were closer to getting some action.

---

[253] Gibbons, p. 70.
[254] Jones, p. 89.

After this meeting, President Kennedy had lunch with New York Times columnist Arthur Krock, who had been a longtime friend of the Kennedy family. Kennedy told him that he was getting concerned with the situation in Southeast Asia and did not want it to turn into a big war. He told him that he had serious doubts about the "falling domino theory" and "that United States troops should not be involved in Asian mainland" in what might merely be "civil disturbances caused by guerillas." He said that "it was hard to prove that this wasn't largely the situation in Vietnam." He told Krock that he had just come from a big meeting on Vietnam and that the Pentagon favored "a recommendation by the Chiefs of Staff to send 40,000 troops there." He told him that he did not want to send such troops "at the time and therefore was sending General Maxwell Taylor to investigate and report what should be done."

Kennedy then held a formal press conference later that day and announced the Taylor-Rostow mission. There were rumors in newspapers of sending US combat troops and in a weak attempt to ward them off Kennedy described the Taylor mission's goal as to "seek ways in which we can perhaps better assist the Government of Vietnam in meeting this threat to its independence."

General Taylor drafted a letter for President Kennedy's signature that included a set of instructions for his Vietnam trip. It included orders for the general “to evaluate what could be accomplished by the introduction of SEATO or United States forces into South Vietnam, determining the role, composition and probable disposition of such forces.” Kennedy took this draft and changed it by striking out any mention of troops from the letter and rewrote it to say that Taylor's directive was to provide Kennedy his views "on the courses of action which our Government might take at this juncture to avoid a further deterioration in the situation in South Vietnam; and eventually to contain and eliminate the threat to its independence." The general "must keep in mind" that his recommendations were to be based on the premise that the Vietnamese people and government had the primary responsibility for their own independence. Kennedy issued a formal National Security Action Memorandum, which stated that Taylor's purpose "was to explore ways in which assistance of all types might be more effective." [255]

President Kennedy clearly did not want to send troops to Vietnam, but in a private conversation with Ambassador Nolting, Diem told him that he now would welcome some American combat troops to South Vietnam. Diem's remark took Nolting by surprise, so he explained that his views had changed due to the worsening situation. His idea was for a "symbolic" US force near the 17th parallel, which would prevent any attacks along the

[255] Schulimson, p. 117-118; Jones, p. 91.

DMZ and free Diem's forces stationed there up for combat operations. He also proposed getting the government of Taiwan to send a division of combat troops for operations too. Nolting passed on the conversation to Washington.

The New York Times reported that "the prospect of United States troop involvement is understood to have advanced a step here in the sense that the South Vietnamese Government is reported to be willing to consider such involvement which it had formerly rejected."[256]

President Kennedy decided to try to stop the momentum for combat troops. The day after this New York Times story, he held a meeting with General Lemnitzer and the Joint Chiefs of Staff. Lemnitzer cabled Admiral Felt of CINCPAC that the "President expressed concern over build-up of stories to effect U.S. is contemplating sending combat forces to Vietnam. He feels that too much emphasis is being put on this aspect and could well result in a tremendous letdown in Vietnamese morale if they expected such action and we decided otherwise. Accordingly, emphasis publicly is being put on fact Taylor will review entire situation particularly to determine if increase[s] in our current efforts are called for. However, you should know (and this is to be held most closely) General Taylor will also give most discreet consideration to introduction of

---

[256] *Pentagon Papers,* p. 81.

U.S. Forces if he deems such action absolutely essential."[257]

The next day, The New York Times published an extended article detailing what the Taylor Mission was going to do. According to the Pentagon Papers, "from the way the Times handled the story it is plain that it came from a source authorized to speak for the President, and probably from the President himself. The gist of the story was that Taylor was going to Saigon to look into all sorts of things, one of which, near the bottom of the list, was the question of US troops at some time in the indefinite future. Along with a lot more immediate questions about intelligence and such, Taylor was expected to '... recommend long-range programs, including possible military actions, but stressing broad economic and social measures."

The Times story said that "military leaders at the Pentagon, no less than General Taylor himself are understood to be reluctant to send organized US combat units into Southeast Asia. Pentagon plans for this area stress the importance of countering Communist guerrillas with troops from the affected countries, perhaps trained and equipped by the US, but not supplanted by US troops."

---

[257] Document 163, *Foreign Relations of the United States, 1961-1963. Vietnam: Volume I, 1961, U.S. Department of State*; https://history.state.gov/historicaldocuments/frus1961-63v01/d163, accessed 5/12/2015

As the Pentagon Papers put it, "in light of the recommendations quoted," and "particularly of the staff papers just described that led up to the Taylor Mission, most of this was simply untrue. It is just about inconceivable that this story could have been given out except at the direction of the President, or by him personally. It appears, consequently, the President was less than delighted by Diem's request for troops. He may have suspected, quite reasonably, that Diem's request was prompted by stories out of Washington that Taylor was coming to discuss troops; or he may have wished to put a quick stop to expectations (and leaks) that troops were about to be sent, or both. "

"The *Times* story had the apparently desired effect," reads the Pentagon Papers, because "speculation about combat troops almost disappeared from news stories, and Diem had never again raised the question of combat troops." However, Taylor and Rostow were going to South Vietnam and both would make more recommendations. They would not be made public, but instead would be "very closely held" and force Kennedy to finally make a decision.[258]

[258] *Pentagon Papers*, p. 82.

CHAPTER VII - A PROVING GROUNDS

In September of 1961, Robert McNamara sent a memo to the Joint Chiefs of Staff saying that "he wanted to make South Vietnam a laboratory for the development of organization and procedures for the conduct of sub-limited war." In 1960, there were around 600 American military personnel serving in South Vietnam. By 1968, there would be over 500,000 Americans there. Millions of Americans traveled back and forth to Vietnam by airplane during the 1960's. They all went for different reasons. Many of them were drafted to go while some of them freely enlisted to join in the battle, because they felt the call of their country and believed that it was the right thing to do, but they all took that plane trip across the ocean with feelings of nervousness, believing that they were going to a proving grounds that would test their courage. And some went with a driving ambition to make their mark.[259]

---

[259] Jack Schulimson, *History of the Joint Chiefs of Staff, The Joint Chiefs of Staff and the War in Vietnam, 1960-1968, Part I.* (Washington, D.C.,: Office of the Joint History Office of the Chairman of the Joint Chiefs of Staff, 2011), p. 121.

On October 15, 1961, General Maxwell Taylor and Walt Rostow left Washington, D.C., by airplane for South Vietnam on the behest of President Kennedy to create new recommendations for him in regards to what action to take in that country. One wonders what they were thinking on the trip. Did Rostow look out the window of his plane as he traveled across the ocean in wonder of what his life had brought him? Riding inside a bomber or transport jet like this made him a passenger of pure power in the skies, but more importantly he now represented the President of the United States and was charged to help him create a program to modernize an entire nation. He had a place now to put his theories to work, and to truly develop and improve man, in a battle for the destiny of the world. Everything that he worked for and believed in was laid out in front of him in what seemed to be a future without limit.

General Taylor also climbed to a pinnacle of power in his career. He had fought insider battles for years and finally came out on top. He had served as the Army Chief of Staff during the Eisenhower administration and ended up defending the interests of the Army against the Air Force, the Navy, and even the President. President Dwight Eisenhower created a strategic policy favoring nuclear weapons over conventional weapons he dubbed The New Look. This policy helped him put a lid on defense spending, but meant threatening the Soviet Union and China with total nuclear war as a means to avoid war. General Taylor emerged as a leading critic of this strategy, claiming that it led to "only two choices, the initiation of general war or compromise and defeat."

The Air Force ended up receiving 46% of all defense spending from 1952 to 1960. By allocating more money to the Air Force than the Army, President Eisenhower threatened the Army with shrinking resources and made its leaders adopt a siege mentality. From 1953 to 1959, the budget for the US Army dropped from $16 billion to $9 billion and troop levels were reduced by a third. General Mathew Ridgway complained that "if present trends continue the Army will soon become a service support agency for other armed services." Eisenhower's Treasury Secretary claimed that "if you gave a nickel to anybody the Army had to have a lot more."

Fewer troops, however, meant fewer Colonels and Generals to lead them and diminished the prestige of the Army brass. General Taylor took up their mantel by coming up with a strategy of "flexible response" that said that the United States had to also prepare to fight "limited" wars in the Third World in which the Soviet and American superpowers would not confront each other directly. This concept was used by Democrats as a way to push for an alternative to President Eisenhower's policies and attracted John Kennedy before he became President. General Taylor got to know the

Kennedys and Robert Kennedy became particularly close to Taylor, even naming a son after him.

General Maxwell Taylor retired from active service in 1959 and came out with a book titled *The Uncertain Trumpet* to push for "flexible response" and bash President Eisenhower. "Flexible response" rescued the Army by giving it a key role in counterinsurgency and potential Third World battles. It also made intervention in Southeast Asia a promised land for the implementation of this doctrine. So General Taylor's trip to South Vietnam on behalf of President Kennedy was of critical importance for him personally.[260]

General Taylor and Rostow were not alone. They had a full entourage with them on the aircraft, because this was a big important trip. On the plane was Brigadier General William Craig on behalf of the Joint Chiefs of Staff Planning Staff, which had completed hundreds of hours of work developing plans of action for Vietnam. General Lansdale was on the plane and so was William Jorden for the State Department Policy Planning Group and over a half a dozen other supporting officials. William Colby, the Saigon Station Chief for the Central Intelligence Agency, was also part of the group.

---

[260] Robert Buzzanco, *Masters of War: Military Dissent & Politics In The Vietnam Era* (United States of America: Cambridge University Press, 1996), pp. 75-79.

Roger Hilsman and Arthur Schlesinger later commented that the entourage was dominated by military officials, because there were no major State Department figures on the airplane. Schlesinger thought that Secretary of State Dean Rusk had made a "conscious decision by the Secretary of State to turn the Vietnam problem over to the Secretary of Defense" and just did not want to get involved. Hilsman thought Rusk saw Vietnam as "essentially a military problem" and "did not want the State Department to play a prominent role in the upcoming decisions on Vietnam."

Kennedy, though, was also doing something interesting by placing General Taylor in charge of the trip. Taylor would later become Chairman of the Joint Chiefs of Staff, but at this moment he was only President Kennedy's personal military advisor. So, by making Taylor in charge of this trip, the President was circumventing the traditional State and Defense Department bureaucracies. The military personnel along for the ride were answering to him instead of the Joint Chiefs of Staff.

Of course, each person on the plane was given a packet of folders with twenty recommendations for consideration created by the Planning Staff of the Joint Chiefs of Staff. The first four proposals were for the deployment of US military units in Vietnam and one of these were to send a combat unit to train the South Vietnamese armed forces. Another one was to send an entire American battalion up to

Da Nang in the northern area of South Vietnam. This idea seemed to derive from SEATO Plan 5 and at the very least would likely lead to its eventual activation. Another plan was to send a combat engineer battalion for humanitarian flood relief. The rest of the recommendations did not involve sending US combat units, but were to increase the number of US advisors in South Vietnam, so that they could be placed at the company level in the South Vietnamese army. Some of these ideas included the use of large-scale helicopters in support of the South Vietnamese army and to further train their Civil Guard units.[261]

But the final product of the trip would be a report written by General Taylor for President Kennedy that would lead to a new executive initiative. The General made it clear that he was in charge before the trip even started, by having everyone going on it meeting with him in his office before they left. "I explained to my colleagues that I felt I had a mandate from the President to give him my personal views and recommendations upon return," General Taylor later wrote. He said that they would be able to include their opinions in his final report, but they would be attached as appendices at the end of it. Walt Rostow was to act as his deputy. Rostow liked this, because it meant the trip would

[261] Schulimson, pp. 121-122.

be "a little like two professors going over the outlines for a series of student term papers."

General Lansdale didn't like this, however, and wrote to a friend that of General Taylor, "he has a mob going." "There are times when patriotism is pretty costly, and I think you know my feelings at being part of a big showy deal with a lot of theorists. Maybe I can snatch a few minutes alone with Diem and others, and make it pay off," he added, "and I'll be damned if I'm about to tuck my tail between my legs for anyone." Lansdale still wanted to play a big role in South Vietnam.

"Immediately after take-off from Andrews Air Force Base," Rostow said, "Taylor and I talked at length with each member of the mission" and handed them assignments. General Taylor gave Lansdale a job that he knew he didn't believe in. He told Lansdale to look into the feasibility of erecting a giant fence across the borders of Laos and Cambodia to stop infiltration. The idea was absurd to Lansdale. Then Taylor insulted Lansdale by telling him that he would not be allowed to visit President Diem with the group.

"Well, I'm an old friend of Diem's," Lansdale replied, "I can't go to Vietnam without seeing him, I'll probably see him alone. Is there anything you want me to ask him?"

As soon as the plane landed, Taylor met with reporters. Diem's secretary noticed Lansdale and told him that he was invited for dinner in the presidential palace that night. Lansdale took off to prepare for the evening, leaving Taylor and the group behind.[262]

Before the evening, though, General Taylor and Ambassador Nolting met with Diem in the afternoon. Diem told them that he did not have enough troops to fight against the Viet Cong and needed more personnel to fill the ranks of his Civil Guard and militia to protect his hamlets and remaining Agrovilles. General Taylor suggested that a more offensive strategy of engaging directly with the enemy might work better, saying that the "Viet Cong find it easy to deviate past GVN units on known trails." Diem claimed that the rebels and North Vietnamese had opened up an offensive in the northern parts of the country to try to make him move his forces away from the South where his programs were having a success.

General Taylor then asked about the possibility of sending US combat troops to Vietnam. He wanted to know why Diem no longer seemed to object to this when he had in the past. Diem explained that the situation in Laos changed the situation. He suggested that American helicopters and air support would be helpful, but did not mention a

---

[262] John Newman, *JFK And Vietnam* (New York: Warner Books, 1992), pp. 130-132.

desire for combat troops. He said that the Vietnamese feared that if American combat troops came that they could simply be "withdrawn at any time."

Ambassador Nolting wasn't sure what President Diem wanted. "It was not completely clear what Diem has in mind at present time," he later reported. As the meeting went on, several times General Taylor brought up a need to create a new overall strategy that combined military, economic, psychological, and political measures to combat the insurgents. Each time he tried to bring this up Diem tried to change the subject until he finally said that he had a "new strategic plan of his own." Taylor and Nolting then pressed for details, but Diem gave only a vague response. Taylor gave up and asked Diem to give him a written copy of the plan as the meeting came to an end. Taylor wrote of this meeting that "it was interminably long...and consisted mainly of a monologue by Diem... [who] smoked cigarettes incessantly and talked in somnolent tones that sorely tested the powers of attention of his overseas visitors, drowsy from too frequent changes of time zones."[263]

The next day, General Taylor and General Lionel McGarr, Chief of the Military Assistance Group (MAAG) in South Vietnam, met with Major General Duong Van Minh (Big Minh) and General

---

[263] Schulimson, p. 125; *The Pentagon Papers, Gravel Edition, Volume II* (Boston: Beacon Press, 1971), p. 84.

Le Van Ty. Big Minh told the Americans that the battlefield situation in South Vietnam had simply gotten worse over the past two years. They said that not only were the Viet Cong increasing in strength, but that the South Vietnamese government was also losing the support of the masses. He even hinted that President Diem was isolated from the people. General Minh complained that, even though General McGarr was trying to urge a unity of command, the military leaders had very little control of the rural Civil Guard and militias, because they answered to province chiefs, who in turn answered personally to Diem.

General Taylor then chaired a conference at MAAG headquarters on intelligence matters and learned that President Diem had seven intelligence groups. William Colby of the CIA told Taylor that Diem thought that intelligence was "power" and by having seven separate groups answering to him no single intelligence head could use that power against him.

General Lansdale also delivered a report on unconventional warfare in South Vietnam for Taylor. He explained that he "was struck by the wealth of ideas, abilities, and equipment which the US has put into Vietnam. Yet, the Vietnamese governmental machinery seems to be bogged down, and somehow things simply don’t get done effectively enough." Lansdale thought that the notion of "just adding more of many things" including people would prove futile. He thought what was needed instead was a "spark" that could best be accomplished by placing "the right Americans into the right areas of the Vietnamese government to provide operational guidance." He said all it would take was a few key people who could work as "helpers not orderers" in Diem's government. He seemed to be lobbying for himself to take a big role.

General Taylor and several MAAG officers then went on a helicopter tour of the DMZ and the countryside. They were shown that the Mekong Delta had just suffered its worst flooding in over thirty years. Taylor thought this could make for a good reason to send a few thousand American troops to South Vietnam. MAAG Chief McGarr sent a wire to Admiral Felt informing him of the "possibility that flood relief could be justification for moving in US military personnel for humanitarian purposes with subsequent retention if desirable. Gen. Taylor and Ambassador evaluating feasibility and desirability."

General McGarr told General Taylor that this idea made him uneasy. General McGarr thought that they would be so few in number that they would not be able to defend themselves if they came under attack. He told Taylor that the Viet Cong were actually growing in strength in the area and if they sent men for flood relief that they would be broken up into small units across thirty different sites. Taylor bluntly told General McGarr that if he was given this mission then it would be his "job to prevent fragmentation and that he would be disappointed in US troops who were unable to protect themselves." General Taylor made it clear that he was not going to listen to anymore critiques when it came to this idea. The planning staff may have first come up with this plan, but Maxwell Taylor was now personally making it his own.[264]

So, General Taylor decided to put General McGarr in his place. He had setup a meeting with Ambassador Nolting and Ngo Dinh Diem at his presidential palace. General McGarr was expecting to go too, but Taylor informed him that there was a change of plans and he was not to come along with him. McGarr said that as the American MAAG commander he should be able to go.

"I do not agree you should," General Taylor responded. McGarr then said that as the representative of the Joint Chiefs of Staff in Vietnam he should go. Taylor then said this was a personal meeting and not for him. McGarr finally gave up, saying, "It is your decision, General." McGarr informed General Lemnitzer of what happened simply cabling him, "Mainly I am particularly concerned about the local loss of prestige in eyes of GVN."

General Lionel McGarr would slowly be ruined, but General Maxwell Taylor would have no possible obstacle when it came to his flood relief idea. It

---

[264] Schulimson, p. 126-128; *Pentagon Papers*, p. 85.

seemed like the perfect way to get some troops in Vietnam as President Kennedy was uncomfortable with sending large numbers of combat troops there. Taylor later said he left for Vietnam "knowing the President did not want a recommendation to send forces." "The last thing he wanted was to put in ground forces. And I knew that. I had the same feeling he had on the subject. But all the way, starting with CINCPAC [headquarters of the commander-in-chief for the Pacific] the feeling was that we'd better get something in South Vietnam," Taylor said. The Joint Chiefs of Staff wanted forces in Vietnam and their planning staff had drawn up various scenarios for them. So taking their proposal for a flood relief mission as his own seemed like a good way to navigate both sides. General McGraw simply did not understand the politics of the situation and General Taylor could not allow him to possibly derail his idea in front of President Diem.[265]

Walt Rostow, though, was able to make it to the meeting General Taylor and Ambassador Nolting had with President Diem. Also with Diem was Defense Minister Thuan. General Taylor presented

---

[265] Schulimson, pp. 128-129; Arthur Schlesinger, Jr., *Robert Kennedy And His Times* (New York: Ballantine Books, 1978), p. 760; Howard Jones, *Death Of A Generation: How The Assassinations Of Diem And JFK Prolonged The Vietnam War* (New York: Oxford University Press, 2003), p. 107.

them with a six point outline of ideas. They consisted of:

> "A. Improvement of intelligence.
>
> B. Joint survey of security situation at provincial level.
>
> C. Improvement of army mobility:...[which included] making available... improved means of transport, notably helicopters.
>
> D. Send blocking [force to limit] infiltration into high plateau...
>
> E. Introduction of US Military Forces...
>
> F. Actions to emphasize national emergency and beginning of a new phase in the war."

General Taylor presented them with his idea of inserting American troops for flood relief purposes. President Diem said he approved of this idea, because now everyone in the South Vietnamese government would welcome some American troops in their country. General Taylor later said that "nothing was formally proposed or approved," but that all agreed that this outline could be used as the basis of more cooperation between their two governments.

The next day, General Taylor had one final meeting with Diem before he left to go back home.

President Diem told him that he needed more aircraft, especially helicopters. The two talked about the points that they agree upon yesterday and then, as the meeting wrapped up, Diem told Taylor that he would like to see Lansdale come back to assist him personally again. General Taylor gave no response to that suggestion, but said that now that they had things they could agree on "life would have to be breathed into it." He promised to go back to Washington to do that. A few pawn pieces were moved as a result. In the next few months General Lionel McGarr would lose his command in South Vietnam and General Ed Lansdale would be placed in charge of Operation Mongoose, a covert program designed to wage a secret war against Fidel Castro. He would not step foot in Vietnam again for the next several years.[266]

However, first General Taylor had to put together his formal report for President Kennedy. He was responsible for the main part of the report, which consisted of twenty-five pages and then other members of his party gave their own opinions in appendices to the report. When they left Vietnam they made a stop in Thailand and then in the Philippines, where they actually wrote the report.

General Taylor decided to prepare Kennedy for what would be in the report before it was finished.

---

[266] Schulimson, pp.128-130.

Before he even left Vietnam, he sent a cable to Washington saying, "because of the importance of acting rapidly once we have made up our minds, I will cable my recommendations...enroute home." He let them know that his ultimate conclusions would consist of a task force of 6,000-8,000 American soldiers for "flood relief."[267]

General Taylor then sent a classified "eyes only" cable to President Kennedy, Secretary of State Dean Rusk, Undersecretary of State U. Alexis Johnson, Secretary of Defense Robert McNamara, and Chairman of the Joint Chiefs of Staff General Lyman Lemnitzer explaining to them why he wanted the troops sent. He said that they would be a "task force largely of logistical troops for the purpose of participating in flood relief and at the same time of providing a US military presence in VN capable of assuring Diem of our readiness to join him in a military showdown with the Viet Cong or Viet Minh. To relate the introduction of troops to the needs of flood relief seems to me to offer considerable advantages in VN and abroad. It gives a specific humanitarian task as the prime reason for the coming of our troops and avoids any suggestions that we are taking over responsibility for the security of the country. As the task is a specific one, we

[267] Ibid, p. 13.

can extricate our troops when it is done if we so desire. Alternatively, we can phase them into other activities if we wish to remain longer."[268]

After he arrived in the Philippines, General Taylor then sent an "eyes only" cable to the President and presented Kennedy with his overall rationale for the troops in it. He said that they faced a "Communist strategy" that "aims to gain control of Southeast Asia by methods of subversion and guerrilla war which by-pass conventional US and indigenous strength on the ground. The interim Communist goal – enroute to total take-over – appears to be a neutral Southeast Asia, detached from US protection."

He saw in Vietnam "a double crisis in confidence: doubt that US is determined to save Southeast Asia; doubt that Diem's methods can frustrate and defeat Communist purposes and methods. The Vietnamese (and Southeast Asians) will undoubtedly draw – rightly or wrongly – definitive conclusions in coming weeks and months concerning the probable outcome and will adjust their behavior accordingly. What the US does or fails to do will be decisive to the end result."

General Taylor seemed to argue that if Kennedy did nothing again, like he did in Laos, then South Vietnam would collapse. He also argued that President Diem's army suffered from "bad tactics and

---

[268] The Pentagon Papers, p. 88.

bad administrative arrangements which pin their forces on the defensive in ways which permit a relatively small Viet-Cong force (about one-tenth the size of GVN regulars) to create conditions of frustration and terror certain to lead to political crisis, if a positive turning point is not soon achieved."

General Taylor claimed that such a turning point could be seized if President Kennedy would "offer to join the GVN in a massive joint effort as part of total mobilization of GVN resources." He wanted to see the US government prepare to "provide individual administrators for insertion into the governmental machinery of South Vietnam in types and numbers to be worked out with President Diem."

This meant a new vision for the American role in Vietnam. General Taylor said, with the President's approval, "a joint effort will be made to free the Army for mobile, offensive operations. This effort will be based upon improving the training and equipping of the Civil Guard and the Self-Defense Corps, relieving the Army of static missions, raising the level of the mobility of the Army Forces by the provision of considerably more helicopters and light aviation, and organizing a Border Ranger Force for a long-term campaign on the Laotian border against the Viet Cong infiltrators. The US Government will support this effort with equipment and with military units and personnel to do those tasks which the Armed Forces of Vietnam cannot perform in time. Such tasks include air reconnaissance and photography, airlift (beyond the present capacity of SVN forces), special intelligence, and air-ground support techniques."

This meant that "MAAG, Vietnam, will be reorganized and increased in size as may be necessary by the implementation of these recommendations." The purpose of the flood task force would be to "provide a US military presence capable of raising national morale and of showing to Southeast Asia the seriousness of the US intent to resist a Communist take-over." They would be able to "conduct logistical operations" and "provide an emergency reserve to back up the Armed Forces of the GVN in the case of a heightened military crisis." And if it came to it they could also "act as an advance party of such additional forces as may by introduced if CINCPAC or SEATO contingency plans are invoked."

General Taylor knew that the idea of sending troops to Vietnam made President Kennedy uneasy, so he sent him another "eyes only" cable to address the arguments against sending them. He acknowledged that "although US prestige is already engaged in SVN, it will become more so by the sending of troops." Taylor also admitted that "if the first contingent is not enough to accomplish the necessary results, it will be difficult to resist the pressure to reinforce. If the ultimate result sought is the closing of the frontiers and the clean-up of the insurgents within SVN, there is no limit to our possible commitment (unless we attack the source in Hanoi.)"

However, General Taylor believed that the size of the US forces "need not be great to provide the military presence necessary to produce the desired effect on national morale in SVN and on international opinion." He argued that his flood relief "force is not proposed to clear the jungles and forests of Viet Cong guerillas. That should be the primary task of the Armed Forces of Vietnam for which they should be specifically organized, trained, and stiffened with ample US advisors down to combat battalion levels." "As a general reserve," Taylor wrote, "they might be thrown into action (with US agreement) against large, formed guerrilla bands which have abandoned the forests for attacks on major targets. But in general, our forces should not engage in small-scale guerrilla operations in the jungle."

"The risks of backing into a major Asian war by way of SVN are present but are not impressive," General Taylor reassured President Kennedy. The reality is that the United States had nuclear weapons while China and North Vietnam did not. This means that "NVN is extremely vulnerable to conventional bombing, a weakness which should be exploited diplomatically in convincing Hanoi to lay off SVN. Both the DRV and the Chicoms would face severe logistical difficulties in trying to maintain strong forces in the field in SEA, difficulties which we share but by no means to the same degree. There is no case for fearing a mass onslaught of Communist manpower into SVN and its neighboring states, particularly if our airpower is allowed a free hand against logistical targets. Finally, the starvation conditions in China should discourage Communist leaders there from being militarily venturesome for some time to come," Taylor wrote.

According to the Pentagon Papers, "these cables, it will be noticed, are rather sharply focused on the insurgency as a problem to fairly conventional military technique and tactics." Looking back on this time later, William Colby of the CIA noted that while General Taylor's theories of flexible response was welcomed as a way to confront wars in the Third World without just responding with nuclear weapons and promised to succeed in fighting against insurgencies, his response to the guerrilla battle in South Vietnam implied conventional large set battles.

As the military historian Andrew Krepinevich put it, "while admitting that the 'new' Communist strategy of insurgency bypassed the Army's traditional approach to war, Taylor offered all of the old prescriptions for the achievement of victory: increased firepower and mobility, more effective search-and-destroy operations, and if all else failed, bombing the source of the trouble (in thought if not fact), North Vietnam, into capitulation."[269]

Some people close to President Kennedy, and who were among the most knowledgeable on Vietnam, were concerned with rumors they were hearing about General Taylor's trip. Senator Mike Mansfield, the chair of the Senate Foreign Relations Committee, wrote the President to tell him that he opposed sending American troops to Vietnam. "It appears to me that the presence of American combat troops in South Viet Nam could be misinterpreted in the minds of millions of Southeast Asians and could well be considered as a revival of colonial force," Mansfield wrote.

Although Senator Mansfield had always been a principal advocate for American aid to Vietnam, he wrote that "while Viet Nam is very important, we cannot hope to substitute armed power for the kind of political and economic social changes that offer the best resistance to communism. If the necessary reforms have not been forthcoming over the past seven years to stop communist subversion and rebellion, then I do not see how American combat troops can do it today. I would wholeheartedly favor, if necessary and feasible, a substantial increase of American military and economic aid to Viet Nam, but leave the responsibility of carrying the physical burden of meeting communist infiltration,

---

[269] *The Pentagon Papers*, pp. 88-92; Newman pp. 135-136.

subversion, and attack on the shoulders of the South Vietnamese, whose country it is and whose future is their chief responsibility."[270]

James Kenneth Galbraith, the US Ambassador to India, also wrote Kennedy a memo telling him that he was against "a military operation in South Viet-Nam which would entail all the risks of the operation in Korea of ten years ago, without the justification of a surprise attack across the boundary, without the support of the United Nations, and without a population determined to fight for independence."

Galbraith advocated going to the United Nations to negotiate a "cease-fire." Then South Viet-Nam "would become a viable independent state" so that "North Viet-Nam would become less dependent on Communist China." "The proposal assumes that our long-run objective in South Viet-Nam should be the creation of an independent, economically viable and politically neutral state, rather than a limping American satellite," he wrote. He suggested as a first step to replace Ambassador Nolting with "someone who can hold his own with both Diem and the United States military, who will insist once and for all on government reform, and

[270] *Foreign Relations of the United States, 1961-1963. Vietnam: Volume I, 1961*, U.S. Department of State; https://history.state.gov/historicaldocuments/frus1961-63v01/d207, accessed1/24/2016.

who will understand the United States political implications of developments there."[271]

A debate over General Taylor's troop proposal also began inside the Kennedy administration as he put together his report. National Security Council staff member Robert Johnson sent a memo to his boss McGeorge Bundy saying that it would be difficult to send a small force of men to Vietnam without expecting them to come under attack and then having to send more. "If we commit 6-8,000 troops and then pull them out when the going got rough we will be finished in Viet Nam and probably in all of Southeast Asia," he warned. He thought that they should not send troops at this time and told Walt Rostow that he shared "some of Bill Bundy's doubts as to whether we will, in fact, be able to convince the neutrals of the justice and our allies of the wisdom of such a course" if their actions meant having to bomb Hanoi.

However, NSC staff member Robert Komer told McGeorge Bundy that "over-reacting, if anything, is best at this point." "Though no admirer of domino theory," he wrote Bundy, "I doubt if our position in SEA could survive loss of S. Vietnam on top

---

[271] *Foreign Relations of the United States, 1961-1963. Vietnam: Volume I, 1961*, U.S. Department of State; https://history.state.gov/historicaldocuments/frus1961-63v01/d209, accessed1/24/2016.

of that of Laos. Moreover, could Administration afford yet another defeat, domestically?"

"I'm no happier than anyone about getting involved in another squalid, secondary theatre in Asia," Komer told Bundy, "but we'll end up doing so sooner or later anyway because we won't be willing to accept another defeat. If so, the real question is not whether but how soon and how much!"

Several people inside the State Department, nonetheless, attempted to push Galbraith's idea of neutralization for Vietnam. Averell Harriman, Chester Bowles, and Abram Chayes, the Legal Advisor of the State Department, recommended exploring it. Harriman told Kennedy that Diem had to be impressed that "we mean business about internal reform" and explained to Arthur Schlesinger that "I am afraid that some feel that military action will cure political difficulties."

Abram Chayes later said that these proposals "didn't fly because we didn't have enough people for it. Bowles was at that time on his way out. He was not a powerful figure. I think Harlan Cleveland (Assistant Secretary of State for International Organization Affairs) was identified with it, also. We had all of the non-power in the Department, and so it just never flew. We talked to the Secretary of

State about it, but it was simply regarded as not within the realm of possibility."[272]

On November 3, 1961, Kennedy received General Taylor and his group at four o'clock in the afternoon in the Oval Office, where they were waiting for him. As the group stood in the room, General Taylor told them that he wanted to soak in every detail inside the Oval Office. He looked around and then sat down in the President's rocking chair at the exact moment that Kennedy walked into the room. General Taylor jumped upright and brought the chair up with his body, as it had been a tight fit for him. Kennedy ignored the General's embarrassment, but General Lansdale lit up in silent laughter.[273]

General Taylor presented the President with the report in a black loose-leaf notebook. According to the Pentagon Papers, Taylor's "evaluation" gave the impression "of urgency combined with optimism. Essentially it says South Vietnam is in serious trouble; major interests of the United States are at stake; but if the US promptly and energetically takes up the challenge, a victory can be had without a US take-over of the war." This document is worth

[272] William Gibbons, *The U.S. government and the Vietnam War: Executive and legislative roles and relationships, Volume II* (New Jersey: Princeton University Press, 1986), pp. 78-83.
[273] Jones, pp. 118-119.

looking at in detail as it is one of the most important papers issued during America's war in Vietnam.

Taylor, with the assistance of Walt Rostow, wrote that "it is evident that morale in Vietnam will rapidly crumble – and in Southeast Asia only slightly less quickly – if the sequence of expectations set in motion by Vice-President Johnson's visit and climaxed by General Taylor's mission are not soon followed by a hard US commitment to the ground in Vietnam."

"Perhaps the most striking aspect of this mission's effort is the unanimity of view – individually arrived at by the specialists involved – that what is now required is a shift from US advice to limited partnership and working collaboration with the Vietnamese. The present war cannot be won by direct US action; it must be won by the Vietnamese. But there is a general conviction among us that the Vietnamese performance in every domain can be substantially improved if Americans are prepared to work side by side with the Vietnamese on key problems," General Taylor wrote.

General Taylor wrote in a section titled "Reforming Diem's Administrative Method":

> "The famous problem of Diem as an administrator and politician could be resolved in a number of ways:

- By his removal in favor of a military dictatorship which would give dominance to the military chain of command.

- By his removal in favor of a figure of more dilute power (e.g. Vice-President Nguyen Ngoc Tho) who would delegate authority to act to both military and civil leaders.

- By bringing about a series of de facto administrative changes via persuasion at high levels; a collaboration with Diem's aides who want improved administration; and by a US operating presence at many working levels, using US presence (e.g. control over the helicopter squadrons) for forcing the Vietnamese to get their house in order in one area after another.

We have opted for the third choice, on the basis of merit and feasibility."

General Taylor, though, blamed the guerilla war being waged in South Vietnam on North Vietnam for most of Diem's problems. He wrote that everyone in his party felt a "common sense of outrage at the burden which this kind of aggression imposes on a new country, only seven years old, with a difficult historical heritage to overcome, confronting the inevitable problems of political, social, and economic transition to modernization. It is easy and cheap to destroy such a country whereas it is difficult undisturbed to build a nation coming out of a complex past without carrying the burden of a guerrilla war."

Taylor also wrote that "with continued infiltration and covert support of guerrilla bands in the territory of our ally, we will then have to decide whether to accept as legitimate the continued guidance, training, and support of a guerrilla war across an international boundary, while the attacked react only inside their borders. Can we admit the establishment of the common law that the party attacked and his friends are denied the right to strike the source of aggression, after the fact of external aggression is clearly established? It is our view that our government should undertake with the Vietnamese the measures outlined herein, but should then consider and face the broader question beyond."

General Taylor also produced an order of battle with intelligence estimates that there were 14,350 guerillas operating in South Vietnam. However, "a reserve force of unknown size and capability is being created in the forests and mountains surrounding the plateau, straddling the Laos (and possibly Cambodian) border which offers a supply base, a relatively secure infiltration route, and safe haven." Taylor's report estimated that these reserves consisted of 4,000 men, but said that the size of this force ultimately was not known and "its capabilities could range from a mere capacity to continue to harass, to a capacity, when surfaced, of producing a Dien Bien Phu."

General Taylor's "evaluation" and program took up twenty-five pages. After that came a series of appendices written by various parties and members of the mission some of which had a difference of opinion with General Taylor in tone and sometimes in substance.

For instance, the first appendix titled "MILITARY APPENDIX," written by General Craig on behalf of the Joint Chiefs of Staff and their planning staff, argued that "it is the consensus of the military committee that intervention under SEATO or U.S. plans is the best means of saving SVN and indeed, all of Southeast Asia." He didn't want to send a small number of American soldiers to Vietnam, but to prepare for a big regional war. "Should this prove impossible for non-military reasons" this appendix then advocated doing everything possible to bolster President Diem's army including sending helicopters and making it so that American "MAAG advisors participate in all planning and operations."

Samuel Cottrell of the State Department expressed skepticism in the next appendix, writing that "since it is an open question whether the GVN can succeed even with U.S. assistance, it would be a mistake for the U.S. to commit itself irrevocably to the defeat of the Communists in SVN." He argued that "since U.S. combat troops of division size cannot be employed effectively, they should not be introduced at this stage, despite the short range favorable psychological lift it would give the GVN."

The way Cottrell saw it, "the Communist operation starts from the lowest social level-the villages. The battle must be joined and won at this point. If not, the Communists will ultimately control all but the relatively few areas of strong military concentrations. Foreign military forces cannot themselves win the battle at the village level."

William Jorden of the State Department then wrote an appendix arguing that President Diem was the real problem in South Vietnam. He claimed that "without some badly needed reforms, it is unlikely that any program of assistance to that country can be fully effective." He thought that they should try to pressure Diem to make reforms and even consider "engineering a coup against the Diem regime."

General Lansdale also had an appendix in which he said part of the problem was that the United States "needs to declare a 'sub-limited' war on the Communists in Viet-Nam and then to wage it successfully. Since such an action is not envisioned by our Constitution, a way of so doing must be found which is consistent with our heritage. The most natural declaration would be a proclamation by the President, which would state U.S. objectives and clearly outline the principles of human liberty involved. The U.S. Congress would vote support of these objectives and principles. Implementing actions would then be carried out by Executive Order."

As for General Big Minh's comments about President Diem, Lansdale wrote to Taylor, "as in any society under great stress, some cracks have appeared. The most apparent one during our visit was the very human one of looking for somebody else to blame for the situation. Big Minh's rather desperate comments to you were an example. This same type of comment was prevalent in many other quarters, including some in which Big Minh was the target. Mistrust, jealousy, and the shock of Communist savagery have contributed to making a none-too-certain government bureaucracy even more unsure of itself. Pride and self-protection still cover this unsureness, but the cover is wearing thin."[274]

General Taylor's report caused an uproar inside the White House. President Kennedy did not want word to get out of the report's recommendations so he recalled some copies of it. He then planted sto-

---

[274] *Foreign Relations of the United States, 1961-1963. Vietnam: Volume I, 1961*, U.S. Department of State; https://history.state.gov/historicaldocuments/frus1961-63v01/d210, accessed 1/24/2016; Pentagon Papers, pp. 92-98.

ries in the press which said that he opposed sending combat troops to Vietnam and that wrongly implied that General Taylor did too. William Bundy said that "almost at once there was dissatisfaction with the half-in, half-out nature of the 'flood relief task force,' and a consensus of disbelief that once thus engaged the US could easily pull the force out."[275]

General Taylor had put President Kennedy in a tough spot. He knew that Kennedy did not want to send combat troops to Vietnam before he took his trip, but the Joint Chiefs of Staff wanted to do so. So, he seemed to latch on to the idea of a small flood relief mission to try to appease both sides. Undersecretary of State for Economic Affairs, George Ball, said, "I knew from experience with my French friends, there was something about Vietnam that seduced the toughest military minds into fantasy." After he got a copy of the report John Kenneth Galbraith wrote in his dairy, "The recommendations are for vigorous action. The appendices say it possibly cannot succeed given the present government in Saigon." He thought it "curious."[276]

George Ball thought that Walt Rostow was a big problem. "The inclusion of Rostow worried me," he

---

[275] Newman, pp. 136-137.
[276] Gibbons, p. 114; Schulimson, p. 133.

later wrote, because he thought of him as "an articulate amateur tactician... unduly fascinated by the then faddish theories about counterinsurgency and that intriguing new invention of the professors, 'nation building.'" He told Robert McNamara that he was "appalled at the report's recommendations." McNamara didn't respond. Ball then told President Kennedy in private, "within five years we'll have three hundred thousand men in the paddies and jungles and never find them again. That was the French experience." Kennedy told him he was "crazy as hell."[277]

President Kennedy told Arthur Schlesinger, "They want a force of American troops. They say it's necessary in order to restore confidence and maintain morale. But it will be just like Berlin. The troops will march in; the bands will play; the crowds will cheer; and in four days everyone will have forgotten. Then we will be told we have to send in more troops. It's like taking a drink. The effect wears off, and you have to take another." "The war in Vietnam, he added, could be won only so long as it was their war. If it were ever converted into a white man's war, we would lose as the

[277] Andrew Preston, *The War Council: McGeorge Bundy, The NSC, And Vietnam* (United States of America: Harvard, 2006), pp. 93-94.

French lost a decade earlier," Schlesinger later wrote.[278]

In their initial review of General Taylor's report, the Joint Chiefs of Staff were skeptical of the notion of sending a small task force to Vietnam. An analysis by the Defense Department said, "The introduction of US troops in South Vietnam would be a decisive act and must be sent to achieve a completely decisive mission. This mission would probably require, over time, increased numbers of US troops; DRV [Democratic Republic of Vietnam] intervention would probably increase until a large number of US troops were required, three or more divisions."[279]

The day after General Taylor presented his report, he met with Secretary of Defense McNamara and several other members of the administration, including General Lemnitzer of the Joint Chiefs of Staff. President Kennedy was not there. General Taylor told the group that Kennedy planned to convene a formal National Security Council meeting in a few days to make a decision based upon the report.

General Taylor informed them that Kennedy "is instinctively against introduction of US forces."

---

[278] Arthur Schlesinger, Jr., *A Thousand Days: John F. Kennedy In The White House* (New York: Fawcett Premier, 1965), p.505.
[279] Schulimson, p. 135.

However, he claimed that his flood relief mission could be carried out over a few months and then the troops withdrawn. McNamara said that "the recommendations in themselves, including the 8000-man force would not save South Viet-Nam from Communism. It is a US commitment to the ground and other forces would be made ready. It is not a temporary commitment; without the '8000-man force', the recommendations will not save South Viet Nam; with it, they might." He said that the forces would need a statement of a clear purpose to "tell the world and the US what our commitment really is" or else they would "not convince anyone of our resolve."

George Ball said, "The placing of the 8,000-man force in South Viet-Nam commits us to unlimited action. Why wait on going at Hanoi? Maybe USSR will be glad to see us engaged in SEA. It is difficult to tell US people we are undertaking a limited series of actions; easier to say we are making a full commitment. If we make such a full commitment-and it is necessary to make the 8,000-man force creditable-we should move fast. A larger force is preferable."

Walt Rostow then said that the "question really is whether we will accept a guerrilla war supported externally as a legal international process. We should take the limited actions recommended by General Taylor, surface the Jorden paper with necessary follow-up, then look to Hanoi. The Vice

President's trip and the Taylor Mission lay on the need for action. There is no soft option. Hanoi and Peking have basic weaknesses which lessen the risk to US action."

Lemnitzer agreed, saying that "employment of 8000-man force will result in combat forces being thinned out in an area in which it is hard to operate. We must commit the number of troops required for success."[280]

After this meeting, Robert McNamara told William Bundy to write a memo for the President to prepare for his National Security Council meeting. In it Bundy wrote that the flood relief mission only had a 50-50 chance of success and depending on the reaction of China and North Vietnam the United States had to be prepared to back them up with up to 220,000 troops.

According to the Pentagon Papers, "the President was being told that the issue was not whether to send an 8,000 man task force, but whether or not to embark on a course that, without some extraordinary good luck, would lead to combat involvement in Southeast Asia on a very substantial scale. On the other hand he was being warned that anything less than sending the task force was very

---

[280] *Foreign Relations of the United States, 1961-1963. Vietnam: Volume I, 1961*, U.S. Department of State; https://history.state.gov/historicaldocuments/frus1961-63v01/d211, accessed1/24/2016.

likely to fail to prevent the fall of Vietnam, since 'the odds are against, probably sharply against, preventing that fall by any means short of the introduction of US forces on a substantial scale (of which the task force would be the first increment)."[281]

Robert McNamara then had lunch with General Lemnitzer, and some other military officials, the next day. The Chairman of the Joint Chiefs of Staff told him that the Chiefs saw the 8,000 flood relief mission as a vanguard for a much larger force and that they wanted assurances from the President that he would be willing to deploy it if necessary. He said that they did not believe that the Soviet Union would respond with nuclear weapons and that North Vietnam had to be warned "that action will be taken against it unless [they] stop support of Viet Cong."[282]

However, an official intelligence estimate said that threats would not stop the North Vietnamese and that they would simply match any American aid sent to South Vietnam. It also said that actual bombing attacks on Hanoi would simply generate a strong response from the Soviet Union and China who would then "regard the defense of North Vietnam against such an attack as imperative."[283]

---

[281] *Pentagon Papers*, pp. 108-109.
[282] Schulimson, p. 137.
[283] *Pentagon Papers*, p. 108.

Secretary of State Robert McNamara had second doubts about his memo. "As soon as I sent the memo to the White House, I started worrying that we had been too hasty in our advice to the President. For the next couple of days, I dug deeper into the Vietnam problem. The more I probed, the more the complexity of the situation and the uncertainties of our ability to deal with it by military means became apparent."[284]

The State Department was also working on a memo for the President at the same time that deferred "the decision on the timing of the introduction of combat forces into South Viet-Nam." Secretary of State Dean Rusk said in a group meeting with Robert McNamara that he supported reinforcing the MAAG advisors in South Vietnam, but was reluctant to send "US forces until Diem makes a 100 percent effort in his area" of internal reform.[285]

According to the Pentagon Papers, "three days later McNamara joined Rusk in a quite different recommendation, and one obviously to the President's liking (and, in the nature of such things, quite possibly drawn up to the President's specifications)."

This new McNamara/Rusk memo for President Kennedy replaced the earlier McNamara/Bundy

---

[284] Robert McNamara, *In Retrospect: The Tragedy And Lessons Of Vietnam* (New York: Times Books, 1995), pp. 38-39.
[285] Schulimson, p. 139.

memo, which supported sending up to 205,000 combat troops. The new memo said that the President "should be prepared to introduce combat forces if that should become necessary for success. Dependent upon the circumstances it may also be necessary for the United States forces to strike at the source of the aggression in North Viet-Nam."

The "loss of South Viet-Nam would stimulate bitter domestic controversies in the United States and would be seized upon by extreme elements to divide the country harass the Administration," the memo warned. The memo stated that "The United States should commit itself to the clear objective of preventing the fall of South Viet-Nam to Communism. The basic means for accomplishing this objective must be to put the Government of South Viet-Nam into a position to win its own war against the guerillas." However, it deferred the decision for American combat troops until later. The President "now had a joint recommendation from his Secretary of State and Secretary of Defense telling him just what he surely wanted to hear," reads the Pentagon Papers.[286]

Walt Rostow found this paper annoying. He wrote President Kennedy, "I appreciate, of course, the difficulty of the decision and the reasons for reserving this move; but I should like to set out as

[286] *The Pentagon Papers*, pp. 110-116.

clearly as I can the reasons for placing some minimal U.S. ground force in Viet Nam as part of the initial package."

Rostow wrote, "Without the troop commitment, the Communists (who have been reading of our fears of white men in Asia and of Nehru's line on Ho Chi Minh) will believe they still have plenty of room for maneuver and to continue infiltration. An ambiguous signal to them is dangerous; and, whatever the rhetoric, they will interpret our policy by deeds, not words. The deeds proposed are, indeed, ambiguous."

Rostow warned Kennedy that "there is a general attitude in the State Department paper which I regard as dangerous. It would inhibit U.S. action on our side of the truce lines of the Cold War for fear of enemy escalation." Rostow believed that offensive action now was needed and Vietnam was the best place to do it. "A final thought," he wrote, "with respect to both Cuba and Laos our legal and moral case was ambiguous. It was impossible in our kind of society to rally the full weight of American authority behind the military enterprises in those areas. The case of South Viet Nam is clean. We know it; the enemy knows it; and, in their hearts, the knowledgeable neutrals know it... If we move without ambiguity-without the sickly pallor of our positions on Cuba and Laos - I believe we can unite the country and the Free World."[287]

The McNamara/Rusk paper became the organizing document for President Kennedy's National Security Council meeting on November 11, 1961. Secretary of State Dean Rusk opened the meeting by reviewing the situation. According to handwritten notes made by General Lemnitzer, President Kennedy said that "troops are a last resort. Should be SEATO forces. Will create a tough domestic problem. Would like to avoid statements like Laos & Berlin."

Attorney General Robert Kennedy then flat out said, "We are not sending combat troops. [We are] not committing ourselves to combat troops." The President said that he was not prepared to make a public commitment to "preventing the fall of South Vietnam" and wondered if such a statement would mean "war with China." He approved the sections of the memo that called to prepare for American troops to assist Diem in his struggle against the guerillas, accepted the proposals in General Taylor's report to assist President Diem, with the exception of the flood relief mission, and agreed to a

---

[287] *Foreign Relations of the United States, 1961-1963. Vietnam: Volume I, 1961*, U.S. Department of State; https://history.state.gov/historicaldocuments/frus1961-63v01/d233, accessed1/24/2016.

section of the memo that tasked Ambassador Nolting with getting Diem to carry out reforms.

However, after this meeting, McGeorge Bundy had difficulty drafting a presidential action memo detailing what was actually approved at the meeting. He called General Taylor and told him that he thought Kennedy "[did] not know what he [was] approving." So, Bundy drew up a draft National Security Action Memorandum (NSAM) for the next National Security Council Meeting on November 15, 1961, for Kennedy to sign off on.[288]

This would be a key document. The release of a NSAM was an exercise in presidential executive power as it would go to the top officials of the national security state to inform them of new official policy. The officials would have to adopt the policy as their own or they would be in violation of presidential authority. "Departments and agencies will always be acting just as fast as they can to respond to the President's directives," Bundy told CIA Director Allen Dulles.[289]

However, the mere act of preparing to draft a new memo moved people in the White House to get into action. So, National Security Council staff

---

[288] *Foreign Relations of the United States, 1961-1963. Vietnam: Volume I, 1961*, U.S. Department of State; https://history.state.gov/historicaldocuments/frus1961-63v01/d236, accessed1/24/2016; Schulimson, p. 139.
[289] Andrew Preston, p.41.

member Robert Johnson told Walt Rostow, "I fear that we are losing a strategic moment for the introduction of U.S. troop units. The world has been made aware of the crisis in Viet Nam as a result of the Taylor mission."[290]

Rostow then came close to demanding that President Kennedy send troops to South Vietnam, writing him, "If we postpone action in Viet-Nam in order to engage in talk with the Communists, we can count surely on a major crisis of nerve in Viet-Nam and throughout Southeast Asia. The image of U.S. unwillingness to confront Communism-induced by the Laos performance-will be regarded as definitively confirmed. There will be real panic and disarray."

"In Viet-Nam the gut issue is not whether Diem is or is not a good ruler," Rostow wrote, "that is important in a variety of ways; but he was doing fine from 1956 to 1959, by the standards we apply to other underdeveloped countries. The gut issue is whether we shall continue to accept the systematic infiltration of men from outside and the operation from outside of a guerrilla war against him which has built up from 2,000 to 16,000 effectives in two

---

[290] *Foreign Relations of the United States, 1961-1963. Vietnam: Volume I, 1961*, U.S. Department of State; https://history.state.gov/historicaldocuments/frus1961-63v01/d250, accessed1/24/2016.

years. The whole world is asking a simple question: what will the U.S. do about it?"[291]

President Kennedy then sent a memo to Robert McNamara and Dean Rusk saying that they should "get their ducks in a row" for the next National Security Council meeting and expressed frustration over Vietnam. He asked them to consider the viability of new proposals by Averell Harriman to try to negotiate a cease fire in Vietnam. Harriman's ideas called for a diplomatic conference including United States, England, France, China, and North and South Vietnam to create a cease fire on the lines of the 1954 Geneva Accords. Kennedy also requested that more be looked into how to actually fight guerilla war. "I think there should be a group specially trained for guerrilla warfare. I understand that the guns that have been used have been too heavy. Would carbines be better? Wonder if someone could make sure we are moving ahead to improve this," he wrote.[292]

Almost everyone around the President wanted him to send combat troops to South Vietnam. His

---

[291] *Foreign Relations of the United States, 1961-1963. Vietnam: Volume I, 1961*, U.S. Department of State; https://history.state.gov/historicaldocuments/frus1961-63v01/d251, accessed1/24/2016.
[292] *Foreign Relations of the United States, 1961-1963. Vietnam: Volume I, 1961*, U.S. Department of State; https://history.state.gov/historicaldocuments/frus1961-63v01/d252, accessed1/24/2016.

National Security Advisor, McGeorge Bundy wrote him, "so many people have offered their opinions on South Viet-Nam that more may not be helpful. But the other day at the swimming pool you asked me what I thought and here it is."

McGeorge Bundy's advice was to send "about onc division when needed for military action inside South Vietnam." "I believe we should commit limited U.S. combat units, if necessary for military purposes (not for morale), to help save South Vietnam. A victory here would produce great effects all over the world. A defeat would hurt, but not much more than a loss of South Viet-Nam with the levels of U.S. help now committed or planned," he wrote Kennedy.

"I think without that decision the whole program will be half-hearted. With this decision I believe the odds are almost even that the commitment will not have to be carried out. This conclusion is, I believe, the inner conviction of your Vice President, your Secretaries of State and Defense, and the two heads of your special mission, and that is why I am troubled by your most natural desire to act on other items now, without taking the troop decision. Whatever the reason, this has now become a sort of touchstone of our will," Bundy wrote the President.

McGeorge Bundy did not think that President Kennedy could take the same route he did with

Laos towards South Vietnam. "Laos was never really ours after 1954. South Viet-Nam is and wants to be. Laotians have fought very little. South Viet-Nam troops are not U.S. Marines, but they are usable. This makes the opinion problem different at home and abroad," he wrote him. For how long and for how many times could the President go against his national security advisors?[293]

A National Security Council meeting was held at 10:00 AM on November 15, 1961, to discuss McGeorge Bundy's NSAM draft for a new American program in South Vietnam. According to notes taken by Colonel Howard Burris, the meeting opened up with "a brief outline of the size and disposition of Chinese armed forces was given. The President then asked what routes of movement are available for these troops from China to North Viet Nam. Mr. Amory pointed out and described the condition of railway and roads of access and cited the generally inadequate aspects of these avenues. Mr. Dulles cautioned that it should not be assumed that the Chinese setbacks as well as the ideological rift were such that the Soviets and Chinese would not be able nor willing to engage jointly any nation which threatened Communist interests."

---

[293] *Foreign Relations of the United States, 1961-1963. Vietnam: Volume I, 1961*, U.S. Department of State; https://history.state.gov/historicaldocuments/frus1961-63v01/d253, accessed1/24/2016.

"The President expressed the fear of becoming involved simultaneously on two fronts on opposite sides of the world. He questioned the wisdom of involvement in Viet Nam since the basis thereof is not completely clear. By comparison he noted that Korea was a case of clear aggression which was opposed by the United States and other members of the U.N. The conflict in Viet Nam is more obscure and less flagrant," wrote Colonel Burris.

"The President said that he could even make a rather strong case against intervening in an area 10,000 miles away against 16,000 guerrillas with a native army of 200,000, where millions have been spent for years with no success. The President repeated his apprehension concerning support, adding that none could be expected from the French, and Mr. Rusk interrupted to say that the British were tending more and more to take the French point of view," wrote Burris.

Secretary of State Dean Rusk then expressed hope that "a strong firmness in Viet Nam in the manner and form of that in Berlin might achieve desired results in Viet Nam without resort to combat. The President disagreed with the suggestion on the basis that the issue was clearly defined in Berlin and opposing forces identified whereas in Viet Nam the issue is vague and action is by guerrillas, sometimes in a phantom-like fashion. Mr. McNamara expressed an opinion that action would become clear if U.S. forces were involved since this power would be applied against sources of Viet Cong power including those in North Viet Nam. The President observed that it was not clear to him just where these U.S. forces would base their operations other than from aircraft carriers which seemed to him to be quite vulnerable."

"The President asked the Secretary of Defense if he would take action if SEATO did not exist and McNamara replied in the affirmative. The President asked for justification and Lemnitzer replied that the world would be divided in the area of Southeast Asia on the sea, in the air and in communications. He said that Communist conquest would deal a severe blow to freedom and extend Communism to a great portion of the world. The President asked how he could justify the proposed courses of action in Viet Nam while at the same time ignoring Cuba. General Lemnitzer hastened to add that the JCS feel that even at this point the United States should go into Cuba," wrote Burris.

In response to this "the President stated the time had come for neutral nations as well as others to be in support of U.S. policy publicly. He felt that we should aggressively determine which nations are in support of U.S. policy and that these nations should identify themselves. The President again expressed apprehension on support of the proposed action by the Congress as well as by the American people. He felt that the next two or three weeks should be utilized in making the determination as to whether or not the proposed program for Viet Nam could be supported. His impression was that even the Democratic side of Congress was not fully convinced," read the notes of Colonel Burris.[294]

President Kennedy closed the meeting by saying that he wanted to speak with Vice-President Lyndon Johnson to get his measure of Congressional interest in Vietnam before making any decision on Bundy's draft NSAM.

After this meeting, Walt Rostow wrote Kennedy, "with respect to American troops, I know of no one who has recommended that American troops take part in sweeps through Vietnamese territory. There are, nevertheless, concrete functions for U.S. forces which might be envisaged if the battle goes badly or if we feel, for other reasons, American troops are necessary: to provide a plate-glass presence at the 17th parallel and to relieve Vietnamese forces for combat; to take over the protection of towns in the open country (either in the plateau or along the coast), and to relieve Vietnamese troops for combat; to provide assistance in road building and in other engineering and logistic tasks; to help cope with the Viet Cong if they move

---

[294] *Foreign Relations of the United States, 1961-1963. Vietnam: Volume I, 1961*, U.S. Department of State; https://history.state.gov/historicaldocuments/frus1961-63v01/d254, accessed1/24/2016.

from their present hit-and-run tactics to open and sustained battle."

"The Viet-Nam situation confronts us with the question of whether we shall or shall not accept the mounting of a guerrilla war across a frontier as legitimate. I wish it were not so; but the New Frontier will be measured in history in part on how that challenge was met. No amount of political jiu-jitsu is going to get us off that hook; but-certainly-our stance in dealing with that issue will be affected significantly by the administrative and political effectiveness of the government in Saigon," Rostow wrote the President.[295]

On November 22, 1961, President Kennedy issued NSAM-111, which expanded American involvement in Vietnam. It stated that the "US Government is prepared to join the Vietnam Government in a sharply increased joint effort to avoid a further deterioration in the situation in South Vietnam." This order did not call for combat troops or demand victory. But it said to "provide increased air lift to the GVN forces, including helicopters, light aviation, and transport aircraft, manned to the extent necessary by United States uniformed personnel and under United States operational

---

[295] *Foreign Relations of the United States, 1961-1963. Vietnam: Volume I, 1961*, U.S. Department of State; https://history.state.gov/historicaldocuments/frus1961-63v01/d274, accessed1/24/2016.

control." It contained most of General Taylor's recommendations except the deployment of the task force. Kennedy also struck out all references to the deployment of US combat forces in it.[296]

President Kennedy saw Vietnam as a guerilla struggle while the Joint Chiefs of Staff also saw it as a potential conventional battlefield and maybe even a staging ground for a regional war as SEATO Plan 5 conceived of. According to Thomas Hughes, who served as an assistant to Undersecretary of State Chester Bowles, when it came to counterinsurgency, "Kennedy is personally involved; he is fascinated with the whole idea, and I think he thinks of it as a way to get out of these other problems with the JCS and the big troops issue. It keeps him in the military framework. Bobby is already keeping a green beret on his desk in Washington at this point. Bobby emerges as the President's foreign policy confidant during this period. He is involved in Cuba operations as well, so he is full of counterinsurgency."[297]

However, CIA Saigon Station Chief William Colby later said of Kennedy's decision, "he had not

[296] *Foreign Relations of the United States, 1961-1963. Vietnam: Volume I, 1961*, U.S. Department of State; https://history.state.gov/historicaldocuments/frus1961-63v01/d272, accessed1/24/2016.
[297] James Blight, Janet Lang, and David Welch, *Virtual JFK: Vietnam If Kennedy Had Lived* (New York: Lowman & Littlefield Publishers, Inc., 2010), p. 85.

articulated any very solid expression of his own ideas or strategy. Consequently, we had produced an agglomeration of the preferences of all the agencies involved, devoid of any strategic concept or inspiration."

Colby didn't blame Kennedy for this. It just came as a result of the collective decision making that they all were a part of. "I frankly gave more thought and effort to ensuring that the station would receive permission to continue the small – but, I thought promising project we had started than to outlining my fundamental strategy for Vietnam. Unfortunately, this was the attitude of most of the other participants in the process," Colby later said. Different people had different programs they wanted to test and prove in Vietnam. Somehow everyone's opinions always seemed to coincide with the interests of the organizations that they represented.[298]

Secretary of Defense Robert McNamara now replaced General Taylor as President Kennedy's point man when it came to Vietnam. Accordingly, Robert McNamara sent an order to General Lemnitzer telling him to revamp the command and control structure in South Vietnam so that "it is understood that such a commander would report directly to the JCS and me."[299]

---

[298] Newman, p. 139.
[299] Schulimson, p. 140.

McGeorge Bundy said decades later in an interview, "Kennedy decided sometime in 1961 that he was not going to send combat troops to South Vietnam." Despite the fact that summer that the President had repeatedly refused multiple calls to send troops and had planted stories in the press to fight the notion, almost all of his key advisors pressed him hard for large scale intervention, even if it meant over 200,000 American combat troops. They were at times almost flippant about it.[300]

After the National Security Council meeting of November 15, 1961, McGeorge Bundy realized that President Kennedy really wasn't getting the type of help he wanted from his advisors. The President had told General Taylor that he did not want to send combat troops to Vietnam before he took his trip over there and he came back with his flood mission. Almost all of Kennedy's advisors were pushing proposals that made him uneasy. So, Bundy thought some changes in the administration might be needed for him. Maybe Averell Harriman needed to have a bigger role. He met with Secretary of State Dean Rusk to discuss this.

He wrote President Kennedy of this meeting, "I've told the Secretary frankly that you feel the need to have someone on this job that is wholly responsive to your policy, and that you really do not get that sense from most of us. I suggested Averell.

---

[300] Gibbons, pp. 63-67.

He said Averell was needed in Geneva and that Alexis would loyally carry out any policy you directed. I don't think this is the same as having your own man-Alexis isn't that dispassionate-or that much of an executive. Averell is your man, as Assistant Secretary."

Bundy also found that Rusk "thinks the good of our actions depends on belief we mean to hold in Southeast Asia. He knows we may lose, and he knows we want no Korea, but he thinks we must try to hold and must show determination to all concerned. He suggests you should let this be a Rusk-McNamara Plan and fire all concerned if it doesn't work." Such words could provide little comfort for a President who was reluctant to get the United States more deeply involved in Vietnam.[301]

President Kennedy's advisors presented him with only grim options as he ordered a new program to support Diem with more aid and American personnel. Kennedy had been to Vietnam when the French were fighting there and saw how futile a conventional war could be there for himself. He fended off a similar drive to war in Laos in which the introduction of combat troops would have led to carrying out a chain of escalation that could have led to the use of nuclear weapons. Some of the

---

[301] *Foreign Relations of the United States, 1961-1963. Vietnam: Volume I, 1961*, U.S. Department of State; https://history.state.gov/historicaldocuments/frus1961-63v01/d256, accessed1/24/2016.

members of the Joint Chiefs seemed to welcome such a possibility

The only alternative to further intervention in Vietnam then was a political solution with the North Vietnamese similar to the one made for Laos. Only a few men in the State Department and ambassadors such as John Kenneth Galbraith promoted this alternative and they did not even have the support of the Secretary of State. All of Kennedy's White House advisors were against such a notion and saw it as cowardice. The Joint Chiefs of Staff would certainly oppose it and they were even more important than Kennedy's advisors. President Kennedy's final decision then was to further US support in Vietnam, but to keep such involvement limited and dependent on South Vietnam's own ability to defend itself and win its own war.

Decades later looking back on the decisions made during these days, Robert McNamara wrote, "we failed to ask the five most basic questions: Was it true that the fall of South Vietnam would trigger the fall of all Southeast Asia? Would that constitute a grave threat to the West's security? What kind of war – conventional or guerilla – might develop? Could we win it with U.S. troops fighting alongside the South Vietnamese? Should we not know the answers to all these questions before deciding whether to commit troops?"

McNamara claimed that it "seems beyond understanding, incredible, that we did not force ourselves to confront such issues head-on." The biggest reason why he said is that, "we were confronting problems for which there were no ready, or good, answers. I fear that, in such circumstances, governments – and indeed most people – tend to stick their heads in the sand. It may help to explain, but it certainly does not excuse, our behavior."[302]

One reason why Robert McNamara and Kennedy's other civilian advisors did not ask such questions is that there was no great incentive to do so. If asking such questions would lead one to conclude that intervention and war in Vietnam could not lead to success then past history taught that one could get in trouble by revealing such information. The State Department had purged such men who doubted the viability of Chiang Kai-shek during the Chinese Civil War over a decade earlier.

Secretary of State Robert McNamara's job was to serve as the head civilian supervisor of the entire American defense establishment and work with the Joint Chiefs of Staff for President Kennedy. He could not simply dismiss the views of the chiefs and their planning staff out of hand.

Even though the United States was not in a shooting war with the Soviet Union, it had been

---

[302] McNamara, pp. 39-40.

placed on a total instant war footing with them. The SAC nuclear bomber command was on constant alert to carry out a nuclear attack against the Soviet Union. President Kennedy himself had run a campaign saying that the United States faced a dangerous "missile gap" with the Soviets that had to be stopped. Every American had been trained by newspapers and movies to be in total fear of the Soviets, world communism, and atomic bombs. Vietnam was a test case in this global confrontation that simply could not be shirked.

Many in government did not personally believe the domino theory, but the domino theory was used to explain America's role in the world and it demanded that the nation never back down or show weakness. No body of men were more important in this environment than the Joint Chiefs of Staff, because they were the watch guards in a nation on a total war footing trusted with the safety and defense of every American in this Cold War nuclear confrontation.

This was not a time to ask questions, but a time to be strong in a good and evil struggle of life and death. As Robert McNamara later put it, "we saw Vietnam as an element of the Cold War. Not what they saw it as: a civil war." This became a problem. The Chairman of the Joint Chiefs of Staff in 2003, General Richard Myers, explained decades later, "You have to be broadly prepared for a spectrum of conflicts. We were not prepared for the Vietnam

War. All the plans pointed to a potential nuclear conflict, not a counterinsurgency." They were prepared to win a nuclear conflict against the Soviet Union and China to defeat global communism, but not prepared to win a civil war in a third world nation. Therefore, the Joint Chiefs of Staff and their planning staff did not think of Vietnam in those terms.[303]

Within weeks of issuing NSAM-111 more American military personnel appeared in South Vietnam, but it would not be enough. The drive for more action in South Vietnam inside President Kennedy's own administration was relentless. The United States had been sending aid to Vietnam for over a dozen years. So, instead of merely responding to statements made by President Kennedy in meetings, almost all of his advisors simply produced proposals that fit with the legacy of the past decisions of the agencies they worked for and the plans they generated. Decision after decision made year-after-year now essentially made further involvement in Vietnam irreversible for them.

Although Walt Rostow worked in the White House for the President, and not in the State Department or the Defense Department, he took it upon himself to act as a spokesman for the entire

---

303 *The Fog Of War*, Dir. Errol Morris, Sony Pictures, 2003. DVD; Myers, Richard, "Voices," Vietnam, February, 2016, p. 18.

war state bureaucracy instead of simply as an assistant to the President. No bureaucracies ever look to diminish themselves, much less disband. All bureaucracies seek to grow in size and influence. By aligning himself in mind and in spirit with the entire war state bureaucracy, Rostow could control the destiny of the world along with it. Action in Vietnam would mean glory for any American infantry men that might fight there and for pilots who might fly planes and drop bombs there or elsewhere if the conflict spread. But it is only planning that makes such action possible and it is the promise of planning that holds the potential to improve man. Nothing was more important than this and nothing could make Rostow more important. Vietnam was a proving ground. President Kennedy's unwillingness to go all the way there stood in the way of total victory.

Years later, General Curtis LeMay said that the military brass were disappointed with Kennedy's decision. He said that they believed that the President's program was "anything except some diplomatic fiddling around." On December 5, 1961, the Joint Chiefs of Staff met with Robert McNamara and Dean Rusk. General LeMay told them that the Kennedy measures were inadequate and declared that all they were doing were delaying decisive actions that would become inevitable anyway. He said they were facing a challenge against world communism and that Southeast Asia was the best place to meet and defeat it. "U.S. military intervention in Southeast Asia, including the use of nuclear weapons, could be followed by many layers of escalation before the ultimate confrontation would occur," LeMay said.

General LeMay then told the other chiefs that they should press for a "high-level" accord to produce a "clear statement of US objectives" from the President and tell him that "timely, positive military actions are essential." He believed that they should send an Army brigade, a Marine division with an air wing, and three tactical Air Force units immediately to Vietnam to get started. In forty-eight hours the Joint Strategic Survey Council completed a study for the Joint Chiefs of Staff, which concluded that "the recently authorized measures, even when implemented, will prove to be inadequate."[304]

On January 27, 1962, the Joint Chiefs of Staff sent Secretary of Defense Robert McNamara a memo on "The Strategic Importance of the Southeast Asia Mainland." It began by reiterating the domino theory. If the United States withdrew from Vietnam it "would mean the eventual communist domination of all of the Southeast Asian mainland." Therefore, Vietnam's key importance "lies in the political value that can accrue to the Free World through a successful stand in that area." To

---

304 Newman, pp. 162-163.

back down from this challenge would be a form of national surrender, because it "would markedly reduce our ability in limited war by denying us air, land, and sea bases, by forcing greater intelligence effort with lesser results, by complicating military lines of communication and by the introduction of more formidable enemy forces in the area."

Therefore, the memo told Kennedy that "the Joint Chiefs of Staff wish to reaffirm their position that the United States must prevent the loss of South Vietnam to either communist insurgency or aggression, must prevent the communist control or domination of the Southeast Asia mainland, and must extend its influence in such a manner as to negate the possibility of any future communist encroachment."

To fail to act would mean, a failure of will to prevent what is "in fact, a planned phase in the communist timetable for world domination. Whereas, control of Cuba has opened for the Sino-Soviet Block more ready access to countries of South and Central America, control of Southeast Asia will open access to the remainder of Asia and to Africa and to Australia."

The memo then cited a list of weaknesses of President Diem's rule, but said there was no alternative to him. It then warned that if the current programs in assisting Diem did not change the situation and "the Viet Cong is not brought under control, the Joint Chiefs of Staff, see no alternatives to the introduction of US military combat forces along with those of the free Asian nations that can be persuaded to participate."

The memo then asked the President to reconsider a "decision be made to deploy US forces to South Vietnam" and stated that "we are the opinion that failure to do so under such circumstances will merely extend the date such action must be taken and will make our ultimate task proportionately more difficult."

Secretary of Defense Robert McNamara passed this memo on to President Kennedy and Secretary of State Dean Rusk with a cover letter in which he stated his opinion that "the memorandum requires no action by you at the time. I am not prepared to endorse the experience with our present program in South Vietnam."[305]

According to Walter Rostow, President Kennedy's relationship with the Joints Chiefs of Staff was "a nightmare. It was just awful." As a strategic doctrine the domino theory claimed that if any nation fell to communism then much of the world would fall under communist domination. As a theory it was more accurate not in its description in the actual capabilities of the Soviet Union, but in describing the importance of the will of American

---

[305] *The Pentagon Papers*, pp. 662-666.

politicians and presidents in maintaining this empire. The American war state operated as a global super-power with bases all over the world and client regimes. If the political will of the American people was not sufficient to maintain this entire structure than losing one piece of it could threaten the whole.[306]

In General LeMay's view, the people in the Kennedy administration were "cockroaches." "Everyone that came in with the Kennedy administration," he said, "is the most egotistical people that I ever saw in my life. They had no faith in the military; they had no respect for the military at all. They felt that the Harvard Business School method of solving problems would solve any problem in the world. They were capable of doing it; they were better than all of the rest of us; otherwise they wouldn't have gotten their superior education, as they saw it. And the fact that they had it entitled them to govern the rest of us, and we shouldn't question their decisions." The implementation of the Kennedy program for a "joint-effort" in Vietnam would prove to be dysfunctional and end with the murder of Diem in a coup, but it succeeded in its primary objective of keeping the

---

[306] Schulimson, p.251.

United States out of a major war in Vietnam for as long as President Kennedy lived.[307]

[307] Michael Swanson, *The War State: The Cold War Origins of the Military-Industrial Complex And The Power Elite, 1945-1963* (North Charleston: CreateSpace, 2013), pp. 254-255.

CODA

The big events that are written about in the history books tend to be moments of conception in time. Movements, forces, and ideas drive history like spokes in a moving wheel, but they are often forgotten about, and like ghosts they are sometimes not even seen by the people living through them, even though they lead up to the big events that are talked about, recorded, and taught years later. Momentous changes can happen so slowly that people just don't notice them until one day they wake up with a sudden realization that things are suddenly different from the way they were before. And sometimes a new idea can take hold and influence things from then on with unforeseen consequences that only a few insiders are able to later understand.

The surrender of the French garrison at Dien Bien Phu, in 1954, to the forces of the Viet Minh not only destroyed French power in Vietnam, but caused officials in the United States to wonder what the implications were for American power in the region too. After the battle, Secretary of Defense Charles Wilson got on an airplane and took a tour of Asia to visit key allies. This was probably one of the most important trips he ever took during his lifetime, but it is not recorded in any history books until now. The trip and the meetings around it would be forgotten about, because the ideas discussed in them didn't immediately go anywhere. They didn't lead to a new public statement or even a secret operation, but sometimes it is things that did not happen that are more important than what did happen. A new conception of American power was born that brought with it a logic that would take on a life of its own.

Seventeen days after the French surrendered at Dien Bien Phu, Secretary of Defense Wilson visited with General Chiang Kai-shek, the president of The Republic of China based in Taiwan, about the world situation. Chiang and Red China were mortal enemies, but Chiang saw big problems if the United States were to simply try to replace the French in Vietnam. According to a cable from the American ambassador to Taiwan, who was in these meetings with Wilson, Chiang told them that if their government intervened in Vietnam the "US inevitably would find itself enmeshed in British and French colonial problems and made to appear to Asians as another champion of colonialism. Nothing short of large scale use of American ground forces in Indochina could check Communists under these conditions," but even that would not be enough. In the end, Chiang said that the "only practicable military means of relieving pressure in Indochina is by threatening coastal flank of Communist China, which is prime mover in Red machinery for aggression in Asia." He proposed a five power pact with Taiwan, Japan, South Korea, Philippines, and the United States form to oppose China.

The next day, thc Joint Chiefs of Staff convened together in Washington and discussed Chiang's proposal and the overall situation along with Assistant Secretary of Defense Robert Anderson. They prepared a memo for Anderson, which he then sent to Secretary of State John Foster Dulles and to Robert Cutler, President Eisenhower's national security advisor for him to distribute to his assistants on a strict "need to know" basis. The memo from the Joint Chiefs of Staff was signed by Chairman Admiral Radford. It stated that if Southeast Asia were to fall that the Joint Chiefs of Staff recommended military action to prevent the fall of Thailand, Burma, and Malaya. It saw two options. The first would be "state defense type (Korea)" and the second would be "an offensive to attack the source of Communist military power being applied in Southeast Asia."

However, the memo argued that the first option held "damaging weaknesses." It estimated that it would take so many men that "it would take a minimum of 12 months to build up the necessary base complex and facilities required to support the forces" and that they would have to "remain for an extended period." The forces would "provide a basis for Communist propaganda to develop and intensify anti-Western sentiment." The "execution of static defense plan would result in maldeployment and seriously reduce the flexibility of employment of United States forces. This could seriously jeopardize the United States of supporting logistically our present war plans." In fact, sending such forces "would contribute to the realization of the politico-military objectives of the USSR vis-à-vis the free world."

The memo concluded, therefore, that "the United States should adopt the concept of offensive actions against the 'military power of the aggressor,' in this instance Communist China, rather than the concept of 'reaction locally at the point of attack.'" It then stated that if a decision was made to go with either option then "it would be necessary to insure the degree of mobilization required to take care of the increased possibility of general war."

Deputy Secretary of Defense Robert Anderson and Secretary of State John Foster Dulles met with President Eisenhower in private to discuss this Joint Chiefs of Staff memo and the views of General Chiang Kai-Shek. They gave Eisenhower the memo and told him that the Joint Chiefs of Staff believed that there was "little use discussing any 'defense' of the Southeast Asia area or any substantial commitment of U.S. force to this area; that United States power should be directed against the source of the peril which was, at least in the first instance, China, and that in this connection atomic weapons should be used."

Secretary Dulles told Eisenhower that, while he "did not question Admiral Radford's military judgment, I did not believe that it was serving our political objectives to present it at this time; that it would lead to U.S. isolation." He just thought that if "there was U.S. intervention as part of a coalition, no one could, of course, tell what the consequences might be or whether the initial theater would be enlarged. However, it was not politically good judgment to take it for granted that any defensive coalition would be found to become involved in a general war with China, and perhaps with Russia, and that this would be an atomic war."

According to Dulles, "the President said he wholly agreed with me and that he was strongly opposed to any assumption that it was necessary to have a war with China. He said that the JCS should not act in any way which would interfere with the political purposes of the government, and that he would try to find an occasion to make this clear."[308]

---

[308] *Foreign Relations of the United States, 1952-1953. East Asia And Pacific, Volume XII, Part I,* U.S. Department of State; pp. 511-517; (http://history.state.gov/historicaldocuments/frus1952-54v12p1/pg_514, accessed 3/1/2020)

Three days later, President Eisenhower held a National Security Council meeting with the members of the Joint Chiefs of Staff and Secretary of State Dulles along with the Assistant Secretary of Defense, as Wilson was still out of the country. According to meeting minutes, "the President said at the outset he wanted to make two general points." While the military should be "entirely frank in expressing their military views," he believed that they "should not appear to be discussing issues from the policy point of view in public, or in negotiations with friendly countries." The President believed that "in Indochina there were certain political prerequisites to establishing a satisfactory basis of operation, and without these prerequisites no purely military victory would prove worth having."

Secretary of State Dulles then held in his hand the JCS memo that advocated war with China and stated that if the US policy were to be guided by this thesis that he would not be able to negotiate alliances in Asia. He told them that "it was necessary to moderate our purely military judgment to take account of political factors, to give the Thai people, the Burmese, the Malaysians some hope that their area would not simply be overrun and occupied until China was destroyed, in order to keep them on our side." He worried that "if our plan were initially to destroy the total power of China, our allies would think we were heading toward general war" and "if we leapt to general war all at once, our allies wouldn't leap with us." President Eisenhower and his Secretary of State shot down the idea of starting a war with China together.

Admiral Radford reacted to them by backtracking. He stated that the JCS memo that Dulles was referring to was simply created out of an analysis of deploying forces to Thailand and of the viability of "making a military defense in Southeast Asia." He said he agreed with Dulles that "it was not necessary in military talk to mention atomic weapons" with allies; "We could just say we would attack military targets which directly support China action against Indochina or Korea without specifying the weapons."[309]

After this meeting, Dulles told President Eisenhower that he thought it "more likely that a Chinese offensive against Southeast Asia would take the form of subversion and indirect aggression rather than open direct aggression. This does not seem to be dealt with at all by the paper and perhaps this is not a type of problem on which the JCS wish to express themselves as it largely involves political judgment." He believed the solution was a strong regional alliance and "some buildup of local forces, as in Thailand, by some token participation of forces of the coalition and by economic and social measures which may cost us some money, but infinitely less than would be required to build a

309 Ibid, pp. 521-526.

major military defense in the area which I agree seems quite unwise to attempt."[310]

In a similar line of thinking seven years later, in 1961, President Kennedy would also decide that it would be wiser to send more assistance in terms of money and advisors to South Vietnam than combat troops, much less go down the road of SEATO Plan 5 with all of its implications. It was a way of looking at Southeast Asia and Vietnam differently than some members of the Joint Chiefs of Staff did. Their way of thinking would return and sometimes influence events at key moments in the years to come. Those who thought this way did so in terms of pure military power, with China as the real threat in Asia with time running out to stop it.

This conception happened as a result of the fall of Dien Bien Phu. The French defeat posed a huge problem for the American Air Force, who out of necessity suddenly needed to try to reinvent its war planning, or be left out with no role to play in the next conflict. The logic of nuclear weapons suggested that they were best used all at once, as quickly as possible, against an enemy if a nuclear confrontation occurred. If you didn't use them, then you risked losing them. From the beginning of the Cold War, Air Force doctrine held that the chief value of air power was as a retaliatory force that

[310] Ibid, p. 528.

would crush world Communism with massive destruction if the Soviet Union attacked Western Europe. President Eisenhower through his "New Look" doctrine advocated for massive nuclear retaliation as a way to prevent war, but, even though this meant more funding for the Air Force, the defeat at Dien Bien Phu demonstrated that it was actually very difficult to use massive air power in practice. During the siege trial balloons to do so were floated and popped.

The Vice Chief of Staff for the Air Force, General Nathan Twining, sent a message to the commanders of the Far East Air Forces, the Tactical Air Command, and Air University warning them of a growing threat to their service. He said that he was disturbed by growing talk that the Air Force can't "do anything other than [take] massive retaliatory action in the event of a major war." Doubts were growing that "contain a fundamental implication that surface forces are more capable of dealing with localized aggression than are air forces." He warned that the Air Force did not "appear capable of justifying increased air power to meet the military threats [of] anything short of major war." He specifically wanted to know: "What can air forces do to resolve the military problem in Indochina?"

The Air University happened to have a man working on this problem of air power. His name was Colonel Raymond Sleeper and he had been put in charge of a major study group called Project

Control. General Twining tasked him to do a quick study of the Indochina question and how to apply the strategies developed by Project Control against China. General Twining had already known of Colonel Sleeper and had been captivated by his work.[311]

Colonel Sleeper was a Harvard graduate who went into the Strategic Vulnerability Branch of US Intelligence before becoming a faculty member of Air University, but his devotion to his study of air power was sparked by an Air Force briefing he attended in 1948 that was given to top State Department officials. In attendance was the influential George Kennan and Charles Bohlen, who were leading experts on the Soviet Union. The briefers went through the Air Force plans to completely blitz the Soviet Union with atomic bombs all in mass, all at once, for total annihilation in the event of war. Kennan and Bohlen didn't think such an attack would be feasible. Kennan said that all it would do is "convince the Russians you are barbarians trying to destroy their very society and they will rise up and wage an indeterminate war against the West." He just thought there would be endless

---

[311] David Dean, "Project Control: Creative Thinking at Air University," Air University Review, July-August, 1984, p.9.

guerilla war, while Bohlen believed that "the negative psychological results of such an atomic attack might endanger postwar peace for 100 years."[312]

Attending this briefing made Colonel Sleeper realize that there was a massive gap between military planning and political planning inside the government. He decided he would work to discover a way to bridge that gap. He wanted to come up with a way to use nuclear weapons that could eliminate the political worries. It was tough. On August 25, 1950, just two months after the start of the Korean War, the Secretary of Navy, Francis Matthews, gave a speech in which he made the argument that the United States needed to consider becoming the first "aggressors for peace."

Matthews advocated for a massive arms buildup, and even attack, to not simply prevent any aggressions, but to take the step of "waging war for peace." He said that he knew there would be a personal cost. "They would brand our program as imperialistic aggression. We could accept that slander with complacency, for in the implementation of a strong, affirmative, peace-seeking policy, though it cast us in a character new to a true democracy – an

---

[312] Dean; Tami Davis Biddle, "Handling The Soviet Threat: 'Project Control' and the debate on American strategy in the early Cold War years," The Journal of Strategic Studies, 12:3, 1989, pp. 273-302. (https://doi.org/10.10180/01402398908437380, accessed 3/1/2020)

initiator of a war of aggression – it would win for us a proud and popular title – we would become the first aggressors for peace."

Matthews's speech had not been cleared by the State Department and immediately Secretary of State Dean Acheson disavowed his remarks. President Harry Truman then called Mathews on the phone and chewed him out. He thought he sent a clear message, but then just a few days later General Orvil Anderson, commander of the Air War College, made a statement to a reporter in which he said, "give me the order to do it and I can break up Russia's five A-Bomb nests in a week. And when I went up to Christ I think I could explain to him why I wanted to do it – now – before it is too late. I think I could explain to him that I had saved civilization." After these remarks were splashed all over the country in print, radio, and television, President Truman gave a speech denouncing the idea of preventive war. A day later, Air Force Chief of Staff General Hoyt Vandenberg informed Anderson that he was relieved of his command and made his own statement that "the Air Force is first, last, and always primarily an instrument for peace."[313]

Colonel Sleeper wanted to find a way to use nuclear weapons without them enduring such wrath. What point did the weapons have if they couldn't be used? And if they couldn't be used what would

---

[313] Biddle, p. 274, 276-277.

that mean for the Air Force? He needed to figure out a way to use them without simply creating total devastation of the Soviet Union. In the summer of 1952, he encountered the phrase "Air Control" while visiting with members of the Royal Air Force on a trip to England. This concept of "Air Control" was conceived by them in the 1920's and used in the 1930's to "control" hostile people in distant colonial territories of the British Empire. It was used successfully in Afghanistan, Iraq, and Somaliland in 1919 against unruly tribes.

What it involved was using air power against rebel tribes and, as the Brits explained it, as an "inverted blockade, keeping villagers away from their crops and stores of gain, or keeping nomads on the run and away from their livestock." Aircraft recon overflights could first be used as a form of intimidation and if they did not bring compliance area bombing could be used until compliance was given. For Sleeper the concept of "Air Control" grabbed him, because he believed that it "puts the air arm literally at the disposition of the political. The air objective and the political objective meld into one."[314]

Sleeper developed a thesis of "control by air and other means." It argued that the United States could use air power and even nuclear weapons to force an enemy to surrender before a conflict led to

---

[314] Ibid, pp. 279-280.

full-scale total war. He labeled his research "Project Control" and turned it into much more than a one-man affair.

On January 5, 1953, he met with Pentagon Brigadier General Hunter Harris, Air Force Director of War Plans, who quickly saw how important it was. The General sent a letter to the Air University requesting that it be turned into a formal study. Soon General Thomas White, Deputy Chief of Staff for Operations, sent a letter to the college informing them that the Air Force considered this project to be "unusually significant" and that it "should be considered high priority against the resources available to the Air University" and promised that he personally would accord it "high priority by this headquarters."

Soon Sleeper had over one hundred men working under him, including civilian consultants from think tanks and the CIA. Among the men chosen were Assistant Secretary of State Dr. A.A. Berle, RAF General Sir John Slessor, and Walt Rostow of MIT. Max Millikan, the Director of the CIS at MIT, told Sleeper that he shouldn't have his study focus only on air power, because the other service branches of the military would have to be let in for project proposals to be supported by them, much less implemented. Millikan suggested that he reach out to Robert Bowie, who served on the State Department Policy Planning Staff, because he thought he would be sympathetic.[315]

Project Control was a massive undertaking in manpower hours and once completed resulted in a three volume work of several thousand pages in length. Sleeper and his team wanted their ideas to have an impact at the top of the national security state, so they created a short summary volume and prepared for Sleeper a concise sixty minute briefing presentation he could present to key people. On May 24, 1954, Sleeper briefed the Air Force World Wide Commanders at Eglin Air Force Base in Florida. In attendance were Generals LeMay, Norstad, White, Twining, and Weyland. This was the exact same day that Secretary of Defense Charles Wilson was in Taiwan speaking with Chiang Kai-Shek.[316]

The first volume of Project Control consisted of two counterfactual histories of World War II. The first one claimed that if the United States had begun air control operations in Asia against Japan as early as 1931 that it would have thwarted Japan without World War II. As far as World War II went, it also argued that if the United States had announced in mid-1944, after capturing the Marianas Islands, that it did not intend to invade Japan, but would bomb it nonstop until it surrendered that it

---

[315] Dean, pp. 5-6; Biddle, pp. 280-281.
[316] Dean, p.16.

probably would have surrendered by February 1945, without even having had to use the atomic bomb. As for Germany, the study claimed that if air power had been used with ultimatums, in 1936, that Hitler never would have invaded Poland.

All of these counterfactuals amounted to Air Force fantasies as none could be proven to have been real. But they led to the rest of the study, which concluded that similar tactics could be used to make the Soviet government surrender. Instead of a mass attack of annihilation, Project Control advocated for a campaign of graduated pressure to force a Soviet surrender or government collapse. The campaign would begin with intimidation air recon overflights, move to ultimatums, and then to covert action support of internal opposition forces inside the Soviet Union combined with a bombing campaign of increasing intensity. If that campaign led to nuclear weapons, they would not be deployed all at once, but in waves, with the expectation that the Russian military or other opposition forces would depose the Soviet state and replace it to negotiate and in time form a democratic government.

However, this plan had to be implemented immediately, because the United States had "until at least July 1957, superiority over the Soviet Union in atomic and nuclear weapons as well as the capacity to deliver these weapons, and that the USSR would recognize and react to that fact." This window of opportunity would close. In order to begin, the United States had to reject the prohibition against striking the first blow. The United States needed to think of itself as if it were a wild-west gunfighter in which certain Soviet "aggressive acts" warranted firing the first shot. Project Control concluded that "any nation that persists in the development and production of military force capable of threatening the existence of the Free World and whose political actions and stated national intent leaves no doubt that she intends to use that military force to conquer or subjugate free countries should be considered as an aggressor who is preparing to commit an aggressive act against the Free World."[317]

The Air Force brass briefed at Eglin Air Force base were captivated by Sleeper's briefing. General Kuter of Air University informed Sleeper, "it was apparent," he believed, "that this presentation did more to increase the stature of the Air University in top Air Force circles than any other single event to date." The attendees were happy to know that "the Air University is not planning to fight World War II 1/2, but that it is apparently doing as well in planning for World War III as the Air Corps Tactical School for World War II."[318]

The Secretary of the Air Force wanted to get Project Control pushed the right way to have an

---

[317] Biddle, pp. 281-291.
[318] Dean, pp. 15-16.

impact. Colonel Sleeper was assigned to temporary duty to the Air Staff where he began a series of briefings to top leaders outside of the Air Force. He got in front of Secretary of Defense Charles Wilson and his assistant Secretary, General Twining, and others at his first event. A memo records that the "comments were sympathetic and lively, but largely noncommittal." The consensus was that the United States had the capability to carry out "Control by Air and Other Means," but "that the essential element which is lacking is the political decision to proceed."[319]

Admiral Radford believed that Project Control's proposals should be taken to the White House. More briefings were needed to build support first. Sleeper briefed CIA Director Allen Dulles and his staff. Dulles seemed to agree with the historical analysis about Germany and Japan. Brigadier-General Jesmond Balmer, of the CIA, said that Sleeper's presentation "agrees well with the thinking in the CIA" and added that the "CIA is the only agency in the government with a plan for the cold war." Dulles, though, was circumspect saying that the project was interesting, but "would absorb a great deal more thought" and offered to have the CIA try to wargame it.

When Sleeper went to the Department of State, however, and briefed John Foster Dulles, he got a

---

[319] Dean, p16; Biddle, pp.290,

hostile reception. Robert Bowie decried that it was just "simply another version of preventive war" and there was no way to predict how the Soviets would respond to an air intimidation campaign and that the theory that the Soviet's would back down was "fallacious." Max Millikan heard what happened and concluded that Sleeper had failed, because he didn't get Robert Bowie involved early at the start of Project Control.

Nevertheless, Admiral Radford remained supportive. In a meeting over it with other members of the Joint Chiefs of Staff he argued that "if the US did not adopt and successfully follow through on a course of action similar to Project Control, that in the period 1957-1960 there would be either an all-out atomic war or the US would be forced into agreement which would mean victory for the USSR." He told them he wanted to brief President Eisenhower and get a high level group set up to develop Project Control further. When General Twining reached out to Colonel Sleeper for ideas on how air power could be applied in Southeast Asia, after Dien Bien Phu, applying the concepts of Project Control against China were given back to him as the answer in a report titled *Project Control Research Memorandum 4.5: Resolution of the Indo-China Conflict through Control by Air and Other Means*.[320]

[320] Dean, p.10-11; Biddle, pp.290-292.

Nonetheless, for many the idea of using nuclear weapons first as part of a conflict initiated by the United States was just too much. When Colonel Sleeper gave a briefing about Project Control to strategists at the RAND Corporation one attendee recalled that "it was received with disbelief, dismay, and alarm." The issue came to a head towards the end of 1954, as President Eisenhower commissioned a formal policy statement to review and define American national security policy in regards to conflict with the Soviet Union, including the use of nuclear weapons. As part of this process a series of National Security meetings were chaired by the President and members across his administration.[321]

In one meeting, General Mathew Ridgway decried the idea of using nuclear weapons to defeat the Soviet Union. He said that even if they won a nuclear conflict "what do you do after you win?" The economic and social costs would be so staggering that you would win nothing. Ridgway thought if war with the Soviets broke out that they wouldn't use nuclear weapons if the United States and NATO didn't use them first, just as Hitler didn't use chemical weapons in the last war.

After Ridgway left the room, Secretary of Defense Wilson noted that there "was a split in views

---

[321] Raymond L. Garthoff, *A Journey through the Cold War: A Memoir of Containment and Coexistence* (Brookings Institution: Washington, D.C., 2001), pp. 14-15.

among the Joint Chiefs of Staff, and that General Ridgway was making a justification for a much larger army. It was quite proper for General Ridgway to advocate larger Army forces, but the Council should recognize what it was hearing." Governor Harold Stassen, who was serving in Eisenhower's cabinet, then said it might be "fruitful to have a special group undertake to make a study of the difficult problem which General Ridgway had underlined" – "namely, how to organize the victory after the end of a nuclear war – how the US could rebuild a shattered world without destroying its own economy." However, he "doubted the entire validity of General Ridgway's thesis that we would draw upon ourselves the hatred of most of mankind if we resorted to atomic warfare. History showed that the great hatreds were engendered in the post-war period rather than during the time of the actual conflict."

President Eisenhower said "that our only chance of victory in a third world war against the Soviet Union would be to paralyze the enemy at the outset of war. Since we cannot keep the United States an armed camp or a garrison state, we must make plans to use the atom bomb if we become involved in a war. We are *not* going to provoke the war, and that is why we have got to be patient. If war comes, the other fellow must have started. Otherwise we would not be in a position to use the nuclear weapons, and we have got to be in a position to use that weapon if we are to preserve our institutions in peace and win the victory in war."[322]

In a follow up National Security Council meeting, Secretary of State John Foster Dulles ruled out preventive nuclear war. He said that it "would almost certainly cause the disintegration of the free world bloc, of which we were the leaders, for our allies in the free world would never go along with such courses of action as these." When it came to Asia, "he was not at all optimistic about the future of Free Vietnam. Laos and Cambodia are also very vulnerable. Yet if one looked at the other side of the picture, these countries are not really of great significance to us, other than from the point of view of prestige, except that they must be regarded as staging grounds for further forward thrusts by the Communist powers. An example would be Indonesia. Happily, the countries which are likely victims of such a Communist forward thrust are covered by adequate defense arrangements."

In this meeting, Secretary of Defense Wilson agreed, "Plainly, we must live for the time being with Communism. While we ourselves can't do very much externally to destroy it, he was sure that ultimately it would destroy itself. The same applied

---

[322] *Foreign Relations of the United States, 1952–1954, National Security Affairs, Volume II, Part 1*, Department of State, pp. 803-806 (https://history.state.gov/historicaldocuments/frus1952-54v02p1/pg_805, accessed 3/1/2020)

in a slightly different way to China. China had been a dictatorship for centuries; so had the Soviet Union. These countries had new kinds of dictators now, but these dictators still faced the problem of how to control their population."

John Foster Dulles did not believe that the Soviet Union or China would militarily attack other countries. "They were not reckless, as Hitler was," he said, "but primarily they rely not on military force but on methods of subversion. This was natural, because the Communist Party was in essence revolutionary and conspiratorial. At the present time they calculate that it is not worth their while to undermine the successful campaign of subversion by indulgence in actions of open brutality." The solution then was "to provide to these vulnerable nations sufficient military and economic assistance as will enable them to provide for their internal security and for the bettering of their economic health. The situation in Vietnam, warned Secretary Dulles, was not a typical case but a special case, and we should not generalize on the basis of Vietnam, where the French had messed up the situation so thoroughly."[323]

[323] Document 143, *Foreign Relations of the United States, 1952–1954, National Security Affairs, Volume II, Part 1*, Department of State (https://history.state.gov/historicaldocuments/frus1952-54v02p1/d143, accessed 3/1/2020)

By the end of 1954, President Eisenhower issued formal policy statement NSC 5440 – a summary statement of US national security policy. It argued that while at the moment the United States had an overwhelming advantage against the Soviet Union in terms of nuclear weapons that window would probably close in five years. That would probably lead to a situation of "mutual deterrence." Nonetheless, it stated as matter of national policy that "large-scale military action" before that time against the Soviet Union would "not be an acceptable course either to the U.S. or its allies."[324]

By issuing NSC 5440, President Eisenhower rejected preemptive nuclear war against the Soviet Union or China as a national policy. The concepts of Project Control would not enter into formal nuclear war planning and instead one shot massive all or nothing strikes would continue to define the nuclear war plans in the years to follow. As for Colonel Sleeper, he would go on to head the foreign technology division of the Air Force Systems Command and after retiring from active service in 1968 became a lecturer on cybernetics at the Space Institute of the University of Tennessee, seeing a future networked computer society on the horizon. However, two ideas that were central to Project Control could not be forgotten.

---

[324] *Foreign Relations of the United States, 1952–1954, National Security Affairs, Volume II, Part 1*, Department of State, pp. 808-822.

The first was that the United States had an overwhelming strategic advantage in terms of nuclear weapons against the Soviet Union and China that was not going to last forever. This was a simple fact. The second idea in Sleeper's study was that this fact meant that if one used nuclear weapons now, in the right way, the enemy may not be able to respond and might instead surrender in defeat. Perhaps not, and perhaps it was all a fantasy, because when government strategists war gamed Project Control they concluded that the Soviet team would never surrender, but that was just a mental exercise. One might not be able to put it on paper, but one could still imagine, and talk, about how a smaller regional use of nuclear weapons – or threat of such use - could create total victory, before time ran out.[325]

In 1955, The Air Force changed its doctrine Air Force Manual (AFM 1-2) to change its focus from one of "air superiority" to "air control," which it defined as "achieved when air forces, in peace or in war, can affect the desired degrees of influence over other specific nations." Previous manuals rejected the use of force except as a last resort. This new manual argued that "any elements of a nation's power, or all elements, may be used, as required, to gain its desired ends through courses of

[325] Biddle, pp.292-293.

action which are consistent with its national policies" in war or peace.

While formal nuclear war planning was for general total war, culminating in the Single Integrated Operational Plan of the Joint Strategic Planning Staff, in 1960, Air Force leaders believed nuclear weapons could be used in a controlled way in a localized conflict. In 1957, the Air Force plans chief, Major General John Cary, explained in a lecture that "the Air Force feels strongly that the best way to accomplish this is to end the local war quickly and decisively and this opinion is reflected in national policy." He claimed that if the Air Force used atomic bombs early in Korea that the war could have ended in days, or weeks, with much lower casualties. One Air University study advocated launching a surprise atomic attack on a Chinese offshore island as a demonstration that "could be decisive in the efforts of the Free World to deter limited aggression."

In a 1957 Department of Defense filmed interview, Thomas White of SAC said that there was no "upper or lower limit to SAC's capability." He saw SAC as a general use force for total war that could be used to operate anywhere on the spectrum of conflict. In an internal staff letter, the SAC commander's office explained that a small "brush war" could be won with a small number of bombers. All the United States would have to do is give an ultimatum before attacking to give civilians time to flee and then drop nuclear bomb after nuclear bomb until the enemy surrendered or could no longer fight.[326]

The Cuba Missile Crisis of 1962 almost resulted in a massive bombing campaign against Cuba with an amphibious invasion of the island bringing with it the threat of nuclear war. When the Joint Chiefs of Staff met with President Kennedy during the crisis, General Curtis LeMay advocated for such a course of action on the grounds that he did not believe that the Soviet Union would respond, because of the nuclear advantage. Army Chief of Staff General Earle Wheeler also argued to "go ahead with a surprise air strike, the blockade, and an invasion because these series of actions progressively will give us an increasing assurance that we really have got the offensive capability of the Cuban-Soviets cornered." As I explained in my previous book *The War State* we now know that things would not have turned out that way, but such thoughts were in line with the concepts of Project Control.[327]

---

[326] Byron Fairchild & Walter Poole, *History of the Joint Chiefs of Staff: The Joint Chiefs of Staff and National Policy, Volume VII, 1957-1960* (Office of Joint History, Office of The Secretary of Defense: Washington, D.C., 2000), p.53-54.; Edward Kaplan, *To Kill Nations: American Strategy in the Air-Atomic Age and the Rise of Mutually Assured Destruction* (Cornell University, USA, 2015), pp. 87,137.
[327] Timothy Naftali & Philip Zelikow, editors, *The Presidential Recordings John F. Kennedy: The Great Crises, Volume II* (W.W. Norton and Company: New York, 2001), pp. 583-586;

And in 1964, war planning against Vietnam would try to take advantage of the nuclear superiority against China in a similar manner. A textbook history of the Joint Chiefs of Staff, used at the National Defense University, explains that they advocated for "a more aggressive, immediate strategy to confront the enemy directly with strong, decisive force. Militarily, the chief's solution had much to recommend it. The United States still possessed overwhelming strategic nuclear superiority and could have used that power as an umbrella for large-scale conventional operations against North Vietnam." President Lyndon Johnson and Secretary of Defense Robert McNamara were skeptical that China could be deterred like that (they weren't in Korea) and by 1965 they successfully tested their first atomic weapon. Instead, McNamara would propose a campaign of graduated bombing against the forces of North Vietnam with limits to avoid Chinese intervention.[328]

Why Vietnam? The more hawkish members of the Joint Chiefs of Staff viewed Southeast Asia as simply part of a conflict with China over who would control the entire region. When they advocated in-

---

Michael Swanson, *The War State: The Cold War Origins of the Military-Industrial Complex And The Power Elite, 1945-1963* (North Charleston: CreateSpace, 2013), pp. 340-358.
[328] Steven Rearden, *Council of War: A History of the Joint Chiefs of Staff, 1942-1991* (NDU Press: Washington, D.C., 2012), pp. 281-283.

tervention in Laos in 1961 their plans were for a regional conflict that carried with it a ladder of escalation, the final step of which was an atomic attack on China if they retaliated, one in which they thought they could break the back of Red China. President Kennedy rejected such intervention in Laos, and their proposals in Vietnam, and instead decided to send aid and advisors to South Vietnam as a comprise, but in the process he opened up a new phase in the history of the Vietnam War that came to an end when President Diem and himself were both assassinated in the fall of 1963. I am now working on a new book about that phase of the Vietnam War that ended with mysteries covered up.

Ironically, North Vietnam was never the Chinese puppet state hawks in the United States imagined it to be. Once the Vietnam War was over, China in fact launched a border war against the Democratic Republic of Vietnam in the Sino-Vietnamese war of 1979. In Vietnam today they call this conflict "The War Against Chinese Expansion." Perhaps men like Archimedes Patti were right in 1945, but their superiors saw the whole world in binary us versus them terms and by 1954 many men in the Pentagon got caught up in the nuclear arms race advantage that would one day come to an end.

Today the rise of China as an emerging superpower in the 21st century is in the minds of leaders in the US national security state. On October 10, 2010, Robert Gates became the first Secretary of

Defense since the Vietnam War to take a trip to Vietnam. When he got off his airplane he shook hands with his communist counterpart and honored his nation's flag in an honor guard review ceremony at the Vietnamese Military Headquarters in Hanoi. He then had meetings to discuss possible arms sales and assistance to their nation to help them block China in their maritime claims.[329]

Today Vietnam is one of the fastest growing emerging economies in the world. The world process continues, but when it comes to the American war state concepts such as full spectrum dominance remain its doctrine and Asia is now set to be a top place for its focus for the next several decades. My previous book *The War State* explains its Cold War origins after World War II and the rise of the military industrial-complex and power elite that came with it.

---

[329] Thom Shanker, "In Vietnam, Gates to Discuss Maritime Claims of China," New York Times, October 10, 2010.

ABOUT THE AUTHOR

Michael Swanson is the author of the book *The War State: The Cold War Origins Of The Military-Industrial Complex And The Power Elite, 1945-1963*. He received a Master's Degree in history from the University of Virginia and then dropped out of the college's Ph.D. program to enter the business world. He ran a hedge fund from 2003 until 2006 and runs the website WallStreetWindow.com, which focuses on geopolitics and finance.

Swanson returned to his study of the past with a book of local history, authored *The War State,* and now is working on a new book about The Vietnam War on the period from the end of this book to the deaths of Diem and Kennedy. It is anticipated to be released in 2023. Meanwhile you may want to read the *The War State* as in many ways it serves as a prequel to *Why The Vietnam War?* Help get the word out on this book, because word of mouth is crucial for any author to succeed. If you enjoyed this book please consider leaving a review at Amazon.com, even if it's only a line or two; it would make all of the difference in the world and be very much appreciated.

BOOKS PUBLISHED BY CAMPANIA PARTNERS

In Denial: Secrets War With Air Strikes And Tanks? By Larry Hancock, Campania Partners, 2020.

Human Time Bomb: The Violence Within Our Nature by Carmine Savastano, Campania Partners, 2020.

Judyth Vary Baker: In Her Own Words by Walt Brown, PhD, Campania Partners, 2019.

The War State: The Cold War Origins of the Military-Industrial Complex And The Power Elite by Michael Swanson, Campania Partners, 2013.

Made in the USA
Middletown, DE
13 May 2023

30555711R00265